'If you've always dream[...] an adventure of a lifetime, this book's for you.' *The Independent*

'Halls blends Bill Bryson-esque contextual anecdotes with a genuine earnestness for the subject matter in a manner that is seldom less than endearing.' *How It Works Magazine*

MONTY HALLS is a writer, broadcaster, speaker, naturalist, former Royal Marine, marine biologist and the President of the Galapagos Conservation Trust. He worked for Nelson Mandela during the peace process in the early nineties, and then left the Marines to pursue a career in expeditions, travel journalism and biology. His experience covers two decades of leading teams in some of the most remote environments on earth and presenting numerous wildlife documentaries.

@montyhalls

@montyhallsfamily

www.montyhalls.co.uk

MONTY HALLS

My Family
and the
Galapagos

HEADLINE

First published in 2020
by HEADLINE PUBLISHING GROUP

First published in paperback in 2021 by
by HEADLINE PUBLISHING GROUP

1

ILLUSTRATIONS
Penguin – © Granger Historical Picture Archive/Alamy
Giant tortoise – © Dn Br/Shutterstock
Sea-lion – © Morphart Creation/Shutterstock
Hammerhead shark – © gameover/Alamy
Blue-footed Booby – © Elena Faenkova/Shutterstock
Sally Lightfoot crab – © 19th era 2/Alamy

Cataloguing in Publication Data is available from the British Library

ISBN 978 1 4722 6884 6

Typeset in Garamond 3 by CC Book Production
Printed and bound in Great Britain by Clays Ltd, Elcograf S.p.A.

Headline's policy is to use papers that are natural, renewable and
recyclable products and made from wood grown in sustainable forests.
The logging and manufacturing processes are expected to conform to
the environmental regulations of the country of origin.

HEADLINE PUBLISHING GROUP
An Hachette UK Company
Carmelite House
50 Victoria Embankment
London
EC4Y 0DZ

www.headline.co.uk
www.hachette.co.uk

This book is dedicated to my amazing mum,
the inspiration for so many of my adventures,
and the rock around which our family swirls.

Contents

Prologue

'Are you absolutely sure?' I asked. 'You're genuinely okay with this?'

'I'm fine,' she said, nodding once and staring resolutely ahead. 'Can we go, please?'

'Well, okay then, if you're happy.'

We made the last adjustments to our kit, and slipped over the side of the boat. The water was cool, making me gasp as it flushed through my wetsuit, bringing me instantly alive to the new world around me. I shouldn't have been too surprised at the chill – we were, after all, entering an environment that had emerged from the deep sea, an upwelling of deep Pacific water rich in oxygen and nutrients. It fed a truly remarkable ecosystem, a clamouring, bustling celebration of life itself.

I turned to look up at the boat, finning backwards a few metres as she too stepped off the stern, before moving quickly forward to steady her on the surface while simultaneously looking into her eyes for any trace of panic. She smiled clumsily behind her mask and snorkel while giving me a thumbs up, her head tilted to one side, green eyes shining behind the glass. She was new to this, and, so far, seemed to be taking to it rather well.

Suitably reassured, I nodded once, and turned away to scull towards the dark lava of the reef. She fell in behind me, occasionally reaching forward to touch my shoulder, or to squeeze my hand. The white sand lay in ripples beneath us, a satellite image of a vast desert, each valley and ridge its own tiny world. The sunlight danced and flickered over the seabed and I could see our own shadows below, gliding across the landscape like two motherships, causing tiny reef fish to flick and dart in alarm. This may have looked like some idyllic, delicate tundra, but it was actually a killing ground, a stark place where a moment of inattention would result in a messy demise, signalled only by a cloud of silvery scales or a puff of silt. In the world of the turbulent shallows, where resources are so relatively scarce and so bitterly contested, very few inhabitants die of old age.

Soon we were at the lava wall itself, dark rocks marked by a white border of high energy as the waves crackled and seethed at the end of their journey, mixing air and water, seeking weakness, a fissure or a crack to work on their timeless and tireless task of shaping the Galapagos islands. Theirs was work that was never completed, a story with no end. As long as the islands existed, and as long as waves dashed up against them, then the change that defined these islands would continue.

To our left was a gap, a gulley just wide enough to admit a single person, yet not of a size that would permit two snorkelers to swim side by side. We moved to the entrance, a gateway to another, more claustrophobic place, a dark canyon that twisted away ahead of us. I cautiously reached back, squeezed her hand, then – without ceremony – pulled her forward, and gently pushed her into the gap. She did not resist, allowing her body to float forward, all the while scanning around and beneath her.

I followed her, the walls closing in on either side, the surge pulsing through the constriction, easing us forward then dragging us back, the very heartbeat of the sea. The light became other-worldly, a dull planktonic glow that seemed to emanate from the ocean itself. It illuminated the narrow strip of sand three metres below, and the unmistakable, sinuous forms of its inhabitants.

Survival in the Galapagos is as much about exploiting every environmental niche as it is about embracing the constant change that characterises the islands. The opening of this gulley over eons of time had proved irresistible to the local whitetip reef sharks, providing a calm, dimly lit haven. They lay beneath us, gun-metal sculptures, one atop another, gills pulsing and mouths gaping. Some were of a decent size too, with the largest about two metres long.

The whitetip reef shark is a monument to predatory efficiency, hunting at night in the shallows, moving in packs, with a battery of senses honed to seek out the weak and the unwary. They have a remarkable sense of smell, and have a flattened head, tough as teak, that they use to chisel into the smallest overhangs. Their bodies drive forward, a pistoning tail to the rear, fins flattening against their flanks like the blades of a pen-knife. All the while they smell the water, see into the darkness, and use jelly-filled pits on their snouts to detect the flicker of electricity that emanates from any living thing. We were hovering just above the wolf pack as they slumbered before the evening hunt, her and me together, constrained and constricted by the ebony darkness and claustrophobic proximity of the lava walls on either side.

I looked ahead, and saw her try to dive towards them, her body jack-knifing at the hips and her arms reaching downwards as she strove to join – even for a moment – the elegant forms at repose beneath her. She was drawn to them, to their proximity, to their potential energy, to their lithe togetherness. She wanted to rest among them, and then to join them on the prowl as the sun set over the reef crest.

I decided that this might be an unwise move, and sculled forward to grasp the tip of her fin, dragging her back towards me and the surface. She glanced around in annoyance, shaking loose her foot from my grasp to once again look down, find the sharks beneath her, and try to dive down towards them.

The result was a rather comical tug of war, with me vigorously hauling one end, and her trying to dive ever deeper with her hands at the other. It was rather like holding on to a large trout, but I was (justifiably) concerned that her arrival among the sleeping sharks might be greeted in one of two ways – considerable enthusiasm, or considerable alarm. Neither was particularly desirable. I had visions of an explosion of dark bodies in the constricted gulley, a scattering of predatory shrapnel with her borne along in its midst as a piece of wide-eyed collateral damage.

I finally managed to haul her back towards me, simultaneously spinning her round so we were face to face. She glared at me, and I glared right back, waggling my finger in front of her mask. There are times when one simply must take charge, particularly where large predators and confined spaces are involved. I needed to show who was boss here, given that Isla – my irrepressible, feisty, fearless, insatiably curious snorkeling companion – wanted to get back down to the sharks more than she wanted anything else in the world. At times like this she really could be quite unreasonable.

Mind you, I reflected, perhaps I should be a little more understanding. You can get a little carried away with your emotions when you're only five.

One

'I look forward to the Galapagos with more interest than any other part of the voyage.'

Charles Darwin's journal from on board HMS *Beagle*, before arriving in the Galapagos in 1835

Ancient History

I pressed my face as close to the window as possible, peering downwards to catch a first glimpse of the islands. My nose bent against the glass, snorting twin blasts of condensation as I attempted to look at the scene directly beneath our descending aircraft. I must have looked completely ridiculous, but I didn't really mind – this was, after all, the end of a journey that had taken several decades, the culmination of a lifetime of dreaming.

And there, thrillingly, between the gaps in the scudding clouds beneath us, was a ragged outline of a dark lava reef trimmed with white as the ocean crackled and heaved against it. My first glimpse of the Galapagos was strangely fitting, an isolated group of rocks fringed by wind and current, with the sea snarling and snapping at its margins. As the aircraft banked on the final approach to

9

Baltra Airport, I was gifted an uninterrupted view like no other on the planet – the great ragged mosaic that are the Galapagos, a volcanic upheaval set in a cobalt sea, 600 miles off the coast of Ecuador.

I was on board the one flight a week that visited the islands. The year was 2001, which seemed to me to be an entirely fitting date to undertake such a millennial trek. Around me were a host of fellow bucket-listers, creating a rising wave of excited chatter as we began our final approach, while behind me were the small team of film-makers and divers with whom I was travelling. With a thump and a squeak, we landed, and I hefted my bag on to my shoulder and shuffled slowly down the aisle of the aircraft. Descending the steps, I set foot on the Galapagos for the first time – a seminal moment in my life, although I was blissfully unaware of it at the time.

The Galapagos Islands cast a truly global spell, one that bewitches from afar, then dazzles up close. For virtually every modern traveller it is one of the few destinations on earth that lives up to the highest levels of feverish anticipation. This is an archipelago one plans to visit for decades, explores for a matter of days, then remembers for ever.

On a superficial level, the allure is simple – the proximity of remarkable wildlife, the stark beauty of the volcanic landscapes, and the remoteness of the destination. When combined with the mystique, scientific significance, and truly unique character of the islands, it creates a potent sensory cocktail. But sadly there is also a fragility, a vulnerability to external forces, that today places the islands in real jeopardy. Remarkably, though, the islands have retained a great deal of their original environmental identity, despite the rampant interests of mankind for the last two hundred years.

For many of the hordes of modern visitors, of whom I was merely the latest, following what was by now a well-worn trail, it is often the initial impression of the islands that lingers long in the memory – a twisted, tortured moonscape that speaks volumes for its fiery birth. This is no lush tropical paradise, and even with all the accoutrements of modern travel there is no denying that you are somewhere remote. Indeed, the very first thing that struck me as I walked away from the aircraft is that, although my feet may have been on dry land, essentially, I was at sea. The breeze I felt upon my cheek was oceanic, carrying with it the scent of salt and spray. It combined with the heat of the earth, and the warm musk of equatorial plants, making my senses come alive – a primal reflex to a new world. This was a shattered volcanic vista inhabited by the Bedouin of the natural world, creatures and plants that have not only survived the journey here – in itself a miraculous accomplishment for any land-based animal – but have also learned to live with the vagaries of wind and wave, of equatorial sun, and of scant resources.

This very landscape is one of the reasons the islands remained relatively unchanged for so long, utterly unforgiving as it was for the first human settlers who travelled there with naïve visions of Eden. For hundreds of years mankind simply couldn't settle in any significant numbers on the islands. This means that, today, 95% of the different species of plants and animals that had made the Galapagos their home before man arrived are still in place – a unique phenomenon among any inhabited oceanic island group.

And now, at the turn of a new century, it seemed that precious integrity was still in place. As I arrived, I was simply another one of 10,000 annual visitors to the islands. When the archipelago was established as one of the first World Heritage Sites in 1978 by the United Nation Educational Scientific and Cultural Origination (UNESCO), the parameters set were that the Galapagos could deal with just over 8,000 tourists a year before the ecosystem would start to be negatively impacted. Walking towards the terminal and joining the back of the queue to passport control, I reflected on the fact that although the visitor numbers were indeed now being exceeded, it was commendable that it was only by a small amount, and this after twenty-three years of having WHO status. It seemed to me that the Galapagos were a model of restraint and effective management, particularly under the increasing pressure of global tourism, and the fact that the islands had transformed from being an extraordinary place to being an ultimate destination. I therefore arrived in the Galapagos with a relatively clear conscience.

I was here to make a film about one of the islands most enigmatic residents – the Galapagos penguin. As an animal it encapsulated so much about the wonder (and indeed the worries) of conservation here as a new century turned – an animal that is entirely unique, a miracle of fast-tracked evolutionary adaptations that have seen it prosper far north of the range of its brethren, and yet is now under huge pressure due to the arrival and ongoing impact of mankind. It was the ideal subject for our film – part of a wider series about conservation and travel – and a neat parable for the times.

We quickly passed through what can only be described as a fairly basic customs procedure ('*¡Buenos días!* Welcome to the Galapagos,' smiled an official with an impressive uniform, but an unimpressive approach to immigration procedure), and waited by the baggage carousel. I glanced up and around at the terminal building. It was large, fabricated and functional, an echo chamber slowly becoming inhabited by the modern airport paraphernalia of ATMs, kiosks and adverts. It looked somehow incomplete, as though unsure of itself, which it certainly shouldn't have been, as it is probably the most important building in the entire island group, being the gateway to the islands for so many.

Like just about everything in the islands, the site of the airport itself tells a powerful story – both ancient and modern. Baltra sits just north of the island of Santa Cruz, which has always been one of the main focal points of human settlement in the archipelago, due to the presence of the harbour town of Puerto Ayora. Baltra itself is a lump of rock – or rocks, a great many of them – that may well have been underwater at some point in its distant history (hence the flat surface beaten down by wave and current), and which has subsequently been colonised by both plants and animals. It stood out for the American engineers who came here in 1941 needing an airstrip. Nowhere else in the archipelago had the same access to a large island nearby – and so to fresh water – and was level enough to land an aircraft.

The US had decided that the Galapagos represented a vital strategic outpost, somewhere to guard the entrance to the Panama Canal, and to act as a warning post of attack from the west. From this moment on, the islands would change for ever – even the name Baltra comes from the call-sign for the base over the

American radios. It was initially called 'Base Beta Beta', which was obviously a little cumbersome, so was shortened to 'B-3', duly translated by the locals as 'B-tres' in Spanish, which, in the finest of Galapagoan tradition, evolved rapidly into 'Baltra'.

There were to be 4,000 American troops based here, and the creation of the base represents a phenomenal civil-engineering effort. As we drove away from the airport in a rickety bus, bags and cases wobbling on our knees, I could clearly see the ghostly outline of parade squares and thoroughfares in the low scrub beside the road, with many of the buildings still standing, albeit as skeletal remains, the gaps of long-gone windows staring out over a landscape that is slowly reclaiming the memory of the activity that once took place there. Created on the principle of 'if you build it, they will come', the occupants waited for the enemy to appear, at first alert, then vigilant, then dutiful, then bored. As it turned out, not a great deal happened in the Galapagos during the course of the war, and on completion of hostilities, the US government handed the base over to Ecuador. But the genie was out of the bottle, and with the arrival of the Baltra airstrip there was suddenly a way for tourists to access the islands. A new chapter had begun, and soon travellers from around the world would be visiting in their thousands. The enthusiasm and devotion to the Galapagos of these early tourists would know no bounds.

Not that this enthusiasm was shared by the first person to ever arrive on the islands. Given that no ancient artefacts have ever been found on the Galapagos, history credits the discovery of the archipelago to one Tomás de Berlanga, Bishop of Panama. To say that he was unimpressed is an understatement.

The bishop was the envoy of His Imperial Catholic Majesty, King Charles I of Spain – essentially the king's representative in South America. He had set sail from Panama on 23 February 1535, on a voyage to Peru – a leisurely affair that should have taken only a couple of weeks. But the ship became becalmed in the doldrums of the equator, and found itself borne on the Panama Current directly out to sea, a situation that persisted for six whole days. This displeased the bishop greatly, but much as he appealed skywards to his superior, nothing could be done. And then, on 10 March, as they drifted through a vast blue vacuum off the edge of the chart, an island appeared. With only two days' water remaining, this was a welcome sight to say the least, and the bishop immediately dispatched a lifeboat with a small crew on board to find fresh water. Mankind was about to set foot on the Galapagos for the first time.

There is speculation that this first sight of landfall was the island of Espanola in the south-east of the archipelago. Having found no water for themselves, the crew set sail once again until they landed on nearby Floreana. Here again they initially found no fresh water, and then, after convening a hasty mass (the sixteenth-century equivalent of calling the emergency services), they finally found the spring that saved their lives.

Not that the bishop was particularly grateful to Floreana (an island that, even by Galapagos standards, would go on to have a particularly turbulent relationship with mankind). On the contrary, upon his return to Lima, the bishop wrote what can only be described as the first ever one-star TripAdvisor review in his report to the king. He didn't mince his words:

'On the whole island I do not think there is a place where one might sow a bushel of corn, because most of it is full of very big stones, so much so that it seems as though at some time God had showered stones. What earth there is like slag, worthless.'

But the bishop had got it wrong. What he had found was actually a veritable gold mine, a motherlode of natural wonders that would generate billions of dollars over the next five hundred years. The Galapagos was the gift that would keep on giving.

This ability to repel human invaders by the simple tactic of being a terrible, terrible place to live served the Galapagos well until mass tourism made its gaudy appearance in the latter half of the twentieth century. That's not to say that people did not display the full creative breadth of their destructive tendencies throughout the archipelago for the period preceding that. For the vast majority of our early association with the islands, the archipelago was viewed as nothing more than a larder, a place to pillage, somewhere to send the least desirable members of society, and a final destination for the foolhardy. Settlements sprang up and then self-destructed. Villains, rogues, whalers, pirates, dreamers and philanthropists all found their way to the Galapagos, and duly staked their claims. Giant tortoises were carted off in their hundreds of thousands to be consumed at leisure. Goats, cats, rats and pigs feasted on ground-nesting birds and slow-growing reptiles. The fur seal population was decimated, along with the whales that had visited the rich waters of the archipelago for millennia.

During the time of this, my first visit, to the Galapagos, many, many years later, the journey was considerably easier, and the reasons for making it were very different. Visitors come now to celebrate these islands, and to experience at first-hand what is widely recognised to be one of the most remarkable ecosystems on earth.

Having caught a bus, then a boat, then a taxi, we duly arrived in the main settlement of Puerto Ayora. Here we found a quaint port that was doing its best to become a town. The bulk of the buildings were clustered around the harbour itself, with the remainder spread along the shore. A short drive into the interior of Santa Cruz quickly saw the settlement thin out, rapidly giving way to arid scrubland. Essentially, this was a place made up of a sparse, colourful cluster of houses, shops and restaurants spread along the coast, with its brassy face to the sea and its seedy innards hidden away behind.

We settled into our accommodation – a basic set of villas built within a compound a stone's throw from the harbour. One of my first actions, on getting to my room, was to ease a large marine iguana to one side with my foot, as it was lying like a large draft excluder across the bottom of my door. It seemed unimpressed by this, and grumpily walked a few metres away before slumping back down on its belly with a pneumatic hiss. As a first encounter with the islands' famously reticent animal inhabitants, it was a pretty good one. Charles Darwin had a somewhat low opinion of the marine iguana, 'imps of darkness' being the less than flattering description he noted in his journal – a record of his voyage which became the spark for his truly seminal *On the Origin of Species*, published a full twenty-four years after his exploration of the Galapagos – but I thought the iguana looked amazing, and stood for some time staring at it with my head on one side. Meanwhile, it was looking straight back at me. My expression said 'I am agog to be in the presence of a piece of living history, a true global icon.' In return, the iguana's expression said 'I am literally so apathetic about you that I can barely keep my eyes open.'

This is an odd sensation for a human being. To be viewed with mild disdain by a member of the animal kingdom is somewhat disconcerting. We are used to being eyed with either transparent fear (most wild animals), occasional aggression (any animal defending itself, which is frequently required, when mankind is on the scene) or unfettered devotion (most domestic creatures). But to be viewed with casual indifference is distinctly odd and, of course, is one of the defining features of the Galapagos. To have an animal regard you without fear is truly Utopian stuff, particularly if you have an interest in natural history. This is one of the reasons the islands can be so life altering, as a realisation dawns on the visitor that they are just another member of the animal kingdom. This conveys a feeling of acceptance, of arrival in a place where our previous crimes against our fellow creatures can be erased (which is deeply ironic, considering our charge sheet in these islands is long and particularly bloody).

Our guide for the week-long shoot was a dashing young man called Maccaron, a fisherman turned diver. This was in itself a sign of the rapid transition that was taking place in the islands – a poacher turned gamekeeper generating income through celebrating the world around him, as opposed to exploiting it for food and financial gain. He had olive skin, jet-black hair, a big smile, talked with his hands, and a manner that brought the environment to life as he spoke. I liked him from the moment I met him, as I suspected most people did.

We spent a week scouring the shallows, diving and snorkeling through a world described by underwater pioneer William Beebe as 'overflowing with surfeit of colour'. The filming of the penguins was completed early, and with great success. However, it was a dive on the final day that revealed yet another side to these islands. It provided a glimpse of the bipolar nature of the Galapagos, of the ancient ferocity beneath the thin façade of modern gentility.

Maccaron had decided to take us to Gordon Rocks, a dive location renowned for big-animal encounters. The reason was simple enough – cleaving the rocks in two was a deep channel, through which the sea was siphoned as the tides turned. This created a constriction that formed what was essentially an undersea river, bringing food and oxygen-saturated cooler water to the reefs and undersea cliffs of the site. As such, marine animals were drawn here from miles around.

We rocked and rolled our way to the site in a local boat that seemed to be a fusion of a fishing vessel and a garden shed, settling in the lee of one of the great, steepling rock faces to kit up. The cliff towered overhead, a sentinel in the surrounding sea, with the waves hissing and frothing at its base, and flocks of birds swirling in a chaotic tornado in the blue skies above. It was something of an apocalyptic scene, thrilling and desolate.

'I'm . . . errrr . . . not too sure about this actually,' said Richard, our main cameraman, who was helping out with some of the underwater filming. He eyed the green waves and white foam that stood in sharp peaks and ran off the base of the cliff in seething torrents. 'You know what? I'm not going in. Sod it.'

Richard had a refreshing honesty, and a commendable approach to plunging into situations that had the potential to get out of hand (i.e. this one).

Although we had completed recording the bulk of the penguin sequences, there were still some fairly iconic animals we wanted to capture on film in our remaining time – hammerheads, mantas, eagle rays – all creatures for which Gordon Rocks is famed. Maccaron, myself and Simon – the team's specialist underwater cameraman – peered over the side. As we did so a standing wave leapt up, a pillar of ocean trying to engulf us all before dashing us against the rocks in an eclectic explosion of flailing limbs and neoprene.

'We'll be fine, just fine,' said Simon, abruptly turning away and busying himself with his equipment.

'You're right,' I agreed, *sotto voce*. 'It's all on the surface anyway. Be fine once we get deeper.'

Maccaron nodded firmly, and we duly began to kit up. This was, of course, a classic 'we've come this far and might as well try it' exchange, the type that has got an awful lot of people in an awful lot of trouble over the years. In a world of natural selection and survival of the fittest, we were about to stress test Darwin's dearly held view that not responding appropriately to your environment is invariably fatal.

At first, the dive went well. We kicked hard for the bottom, a strip of white sand beneath us akin to a runway. Settling on the seabed, we took a moment to check our gear, signalled to each other that all was well, and rose as one to glide along the rock wall alongside us. This was pitted and cracked by wave action, scoured by millions of years of moving water and barrelling tides.

Looking out into the channel, I immediately saw one of the most distinctive silhouettes in the natural world – the metronomic progress of a hammerhead shark through the water column, with that flattened head rocking gently from side to side as it patrolled the channel. There are a great many theories as to why this extraordinary adaptation has developed – as an aquaplane to aid manoeuvrability, as an underwater radar to scan the sea bed, or as a way of assisting the senses by spreading the eyes and nostrils. The truth is that nobody really knows, which in itself is a rather wonderful thing in this day and age. Whatever the reason might be, an approaching hammerhead is one of the most unmistakable and bewitching sights of the sea.

We hung close to the wall and watched the shark for a moment, and it was soon joined by several others. We drifted with them, the cliff passing alongside in a glorious moment of underwater flight as we hugged its contours on undersea thermals. I glanced across to see Simon behind the camera, the red recording light glowing like a firefly in the viewfinder.

The combination of the depth and the current, detectable even though we were thirty metres below the surface, meant that we were working hard and soon ran low on air. Maccaron signalled that our time was up, and as a group we moved away from the wall into the blue and ascended to hang just below the surface – a decompression stop on the way back to the boat. As we smiled at one another – feeling very much like mighty ocean pioneers – I saw something rather odd in the distance behind Simon. It looked rather like a column of bubbles, writhing and spinning towards us, stretching from the surface all the way into dark water beneath. I'd never seen anything quite like it, and as it came closer, I tapped Simon on the shoulder so he too could turn and watch its progress. And then, in a moment, it was upon us, and all hell broke loose.

This spinning sirocco of bubbles was, in fact, an immensely powerful localised whirlpool that was barrelling through the narrow channel between the rocks. This great pulse of water, a sonic boom of energy and mass, picked us up and hurled us through the water column. We were contorted and twisted, completely out of control as we accelerated towards the open sea, the rock face passing in a blur alongside us. Alarmingly we were also being driven deeper, and I looked up to see Simon hanging on to the bulky camera housing with one hand, while trying to grab a passing rock with the other. Maccaron also hove into view, looking remarkably calm for a man who was upside down and gyrating in a carousel of dive fins and bubbles.

All of this would have been disconcerting at any time of the dive, but as it had happened at the end, none of us had much air left. This was a singularly distracting thought as we hurtled deeper, and I glanced at my gauge to note that I had only minutes remaining in my cylinder. If the current didn't release us, we would all be in genuine trouble, as there was absolutely no way we could fight our way to the surface against it. Down currents are something every diver dreads: underwater waterfalls that drive you deeper and deeper into the blue. I looked around me to see that the bubbles of my exhalations were going sideways, hanging motionless, or disappearing beneath me. They were going anywhere but upwards, and as the light of the surface faded from view our situation was becoming very, very serious.

And then, just as swiftly as it had started, the water stilled.

The whirlpool had travelled beyond the narrow channel and out into the open ocean, and without the constraints of the rock walls on either side, its power had dissipated, melting away into the blue spaces of the Pacific. By now I was alone, and pushed hard for the surface, breaking through just as the regulator tightened in my mouth with the last breath of air. In the distance I could see Maccaron, waving an arm at the boat to collect us. But there was no sign of Simon.

The boat clattered towards us, a rolling mother duck bustling urgently to her offspring. We clambered aboard, and immediately began to scan the surrounding water for Simon, and then – to my immense relief – I heard Maccaron shout 'There!', and, following his outstretched arm, saw Simon's head bobbing at the surface. The boat turned towards him, and soon we were alongside.

It would seem that we had escaped unscathed, but as the boat slowed to pick him up, I could see that his face was contorted in pain. As we helped him aboard, he grimaced and pointed at his ear, shaking his head before gingerly sitting down.

In that initial violent surge, driving us uncontrollably deeper, the abrupt change of pressure had ruptured his ear drum. He was in excruciating pain, and, although he was subsequently treated at the decompression chamber at Puerto Ayora, his diving for that trip, and indeed several months afterwards, was over.

Whenever one dives in the Galapagos, there is always a nagging thought that a brush with a big current is a possibility – no one jumps into the sea here without knowing that. Bruised, battered and somewhat chastened, I reflected on the fact that we had just encountered perhaps the most significant force of all in the islands, a truly defining factor in the unique Galapagos ecosystem.

The great ocean currents that meet at the archipelago, made up of billions of tonnes of seawater in motion, are one of the major forces that shape the Galapagos Islands' character. The islands are a junction for five major currents, and every one of them brings a different element to the shoreline against which they fetch. This is one of the reasons the Galapagos were christened 'Los Islas Enchantas' – The Enchanted Isles – by the early mariners, baffled as they were by the unpredictability of the tides, the startling difference in water temperatures, and the swirling eddies that danced and chuckled around their wooden hulls. Such differences in water temperature also created swirling mists and shifting fog banks that swept in to cover islands that only moments before had been crystal clear on the bows. Surely only witchcraft could create such a bizarre place, with vanishing islands, with water that came to life, and where even the land was populated by hordes of hissing reptilian forms.

The reality might be slightly less supernatural, but it is nonetheless just as wondrous. The climate and ecosystem of the Galapagos are anomalous to the archipelago's position straddling the equator, and indeed the characters of the individual islands vary to a considerable degree from west to east and north to south. All of this is down to seas brought from distant climes and rising from deep water, different habitats transported magically to this one location far off the Ecuadorian coast.

From the south-east comes the Humboldt Current, bringing not only cold water but also residents like the penguin. From the west the Equatorial Undercurrent rises from the nutrient-rich deep oceanic plains, bringing cool seas full of oxygen to wash the coast of Isabela – hence the reason this island has water temperatures as much as ten degrees colder than the rest of the archipelago. Then there is also the confluence of the Peru Ocean Current from the south and the Cromwell Current from the west, the Panama Current from the north-east, the South Equatorial Current from the east, and, just to complete the thoroughly chaotic mosaic of different water bodies, of different temperatures, going at different speeds and coming from different directions, there is the North Equatorial Current and its sibling, the North Equatorial Counter Current.

The result is a layer cake of differing temperatures throughout the island group, from east to west, from north to south, and from deep water to the shallows. This mind-bogglingly complex picture is further complicated by climate events such as El Niño, the periodic warming of the waters that occurs every three to six years. This can have a catastrophic effect on the array of creatures that rely on feeding from the shallows, including iconic Galapagoan animals such as penguins, sea lions and iguanas, with only the strongest surviving as their food source either vanishes completely or moves into colder, deeper water. This is evolution in fast forward, natural selection at its most uncompromising.

I had experienced being in the grip of these momentous factors that drive evolution here, had been a helpless planktonic presence in a violent ocean, held in its grip like a leaf in a storm. It had a profound effect on me, giving me a sense of scale, of my own mortality, and of the elemental forces that shape the islands and their inhabitants. And so, as I departed the islands in 2001, I did so an altogether wiser man, my perceptions of the world around me altered irreversibly.

This basket-case of an archipelago, where the animals ignore you, the ground beneath your feet is convulsed in volcanic folds, and the sea spins you round before spitting you out, had me in its grasp. My impressions were of something uncompromising, stark and utterly compelling, and as I mounted the steps of the aircraft at Baltra to begin the long journey home, I vowed to return.

The Tree House in the Cloud Forest

Once again I had my face pressed against the aircraft window as we banked over the Pacific, trying to catch a first glimpse of dark rocks in a blue sea. Sixteen years had passed since my first visit, and although I had travelled to the Galapagos twice more in that period, I had done so only for short periods guiding groups of tourists. This in itself was rewarding, as there are few experiences more satisfying than witnessing the transformative effect the islands can have on those visiting for the first time, but although I had studied the islands from afar and become involved in raising funds for their conservation, I still felt that such knowledge remained superficial, and a real period of study was required.

Such a study would surely mean an immersive stay on the

islands, and, in early 2017, just such an opportunity had presented itself. After nearly two decades of belonging to a conservation group that specialised in working in the islands – the Galapagos Conservation Trust – I had ascended the greasy pole to the degree that I was now its president. This role is a largely symbolic one, and is more than anything a reward for turning up, however it is also a lifetime commitment. I was reassured by the fact that one can only be edged aside by assassination or a coup, but nonetheless also felt that, in order to earn my spurs, I really should try to understand not only the work being undertaken by the trust itself, but also the nature of the challenges faced by the islands.

As such I was travelling to live in the Galapagos for three months, and was not doing so alone. In stark contrast to any of my other Galapagos experiences, this time I had my family noisily in tow.

To the fore was Isla – five years old, and with a great deal to say for herself. I do appreciate the (entirely justified) insinuation of bias here, but Isla is rather splendid in a number of ways. First off, she's nice. Just a decent, all round, good-egg kind of nice. She tries hard, is polite (to strangers and figures of authority – not to me, obviously), and is also a compassionate soul. And she loves animals and what she broadly describes as 'the nature'. She is also – just out of interest – freakishly strong. One bored and sleepless morning I took her to the local gym, the idea being that she would play with a yoga ball while I huffed and puffed ineffectually on various whirring machines. But she was having none of it, and worked her way systematically along the rack of dumbbells, hefting each one from its place and lifting it to chest height. I intervened when she got to the 25kg weight, and effectively banned her from lifting any other ones, much to her noisy chagrin. It was only as I lifted the dumbbell back into the rack that it dawned on me that it might be unusual for a five-year-old girl to be chucking about things that weigh, in old money, 55lbs. She also shows admirable restraint in not using her formidable strength to systematically dismantle her younger sister, the carrot-topped, blue-eyed, alabaster-skinned Celtic warrior who is Molly.

Molly is three, and quite reasonably has yet to develop many emotions beyond those at the most elemental level. But there is one sense of hers that has evolved way beyond her tender years, and that is protocol when it comes to dress sense. Dressing down for Molls, what she might term 'smart casual', if she knew the term existed, is a three-quarter-length chiffon dress. But as a rule, for day-to-day wear, she prefers a full-length ballgown and a tiara. This applies to every situation and environment, from a sandpit to nursery school. True, it can make scaling certain obstacles at the local adventure park near our home in Devon a tad challenging, but standards are standards. She also has a wicked laugh, an absurdly well-developed sense of humour, and plays me like a cheap violin.

Finally there is Tam, their mum and my wife. She is very much the still point in our turning world as a family, being resourceful, serene, gentle, calm and – for the vast majority of the time anyway – easy going. Although born in London, she has Irish ancestry, with a hint of red hair, a glimmer of emerald in her eyes, and an occasional combative streak – a characteristic of which the other 75% of the family are well aware. As such we do our collective best to avoid seeing the glint of battle appear in her eye, and settle instead on trying to stay on her good side, which is very good indeed. Failing that, we immediately blame the others when things go wrong. She too is passionate about the natural world, and indeed we had cemented our relationship on a trip to the Maldives, where I watched her dance and pirouette with a giant manta ray during a dive, two figures twisting in complete harmony within a sapphire stage. 'Now that's the girl for me,' I thought.

It is said that there is never a good time to change jobs or move house and I had the distinct feeling that we were combining both in a perfect storm of discombobulation as we had packed up the week before. The children had some very clear ideas of their own about what would be required for our placement on the islands, which included a number of favoured toys – Woof, Jingles, Wobbly and Cobbler, to name but four – as well as key items such as princess outfits and paintings from school. Every time I packed a piece of diving equipment or photography gear, I would find it surreptitiously removed, to be replaced by a wooden unicorn or a toy hairdryer. As such packing had proved emotional, but somehow we had all reached an uneasy compromise, one that seemed to involve a colossal number of bags, the contents of which were a complete mystery to me. I just knew they were heavy, and it was my job to carry them.

As the aircraft banked on the final approach, I glanced across at Tam, and noted that she too was now looking out of the aircraft window, with Isla using her own head as a woolly battering ram to get her eye up to a section of glass so she too could get a first glimpse of the islands as they appeared beneath us.

In 2001, I had flown here on one of only four flights a month

– now we were arriving on one of the forty that landed at Baltra every week. The archipelago had a population of 7,000 on my first visit, and was now home to 30,000. I was about to enter a world transformed.

I walked slowly down the steps of the aircraft, a moment of arrival that proved too much for Molly, over-tired and fractious. She made her feelings plain, bellowing at the indignity of it all as I tucked her under one arm and stepped down on to the warm tarmac. I could hardly blame her. It is a very long way indeed from Dartmouth to Baltra, after all. Isla followed, clutching the railing and looking thoughtful as that warm equatorial wind raced unfettered across the runway, ruffling her hair and carrying with it the scent of a different world. In a parallel reaction to my own all those years previously, I saw her lift her head and breathe deeply, the primal response of a young animal to an entirely new environment. Tam followed at the rear in her role as 'tail-end charlie', watching warily for anyone attempting to make a break for it.

As we walked along the gravel path that led to the terminal, I reached back and held her hand.

'Welcome to the Galapagos,' I said. She smiled, and squeezed my hand in return.

Here we stood, the latest pilgrims to cross the world to pay homage. Such moments are precious and important, and should be appreciated as a family – however our arrival was about to go a tad pear shaped. Directly in front of me, held in the crook of my arm at chest height, was Molly. Directly behind me, wheeled along the floor, was my cabin bag. Both were about to have a significant impact on my arrival.

Molly loved this bag very much, and was wont to empty out the contents and fill it with hay when we were at home. This provided a nest for her toys/animals/self. Despite my rigorously policing this activity, Molls was capable of moving entirely covertly when required, and had done so as I had packed for this trip. As such there was hay in my bag. Just enough to provide a comfortable refuge during the trip for a small teddy bear. This, as I was about to find out, was a not insignificant amount.

Biosecurity in the Galapagos has moved on exponentially since my first visit, a recognition of the scale of the threat invasive species represent. Gone was the laid-back local, to be replaced with a formidable team of officials who minutely examined numerous bags, and scrutinised every passing visitor. That one of them happened to have brought what was essentially a small bale straight from Devon was not, as it happened, destined to go down well.

A smiling man in uniform welcomed me warmly to the islands, then gestured that I should place my case on the desk in front of him. He duly opened the lid, to reveal the contents. Granted, there were lots of other things in the bag, but straw definitely featured strongly, poking out between spare underwear, books and camera gear. The equivalent to this might have been, for example, my proudly presenting the official with a sack of ferrets, or perhaps going 'Ta-da!' as I lifted a pair of vigorously mating racoons on to the counter.

During the following hour, the customs official displayed the complete range of emotions. From a brisk start of warm welcome, we accelerated through to furrowed concentration, galloped straight into mild concern, and then streaked into the final furlong of 'What were you thinking?' annoyance. Throughout I stood before him as a broken man, rumbled, busted, and then lavishly told off. I was eventually allowed in, chastened and shuffling, which was preferable to being horsewhipped back on to the aircraft, which had at one point seemed a distinct possibility.

All of this fuss was entirely justified, as what might seem an entirely innocent mistake could have had lasting consequences. Introduced and invasive plants and animals are probably the number-one threat to the Galapagos. Although Herculean efforts have been made to control the arrival of species from the mainland and the rest of the world, it is a constant battle. There are at least thirty species of vertebrates that have been introduced to the islands by people, either deliberately (goats, dogs, cats, cows, horses) or inadvertently (rats, mice). There are also a staggering 870 species of plants that have been introduced (there were only 600 or so native species here in the first place). To understand the importance of this and the threat it represents, one must first understand the different types of invaders, and indeed the broad classification of every creature that calls the Galapagos its home.

In terms of their origins and behaviour, there are essentially four different types of living things on the islands. The first – and some might say the purest category – are the 'endemic' species. These are found here and nowhere else on earth: marine iguanas and flightless cormorants, for example. The Galapagos has a huge percentage of endemic species compared to anywhere else in the world. We then have 'native' species, found on the islands as original inhabitants, but also found elsewhere in the world: red-footed boobies and frigate birds are good examples, in this case. We then have 'introduced' species, not necessarily a bad thing, but nonetheless not native to the islands, having been brought over by man either deliberately or accidentally: coffee, orange trees or pineapples (you'll notice that most introduced species are edible, or benefit man in some way). Finally, we have 'invasive' species, which are bad news all round, looking for trouble, and keen on dominating their particular niche. They are the Vikings of the environment, with aggressive strategies that broker no competition. Examples of these include goats, pigs or the more virulent plant species, such as guava.

By way of an illustration, imagine you are a farmer in the highlands of Santa Cruz who wants to tend a crop of cucumbers on the island. You'll bring some over from the mainland, plant them in the fabulously fertile soil, and sit back happily to watch them grow. You tend them, guard them, and make sure they don't spread. This is a classic introduced species – not ideal, obviously, as in a perfect world no one at all would live on the islands and cucumbers would not be required, but where there are people, there will be farms, and where there are farms, there will be crops, and (at a basic level) that's all there is to it.

But suppose that same farmer tires of cucumbers, and wants to make jam? Then we have a problem. He decides to introduce Hill Raspberry to his little plot, and sits back once again, gleefully anticipating all manner of tart-based excitement (steady now) over the coming months.

The snag is that Hill Raspberry, unlike the mild and mellow cucumber, has an attitude problem. It's rather like introducing a tiger to your back garden and expecting it to sit tight when there are vast tracts of forest nearby to explore. Hill Raspberry – or *Rubus niveus*, if you want to be scientific about it – has a highly aggressive life cycle when it comes to invading neighbouring territory. Under the horrified gaze of the farmer and his cucumbers, the raspberry sends out tendrils, covered in thorns, and duly strangles, tangles and covers the surrounding plant species. The farmer can't keep up, and before he knows it the brambles are running amok, a viral presence spreading up and over the hills around him. And, from a simple desire to have something different in the diet, we suddenly have a species that threatens entire orders of native and endemic plants.

This is an example of an invasive species that has been deliberately introduced, but the majority nowadays come into the islands accidentally. These will be in the form of seeds in travellers' clothing or luggage, insects hidden away in imported food, or marine creatures and plants on ships' hulls or in their bilge water. Or perhaps in the form of straw from Devon in the luggage of an imbecile.

Therefore, it was a rather quiet trip from the airport on Baltra Island to what was to be our home for the next three months. I sat fuming in silent indignation, glancing reproachfully into the rear-view mirror at Molly as she peered out of the car window, looking angelic and innocent.

To travel from the airport to our home for our stay in Galapagos required a short ferry trip from Baltra, the island on which the airstrip is located, to the much larger island of Santa Cruz. Once there, we loaded our bags into a waiting hire car, and commenced the drive along the main highway that runs all the way from the northern tip to the main town of Puerto Ayora, a ribbon of tarmac that stretched ahead of us into the highlands and beyond. This lofty, rich, mystical world at altitude in the Galapagos is one that bewitched Darwin, and has held a powerful attraction for every biologist, botanist and geologist ever since. From the road at the coastline – an arid, relatively barren landscape – we could see our route ahead, with the road seeming to travel directly into the clouds themselves. This stirred something in all of us, jet lagged and bone weary as we were, creating the seductive thought of traversing a route snaking up the flanks of an old volcano into a forest shrouded in thick mist – faces were duly pressed up against the car windows, eager for the show to begin.

It swiftly became obvious that we were indeed entering another world, with the transition from the arid coastal plain to the fertile forests of the highlands happening at bewildering speed. The Galapagos Islands are basically five different ecosystems, from sea level to mountain-top. This dizzying complexity is part of the unique nature of the islands, and is the engine that drives such fundamental changes between similar species on the different islands. Add to the picture the prevailing winds and occasional large-scale climatic events, and of course the ocean currents, and one can begin to see why scientists have been so drawn to the Galapagos over the years. The proximity of such wildly variable environments, frequently inhabited by species that appear superficially similar but have actually had to develop subtle adaptations to cope with the unique ecosystems around them, make the archipelago an evolutionary biologist's dream.

In terms of altitude, from sea level to mountain-top can be broken down into five distinct regions. The first of these is the tidal zone – perhaps the harshest of all in terms of rapid change. Animals and plants don't particularly like change, as it requires them to adapt quickly and makes life rather stressful. And nowhere changes more rapidly than the space between the tides.

During the course of a single day, an animal or plant might be underwater (as the tide rolls in), then exposed to the air (as the tide goes out), dealing with the searing heat of the midday sun, and then the frigid waters of a cold current. Then there is the high salinity of the ocean, followed by the freshwater of the rain. Essentially, anything that lives in this region is a specialist – the mangrove, the Sally Lightfoot crab, the marine iguana – and has developed a battery of physiological adaptations to deal with the extremes of daily life.

The second environment is infinitely more stable, and makes up the bulk of the Galapagos Islands. This is the dry zone, home to cactus and land iguana, beyond the direct reach of the ocean and yet still under its influence. Higher still is the transition zone, where the prevailing conditions are dry, which means that the plants here are drought tolerant. The next layer – the humid zone – is the zone with regular rainfall, and as such most closely resembles what we would think of as a forest. These forests consist in the main of Scalesia trees, which are essentially daisies that are ten metres tall (which seems to be a classically eccentric Galapagos approach – why have a normal forest when you can have an entirely unique one?). Only seven islands in the whole archipelago have enough altitude to create a humid zone. And, finally, there is the high-altitude dry zone, which bears an uncanny resemblance to the dry zone by the coast, and is inhabited by very similar plant species that have a head for heights.

We had arranged to take over a house on the southern side of the island – the airport is just off Santa Cruz's northern tip – and so had to traverse all the way through this fertile, emerald wilderness. As we entered the cloud base I turned the wipers on, our progress punctuated by the regular thunk of the rain being whipped off the windscreen. Feverish anticipation demanded that we should see – at least – several giant tortoises and possibly a volcanic eruption or two, but a steady twenty-minute drive actually revealed two horses and a damp cow. Somewhat deflated, the children sat back and looked sullenly ahead with hollow eyes, adrenaline giving way to fatigue. Tam turned to me and smiled wearily.

'I was kind of expecting it to be a bit more . . .'

'Sunny? Tortoisy? Iguanay? I know what you mean,' I said. 'Don't worry, we've got a lot of islands to explore, and lots of time to do it. Let's see what the house is like first.'

We were living just outside a village called Bella Vista, five kilometres away from Puerto Ayora. Our route soon took us off the main highway, and along a dirt road, a deep ochre track meandering through shining jungle. This was a bit more like it, and morale perked up in the car once again. Soon the track turned to a narrow lane, with the undergrowth brushing and snatching at the car as we rattled along for the final few hundred yards. It was akin to burrowing through the jungle itself, creating our own tunnel like some colossal metal beetle.

Soon a pair of large wooden gates appeared – truly journey's end. We climbed out of the car and I opened the gates. Leaving the luggage, we made our yawning, stumbling progress up the path to our home for the next few months. I had booked this through a local contact on the islands, and had no idea what it might look like. I held my breath as we walked through a garden crowded with tangled undergrowth, and up a dark path of lava rocks that weaved erratically up a gentle slope.

The house slowly revealed itself before us, and to our collective delight turned out to be a vast, impossibly splendid tree house. When you're five and three years old, to discover that you'll be living in a tree house for several months might be the greatest thing that has ever happened to anyone anywhere. It's pretty exciting if you're fifty as well, actually, and after gawping at it for a few awestruck moments, I turned the key in the lock and pushed the door open.

Molly and Isla ran in before me, their feet pattering on the wooden floors. Facing us was a huge area of balcony, with a view that showed the island falling away before us all the way to the distant coast and Puerto Ayora itself. The main structure was set out from the hill slightly, with the arthritic old boughs of the trees into which it was built twisting through its framework, making it an integral part of the forest around it. One look at it made me realise that we would be far from alone during our residency – there was no doubt at all that we would get to know the huge huntsman spiders native to the forests that surrounded us, as well as (exhilaratingly) the fire ants, scorpions, black widows, and, best of all, the giant centipedes. The latter is a nightmare of scuttling nastiness – 30cm long, with large fangs, a toxic bite and a bad reputation. I had researched these extensively before coming out to the islands during an ashen-faced lonely late-night Google horror show, and had developed visions of Molly being carried off wriggling into the undergrowth. She had a habit – as a curious three-year-old raised in the amiable surrounds of the English countryside – of picking up every insect she sees. As some of the insects she was going to be meeting for the next few months had a battery of chemical weapons, or could simply tear your arm off and beat you to death with it, then this was a habit that I imagined was going to be short lived. Or she would be. This house – crawling with hairy and scuttling life – was going to be a perfect setting for this noisy and entertaining drama to be played out over the next few months.

The view from the balcony, glimpsed through huge trees with dark canopies that reduced the space beneath to a gloomy, atmospheric cavern, allowed us to see all the way down the gently sloping landscape to the coast. This presented a finches' eye view of the different zones that typify the Galapagos Islands' land-based ecosystem, with the highlands (green and fertile) leading into the inland plains (arid and scrub strewn), before the coast itself (wild, beautiful, dark, impossibly dramatic).

But any excursions into these environments would have to wait. For the time being, we decided to use the last remaining vestiges of the family energy to unpack and settle in. Tam and I spent the next hour carefully removing everything from the cases, while Isla laid out her dolls on her bed and Molly, for reasons best known to herself, vigorously bounced on our double mattress while bellowing at the ceiling.

I would love to say that we spent the rest of that evening sitting on the balcony, with me carefully identifying the local birds through their song, and with Tam weaving a hammock out of banana leaves and rattan. Sadly, this didn't happen – instead we slept in our clothes, all waking simultaneously at 3am to pace the house like pale spirits, eagerly awaiting dawn and breakfast.

The islands straddle the equator, so dawn arrives every day at 6am pretty much on the dot. At the other end of the day, you might be working in the garden in broad daylight at 5:45pm, only to find yourself fumbling your way back to the house in complete darkness at 6pm. The sun doesn't so much rise and set, as leap out of the sea, race across the sky, then plunge back into the water precisely twelve hours later. This is actually rather lovely, as it means your body clock becomes completely diurnal, and we would rarely make it past nine o'clock in the evening throughout our time in Galapagos, and would always be up at six.

For this first morning, we were all lined up on the balcony wearing a singularly eccentric collection of clothing, watching the first light of dawn touch a distant horizon. Within moments this pale gilding of the sky had turned into a luminous glow, and before us the forest started to come to life. A mockingbird stirred itself in the wide spread of a huge balsa tree in the middle of the garden, settling on a high branch, ruffling its feathers, and greeting the day with a clear, high song. The golden light sped across the tree tops and raced through the plain beneath, and even Puerto Ayora, for a brief moment, looked appealing in the forgiving sun of a new equatorial day. And then, even as we watched, daylight was upon us, and the children stirred and shifted in what seemed like an ancient response to the sudden security of light and warmth, a celebration of the survival of another night.

It was time to go exploring.

Some things are truly universal, and one of them is the bedlam that ensues before departing a house with small children. It felt strangely comforting to go through the familiar routine of lost shoes, fights over sun hats, and adamant refusal to wear sun cream. As we finally ushered the girls out of the door, I took in the view one last time. Puerto Ayora, now in the full light of day, clearly showed through the leafy canopy as an untidy sprawl of concrete buildings scattered along the coastline. Even from this distance, it had the look of a boom town, a frontier settlement built in haste and populated without planning or forethought. From our lofty viewpoint, it seemed to be spreading into the forests and foothills surrounding it, rampant and unfettered. In the midst of a view of staggering drama and beauty, it was a vivid scar, a lesion announcing man's presence in the islands.

This seemed as good a place as any to begin our acquaintance with the islands, and so the yawning, scratching, bleary-eyed Halls stumbled out of the front door and made our way through the overgrown garden to the car.

This turned out to be my first brush with one of the most pervasive, insidious and threatening of any of the invasive species making themselves at home in Galapagos. All of them are, of course, bad news, but some of them are spectacularly so. I was about to meet one of the most alarming.

Molly, as was her wont from time to time, vigorously protested about being put into the child seat in the back of the car, noting at some volume that she wanted to be in the front or (ideally) driving. Molly's tactic during these situations is to arch her back and brace her legs, in effect becoming a banana-shaped arc of sinew and tensed muscle of surprising resilience. As I wrestled and cajoled her into the seat, I became aware of an exhilarating prickling sensation on my (flip-flopped) feet. This sensation appeared to be working its way up my ankles, and glancing down I noticed that I was standing on a trail of ants. They had taken exception to this, and were attempting to devour me.

This situation – braced toddler at the top, livid insects at the bottom – resulted in a series of vigorous bodily convulsions on my part. Molly was soon strapped into her seat, slightly stunned at the vigour with which her dad had bundled her into the car, and was now watching him prance in the road slapping his ankles, a scene that cheered her up no end.

The reason for all this merriment was that Dad was being attacked by tropical fire ants. This tiny ant, only a millimetre or so in length, was first reported in the islands as long ago as 1891, and even for the keen entomologist there is pretty much nothing nice you can say about it. One can admire, in a grudging type of way, its remarkable ability to dominate its environment, but when that domination includes feasting on turtle eggs, tortoise eggs (and the young of both species), bird hatchlings, as well as other insect species – and indeed my feet – then the enormity of its destructive impact becomes apparent. A 2014 report by the Pacific Coast Entomological Society found it in seven islands and eleven islets around the archipelago, occupying 115 different locations (up from only three in the 1980s). That represents a terrifying rate of dispersion, and once in place it has proved to be very, very hard to shift. The impact on human populations has been marked – no one works the land or their gardens in sandals in the highlands of the Galapagos – whereas the impact on the resident animals, birds and insects is yet to be realised, but has the potential to be somewhat apocalyptic. I reflected on this rather sombre fact as I itched my way down the large road into Puerto Ayora.

After an exhilarating drive through the outskirts of the town (through a one-way system of such fiendish complexity that I seemed to be approaching the seafront like an airliner in a holding pattern) we finally made it to the harbour, and I parked the car. I removed my ashen-faced family and announced that – in the finest traditions of British visitors anywhere overseas – we were about to promenade along the seafront.

In line with the theme of the day, this saunter along the bustling walkways of Puerto Ayora led us through the technicolour heart of the most pervasive of all invasive life-forms in the islands – people. There is much speculation about which species is most significant here, but it is a largely theoretical one. It is man alone who will decide the future of the Galapagos. Such a future will only be positive if we begin to show restraint, to curb our worst excesses of greed, and to understand that sometimes the most important decisions are the least popular ones.

The sea front at Puerto Ayora is not perhaps the optimum location to entertain such philosophical thoughts, for here is a town that has seen a rush of speculators that would have graced any clapperboard community in the Wild West, with exponential growth that now mines a rich seam of tourist gold. We were walking through what was essentially a theme park celebrating what has made these islands so special, full of tired vendors who peddled an approximation of the Galapagos through the medium of t-shirts and stuffed sea lions. Most did so with the weariness inspired by having an entirely captive customer base, raising a half smile as I handed over a fistful of dollars for a cheap (in quality, not price) souvenir. It is difficult to comprehend how a town of 18,000 people could have grown up so quickly in a World Heritage Site, unfettered, it seems, by regulation or sanity. Today 90% of the population of Santa Cruz island, of which Puerto Ayora is the capital, are not native to the islands. When I visited in 2001, the town was still relatively small and self contained, confident in its identity as a fishing harbour first, and a tourist centre second. Now it is a sprawling, noisy, bustling metropolis, with taxis plying their trade along the seafront and bars blaring out tinny rap music that is whisked away on the warm sea winds towards a horizon filled with an armada of tour boats – white-hulled invaders massed for constant action.

Population growth on the Galapagos is a matter of huge concern, and yet there are two over-riding factors that provide a glimmer of hope. One is rather prosaic, and the other is absurdly miraculous.

The first factor concentrates not so much on population growth as population density. The glorious hostility of these islands – in the main rocky, waterless, arid and barren – mean that human settlement has historically been almost impossible on all but four of the islands: Isabela, Santa Cruz, San Cristóbal and Floreana. This leaves the rest of the islands without any form of human settlement whatsoever. Add to this the fact that the Ecuadorian government has had the foresight to declare 98% of the total land area of Galapagos a National Park, and we have the unique situation of a substantial archipelago in the modern world that remains the realm of plants and animals, and not of man. Even with a current population of 30,000, if one takes the entire surface area of the islands – about $8,000km^2$, thanks for asking – the density of human population throughout the entire archipelago is only 3.5 people per square kilometre.

To give this context, it is necessary to examine other oceanic islands throughout the world. Let's take, for example, Hawaii. Here, there is a population density of 48 per km^2. It is no coincidence whatsoever that, while the population has boomed, 114 species have become extinct throughout the Hawaiian island chain since 1973, giving the islands the unofficial, and unwelcome, title of the extinction capital of the world. And it is not alone – Mauritius is another volcanic island group, with a surface area of only 1,865 km^2 and yet a population of 1.3 million (that's 466 people per km^2, by the way). It has lost 130 species since it was colonised. As such, you begin to see why, in a crowded modern world, the Galapagos Islands are such a gem.

The second factor is the ever present and much lauded fact that the resident animals have not twitched a whisker or ruffled a feather as man has moved in. They have simply moved slightly to one side, glanced at us in annoyance, and got on with their day-to-day routine. Here is an archipelago where man and animal can (and do) live in harmony – it is just a question of figuring out the most effective way to make that happen for future generations of them, and of us.

In perhaps the most miraculous demonstration of this tolerance of mankind, in Puerto Ayora the sea lions, iguanas, boobies, pelicans and frigate birds have all remained firmly in place even as the town has grown so rapidly around them. What was once lava rocks next to green mangroves might now be a pavement next to a bistro, and yet the iguanas still crouch in the warmth of the sun – stolid, immovable, indifferent. The benches on the jetty are ideal haul-out points for sea lions, who plainly feel that they have been put there specifically for them (and when you see one stretched out, eyes shut, snoring, and scratching blissfully, it does make you reflect that the shape of your average bench is pretty much spot on for the flippers and flatulence that are an essential part of sea lions' make up). A steady stream of tourists and traders bustle along the jetty, essentially walking straight through what was once their colony, and yet the sea lions don't move a muscle beyond occasionally opening one eye in annoyance should the noise levels become excessive.

For Isla and Molly, this was a land from a fairytale, a place where pelicans waddled, dinosaurs sun-bathed, and giants slept. The proximity of these animals was at first frightening, and I felt a small pink hand slip into mine as we began to walk. Then it became intriguing, then wondrous, then truly, truly joyful. The hand duly slipped out of mine, and a patter of bare feet made their way to the edge of the jetty.

'I can see a shark!' bellowed Molly. 'I can see two sharks!'

Sure enough, as she leaned on the creaking wooden rail, below her circled two blacktip reef sharks, two sine waves of muscle and motion moving through the shallows. This was a less than desirable turn of events, as it caused Molls to lean so far out that her toes left the clapperboard floor, which would have been potentially calamitous had the sharks not been about eighteen inches long. I restored her to a more standard upright position and glanced again at the sharks. The wide natural sweep of the harbour – built around the edge of Academy Bay, itself named after a scientific survey vessel – had been a nursery for young marine creatures since time immemorial. It seemed it was not just the land-based creatures who stubbornly refused to leave their home.

We returned to the seafront, and continued to walk, the town stretching ahead of us. I had arranged to meet up with Maccaron once again – our first reunion since the near calamity at Gordon Rocks – and was delighted to see him outside his dive shop. He was telling a story, quite possibly the same story he had been telling when I had last seen him sixteen years before, as the gestures looked remarkably similar. He looked a little older, a little shorter, and a little stouter – like the Maccaron of 2001 if he had been hit by a lift – but there was no mistaking the energy. He turned and spotted me, and raised both arms into the air.

'Ahhh, Monty!' he shouted, and walked swiftly forwards to embrace me. 'My friend. Look at you!' He held me at arm's length, then hugged me once again. 'Welcome back, welcome back!'

After introducing himself to the family – 'Ahh, ¡bonito rojo!' he muttered, looking at Molly's copper-red hair. He bent down to say hello, chuckling as Molly hid herself behind my legs.

'Come, come inside. There's much to talk about.' He paused, shaking his head for a moment, 'Some of it is not so good, my friend.'

He led me into the dive shop, and we sat at a low table. Tam continued to walk with the girls, the lure of the souvenir shops too much for them to resist.

'Have you heard the news?' asked Maccaron, as he poured me a cup of sweet tea. 'It is too much. Too much!'

I was surprised to see his eyes glistening with tears.

'It's a good time for you to come back, as it's now or never that we need to act,' he said. And then, more slowly, 'The whole world needs to know about the *Fu Yuan Yu Leng*.'

Just a few weeks before, on 13 August, the Chinese-registered fishing vessel *Fu Yuan Yu Leng 999* had been steaming south-east through the midst of the archipelago. She was approximately forty miles north of San Cristóbal, and given a few more hours would have been clear of the islands and beginning her journey home.

Unluckily for the *Fu Yuan*, and fortunately for the Galapagos National Park, she had her Automatic Identification System switched on. The AIS transmits not only the position of a vessel, but also her identification. Given the nature of her work, and where she was, it was extremely unusual that the *Fu Yuan* had her AIS activated (there is every chance it had been switched on by accident), it was also doubly unlucky for her that the wrong man happened to be passing in a Galapagos National Park vessel.

Marine ecologist Pelayo Salinas was on his way back from a twelve-day research trip when he was alerted by the skipper to what seemed an anomalous vessel on the radar. Repeated attempts to call the ship on the radio went unanswered, and heightened his suspicions. Not being the type of man to be intimidated by a challenge, he jumped into a thirteen-foot inflatable boat with three crew members and set off in hot pursuit. The *Fu Yuan* is an ocean-going commercial fishing vessel, over a hundred metres long, and quickly outpaced their pursuers, but Pelayo was not to be thwarted. He alerted the Ecuadorian authorities, and a coast guard cutter and helicopter were dispatched. The *Fu Yuan* was finally brought to heel.

Salinas boarded the vessel, to be met by a sight that beggared belief. Filling the immense caverns that made up the holds of the *Fu Yuan* were the silent, gaping, sightless corpses of sharks, piled atop of one another in a hideous mosaic of grey skin, white flesh and scarlet wounds. The latter were all that remained after the fins had been hacked off, a process that takes place as the animal still lives. Death had come to the Galapagos on an industrial scale, in defiance of every international law of conservation, driven by nothing more than an insatiable desire for short-term financial gain.

'There were thousands, if not tens of thousands, of sharks,' Salinas recalled. 'It was the biggest seizure of sharks in the history of the Galapagos, for sure.'

Salinas was looking at a haul of 6,600 sharks, including hammerheads, Galapagos sharks, silkies, and even a young whale shark – every one of these species on the Convention on International Trade in Endangered Species (CITES) threatened, vulnerable, or endangered lists. The *Fu Yuan* was a refrigeration vessel, essentially a place for other boats to store their catch before returning to their grisly work. This was the final destination of a coordinated assault on one of the most precious and delicate marine environments on earth, a ruthless harvesting of a dwindling resource.

To understand why such a substantial vessel – the *Fu Yuan* had a crew of twenty – would sail halfway across the world to fish illegally, it is worth understanding the economics of shark fishing. This is a high-stakes game, and the skippers know perfectly well what risks they run. But there is also strong evidence that these are state-funded fishing operations – these fleets certainly do not operate in isolation.

Their motivation for running such high-cost vessels, and in the process flaunting international law, is a simple one: money. Although the flesh of the shark might only sell for eighty cents a kilogram, this is not what drives the market. Sharks' fins might comprise only 5% of their bodyweight, but they add hundreds of dollars to an individual shark's value, and can be sold for up to $650 per kilogram. The massive fins harvested from iconic species such as whale sharks can be sold for up to $20,000 individually.

All of this feeds the market for shark's fin soup – a prestigious foodstuff in the Far East. It's worth putting this into context: our generation has systematically eradicated one of the most beautiful animals that has ever lived, one that swam in the oceans before dinosaurs roamed the land, in order to make *soup*. And it is soup that is tasteless, odourless and needs additives to make it palatable – the fins provide texture, nothing more.

And yet the desire for the soup, and the prestige it brings, has resulted in one of the fastest and most brutally efficient mass culling of an animal in the history of mankind. The clamouring hordes of passenger pigeons in America, hunted to extinction in a single generation, and the obliteration of the horizon-to-horizon herds of buffalo on the Great Plains, will shortly be joined by the shark on the roll call of our greatest acts of environmental lunacy.

A report by CITES in 2010 noted that we are annually catching 6.4% to 7.9% of all sharks in the sea, with the estimate being that about 100 million individual sharks are being killed per year. It doesn't take a genius to figure out that very soon sharks will be functionally extinct, and now – ten years after that report was written – a great many species do indeed tremble on the brink of complete annihilation. For several it is already too late.

No one knows precisely what the impact will be when we lose sharks from the sea, but all studies agree on one thing – it will be profound. Virtually every study notes that general marine diversity (i.e. the number of different species in one particular environment) will be negatively impacted. We are systematically and ruthlessly removing a keystone animal – one that influences innumerable aspects of the world in which it lives – and will continue to do so until they are functionally extinct. Once they have gone, they will be gone for ever, and already evidence is emerging that some of the larger species, such as oceanic white tips, now have too small a gene pool to ever maintain stable, genetically diverse populations in years to come.

It seemed inconceivable that this scale of destruction was happening here in the Galapagos, but already it was apparent that the apprehending of the *Fu Yuan Yu Leng 999* might just be a seminal moment. The sharks that lay dead in the hold, their role as key controllers in a delicate marine ecosystem now over because mankind requires a thickening agent for soup, may have represented only a small percentage of the daily global catch, but they could prove to be an important one. The gruesome images had been flashed around the world, and already there were stirrings of outrage.

'There is a demonstration tonight,' said Maccaron. 'Would you like to come? I think you should – everyone will be there.' He looked genuinely distressed, his voice wavering. 'It's a message to everyone, the whole world.' He looked helpless for a moment, before going silent. He then quietly said. 'It's now or never.'

That evening I made my way to the main plaza at the seafront. I was not alone. The impounding of the fishing boat and its grisly cargo had galvanised the island, and hundreds of people were making their way to the demonstration. There was authentic anger here, not some manufactured demonstration of passion for the assembled press. Protests can sometimes have a carnival atmosphere, but this was no colourful fiesta. It was a wake, a howl of protest at the violation of sovereign territory, and a lament for the death of an animal that should be sacrosanct.

By the time I arrived at the seafront, the demonstration was a full-throated roar of protest. Conservationists, scientists and local politicians all took to the stage to express their outrage. As they spoke, the enormity of the act seemed to loom ever larger for the crowd. I sensed an impotence amongst the anger, a frustration that, although the intent was genuine, and the passion was high, everyone knew that there was little they could actually do. This was a battle that would be fought at the highest levels of government, as Ecuador tried to balance its need for Chinese investment – already taking place on a massive scale – with a desire to protect its most precious natural resources.

I spotted a group of schoolchildren beneath a set of brightly coloured banners and papier-mâché sharks. They looked bewildered, confused at the merging of a late-night gathering – normally a cause for celebration – with so much anger and frustration from the adults around them. In their midst was the distinctive figure of Roberto Pepalos.

Roby was a man of all trades, most of them centred around the sea. He was a wildlife guide, a diver, and a man who knew everything about everyone. I had been put in touch with Roby as our 'fixer' prior to arriving in the islands, and when I had asked if he could help us out, he had immediately accepted, blissfully unaware of the implications of dealing with red-heads on the equator. He saw me and raised a friendly hand, beckoning me over.

'*Hola*, Monty, *gracias* for coming out tonight. It means a lot that you're here.'

Roby looked precisely like someone who has brine coursing

through their veins should. He was medium height, but lean as a strip of dried kelp. He wore a bandana, giving him the look of a buccaneer, and walked with an economy of movement that spoke of decades working on boats. He perpetually wore a kindly expression, as though recalling a fond memory, and it was absolutely impossible to imagine him angry. He had met us at the docks as we landed on Santa Cruz from the island of Baltra, and was precisely the sort of benign, slightly raffish figure that should meet anyone arriving anywhere. You always felt that things were under control when Roby was around.

One of Roby's key initiatives was to introduce the young people of the Galapagos to the wonders around them. As is so often the case in the most iconic tourist destinations, the natural riches are only revealed to tourists, with locals (particularly children) never having the opportunity to head out to explore the archipelago on the fleet of gleaming alabaster cruise vessels that rocked in the harbour. Roby had made it his mission that every child in the Galapagos should have the chance to head out to sea for at least a day in the company of an experienced guide. If anyone could lay claim to the islands, it was probably them, so this was indeed a noble concept and Roby was making great strides to see it become a reality, one child at a time.

It was therefore entirely appropriate that he was accompanied by his two sons at the demonstration – one a long-haired boy in his early teens, the other slightly younger, with blond hair and the deep tan of someone who spends inordinate amounts of time outside. Rob introduced them to me, and explained that the younger was something of a champion surfer.

'Great,' I said, 'you can teach me to surf while I'm here.'

He looked utterly horrified at the prospect, which, on reflection, was fair enough. I can't imagine that his position in the complex social strata of being a cool young island surf dude would be enhanced by the presence of a gangly, uncoordinated, pale-skinned, middle-aged bald man.

'Don't worry,' I said, 'you can teach me in the dark.' This attempt at a joke didn't make things better, instead making me look not only un-cool, but also slightly sinister. I gave up, and turned to the older son.

'It's so good you've turned out. Are you leading the charge for the next generation?' I asked him.

He looked thoughtful for a moment.

'I guess you could say that all kids are,' he said after a while, which I thought was a splendid answer. One the most heartening aspects of the world today is the mobilising of an entirely new generation of conservationists, motivated as much as anything by the fact that it is their future on the line. It is one of the reasons for genuine optimism, this new cohort who are more aware of environmental issues than we ever were, who communicate on a planetary scale, and are so resolute to engineer positive change. Perhaps there is a glimmer of hope, as they will all be of voting age soon enough, and the engine of our democracy, the one that drives the bulk of our decisions, will become about preservation not profit.

The demonstration soon began to dissipate, the main focus of the speeches in the main plaza having drawn to a close. There was a sense of anti-climax, of impotence, borne from a knowledge that the sound and fury were all for naught if meaningful change was not forthcoming.

'It's difficult,' said Roby, as we walked away from the seafront.

'Ecuador is not a wealthy country, and the Chinese are investing a lot here. You see the main road there . . .' he gestured at the highway leading out of town, a ribbon of lights in the darkness heading up the flanks of the volcano, ' . . . well, the Chinese paid for that. I have a real concern that politics will trump justice here. That's the reason we all came tonight.'

By now we had reached his car, and he turned to shake my hand.

'Well, *buenas noches*, Monty. We keep fighting the fight, hey? See you soon.' He smiled in the gloom of the night, defiant and entirely ready to make his own mark in the conservation of the islands, a heathen king at the head of a new generation.

Darwin – The Curious Boy
from Shrewsbury

It takes no time at all on the Galapagos to make the acquaintance of Charles Darwin. Nowhere is this more apparent than in Puerto Ayora, where any stroll along the seafront is essentially a collage of his classic portrait taken in later life – big beard, stern countenance, and domed forehead. Every sweatshirt, every banner, every shop front seems to have Darwin on it. I was not surprised to see that he is glowering in the majority of the images – I too would be fairly unamused to have my face used to peddle overpriced, badly stitched clothing that hangs next to numerous 'I Love Boobies' t-shirts. This tends to belittle a colossus of a man, someone who bestrides the world of natural science like no other.

We think we know Darwin – a frock-coated gentleman scientist, walking over lava fields, all mutton-chop sideburns and leather journals filled with world-tilting observations. But the reality was a man so driven, so focused, and so energetic that he would have been a giant in any age. Perhaps a reasonable modern context would be combining Ranulph Fiennes, David Attenborough and Stephen Hawkins. It might also be worth throwing in a touch of Steve Jobs and Michael Palin for good measure. As a young man he was physically completely fearless, had phenomenal endurance, was possessed of a curiosity that burned like a furnace throughout his life, and was a fine wordsmith to boot. The latter meant that, during the course of his life, he sent and received a prodigious number of letters, 14,500 of which still exist. This has allowed historians to piece together a very precise picture of his life, and it is full of surprises.

One of the main ones is that, despite his extraordinary range of abilities, he might well have ended up as only a notable figure of his time, not a defining one. The route to such great renown was anything but a simple one.

It is not unreasonable to say that the early days of young Charles were short of promise and long on family conflict. Born into privilege, he had a feckless youth dominated by collecting shells and insects, and what can only be described as 'tinkering' in the garden shed. He was also an amateur chemist with lots of youthful enthusiasm but not a great deal of knowledge. He was joined in this pursuit by his brother Erasmus, five years his senior, who was to remain a great confidant throughout his life.

At Shrewsbury School, surrounded by the sons of the landed gentry, such a past-time earned him the name 'Gas'. This was not a good thing. The formidable headmaster of the school, the Reverend Butler, called him a '*poco curante*', which translates as a 'trifler'. The deep irony of this was, of course, that it was precisely this sort of trifling, that insatiable curiosity and quest for answers, that drove him to such great heights in the years to come. But it was not seen as commendable in the world of a minor public school in the early nineteenth century – classics made the man, not fettling about with chemicals and rock pooling.

Much the same could be said of the situation at home. His time was spent going on shoots on the local estate, collecting beetles, and going rambling with his friends. A love of shooting was ultimately to greatly aid his collecting of specimens – and, indeed, ensure his safety and survival – on the voyage of the HMS *Beagle*, but once again the relevance of such skills in the future were not to be imagined. This apparent lack of direction frustrated his father greatly. The Darwins of Shrewsbury, with his father, Dr Robert Darwin, at the head as a stern and omnipotent controlling patriarchal figure, were expected to have some social heft and not be gadding about in the countryside. Dr Darwin was not the type of man to withhold his disapproval, and there are numerous records of him lambasting his errant son.

The impact of this on young Charles can only be imagined. It is not unreasonable to speculate that such criticism, and many further searing encounters with his father, drove Darwin until the end of his days, manifesting itself in the form of endless attempts to gain paternal approval. He would not be the first or the last great man to have quailed under a domineering and scornful fatherly presence, although even Robert Darwin basked in the national acclaim Charles received on his return from the voyage of the *Beagle*.

Things came to a head when Darwin senior – known to all and sundry as 'The Doctor' – took his son out of school two years early, and gave him an unofficial role as his apprentice. He then sent his son to medical school in Edinburgh, where the only ray of light for Charles was that he would be there with Erasmus.

Plainly, this was an attempt to knock the rough edges off him, and make him a man of note. It failed dismally, as Charles found that he had a strong aversion to blood. After witnessing a botched operation on a child – a scene so barbarous it caused him to flee the room – he vowed never to set foot in an operating theatre again. Medicine in the early nineteenth century was frequently lethal for the patients, but also dangerous for the practitioners, and the loss of his uncle and also his namesake in a 'dissecting accident' (the mind boggles) simply cemented his resolve that he was not cut out to be a doctor.

But his time in Edinburgh had not been completely wasted. It is important to understand the context of the age: this was a period of unprecedented social upheaval, of Whigs and Tories battling to control the moral as well as the political direction of the nation. The French Revolution had happened only a few years previously and already there were stirrings in the lower orders of British society, with the Poor Laws a resultant attempt to quell the restless masses. This atmosphere of ferment, and of challenging previously sacrosanct truths and structures, extended into the world of academia, and the young Charles fell in with Robert Edmond Grant. Grant was a popular mentor among the students at Edinburgh, and was precisely the sort of firebrand academic that has shaped many a young mind over the course of history. Twelve years Charles's senior, he was also an expert in marine sponges. It might be said that his gift to Darwin came in two forms: the first was the lasting impression that nothing is sacred, and the second was an abiding love of the marine environment. Opinionated, eloquent and utterly fearless, Grant showed the young Darwin that there was another path beyond strict conformity and duty to an established order.

Further soul searching saw young Charles enrol at Cambridge University in order to take Anglican orders as a country parson. This was effectively a compromise, the classic refuge for the well-heeled young men of the times who could not find another profession. They would conform to the University's strict protocols, they would take a wife, find a parish, and devote their time to maintaining the moral, religious and political order of the age. For a man who would ultimately tear asunder the very fabric of the church's relationship with the natural world, it was in hindsight an ironic choice. But, once again, lost and restless though Charles undoubtedly was in his 'chosen' degree at Cambridge, it would expose him to some of the most brilliant minds of the age.

It also proved to be a place and a time where the young Charles's obsession with 'trifling' would suddenly became relevant, as a new generation became obsessed with beetle collecting. This rather eccentric past-time had become all the rage with many of the young men, and a few of the young women, of the age, and was a manifestation of the wider rise of interest in the natural sciences. The quest for new species became all consuming, as did the urge to amass vast collections. Darwin suddenly found his métier, and what was once was regarded as a trivial past-time became a social badge of honour. It also became something approaching a competitive sport. Famously, when having a particularly good day of collecting out on the Fens, Darwin faced the dilemma of having a beetle in each hand, and a rather splendid one on the plant in front of him. As a much-fêted intellectual giant of history, his next move might come as a surprise to us Darwin fans, but it is also a mark of just how far he would go to get his hands on any new specimen. He popped one of the beetles into his mouth, in order to pick up the other one. While this showed commendable enthusiasm, it also displayed a worrying lack of beetle knowledge, as the beetle now considering its next move as it sat on Darwin's tongue was a bombardier beetle. These display their displeasure at being mishandled by creating an explosion of noxious fluid out of their rear end (hence the name), and so Darwin spent the next few moments spitting, coughing, dropping the other two beetles, and (I'm sure) resolving to think things through a bit more in the future.

It was through beetling that he met two other figures who were to be defining forces in his early life. The first was William Darwin Fox, who belonged to the Derbyshire branch of the Darwin family. Fox was something of a galactico in the beetle-collecting world, and Charles worshipped him from the moment they met. They became inseparable, and throughout the five long years of the *Beagle*'s voyage, Charles would write to him assiduously.

The other was to be even more significant. The Rev'd John Henslow was the figure Charles turned to when he had a beetle that needed identifying – he would have been a useful companion, for example, when about to store a bombardier beetle in your mouth – and he was already in his third year as a professor of botany. From his letters of the time, it appears that Darwin had what can only be described as a monumental man-crush on Henslow. He described him as 'quite the most perfect man I ever met with', and the two of them shared walks, discussed the great issues of the day, and became the closest of friends.

Henslow was to be a truly pivotal figure for Darwin, and two centuries later we have a great deal to thank him for. After Darwin passed his final exams in 1831, and looked ahead to a mundane life as a country parson – 'the time when I must suffer', he wrote to Fox – it was Henslow who provided a glimpse of a different future, one of academe, and of studying the natural world. Darwin had the restlessness of the young, and the energy and curiosity to look beyond the shores of England to a wider world. 'It strikes me,' he wrote, 'that all our knowledge about the structure of our Earth is very much like what an old hen would know of the hundred-acre field in a corner of which she is scratching.' Young Charles, in other words, wanted to spread his wings and soar to pastures anew. He didn't have long to wait, for on 29 August 1831, Charles found a letter from Henslow waiting for him. It was to tell him about a berth on a vessel sailing round the world – the HMS *Beagle*.

Darwin's role on the *Beagle* was to be the constant companion of its new captain, James Fitzroy. This would involve dining together night after night for years on end, so Fitzroy, also a young man at only twenty-six years of age, suggested that he and Darwin spend some time together in London. This went well, with the two men stocking up on supplies, including, for Charles, a £50 rifle (for the collection of wildlife) and a pair of 'good pistols to keep the natives quiet'. Reading these comments today, one's image of the quiet, learned man of letters does fade somewhat, but these were of course different times. Darwin was virulently anti-slavery, and had indeed been taught taxidermy at Edinburgh by John Edmonstone, a freed slave and a man he held in the highest regard. He believed strongly in the dignity of all men, but as a young man who had just bought three shiny guns with his new best friend, we might charitably assume that testosterone levels were high at that point and he forgot himself.

Fitzroy then took him to see the *Beagle* for the first time in Devonport dockyard. Charles was horrified.

To give the ship (or, more precisely, the boat) context, one must remember that this was to be Charles's home for the next five years, and what's more, it was to be a home eternally pitching and heaving as it charted the treacherous coastline of South America and beyond. And Darwin was no sailor – this was to be his debut voyage.

The *Beagle* was thirty metres long, and eight metres wide. On board were only two cabins, as the rest of the crew slept in communal spaces in the holds. One of these cabins was three metres by four metres, and the other much smaller. Both were, in effect, monastic cells with a few inches of planking separating the occupants from the maelstrom outside. And what's more, Charles would have to share his cabin with another officer on board. As a lanky six-footer, Darwin had to eternally stoop as he viewed the ship, and his sleeping quarters would be a hammock above the chart table. He was undeniably daunted, but determined to go through with the voyage, although the prospect of such close confinement for so long haunted him. 'The absolute want of room,' he wrote, 'is an evil that nothing can surmount.'

With the departure date postponed again and again, his anxiety grew. A sailor from the *Beagle* slipped overboard and drowned on 21 November, filling him with dread. If this could happen in the tranquil waters of the harbour in Plymouth, then what chance did he have off the coast of South America? He began, not unreasonably in the circumstances, to develop palpitations.

Finally, after numerous false starts, on 27 December 1831, the *Beagle* set off on her global odyssey. Darwin began puking as they passed Plymouth Breakwater and essentially didn't stop for the next five years. As anyone who has suffered from seasickness will quickly inform you, this alone marks him out as an emperor amongst men.

The next few years were a litany of adventure, subterfuge, treks of great scope and extraordinary endurance, insurrection, and raw, unrivalled adventure. The voyage of HMS *Beagle* is one of the greatest voyages of discovery ever undertaken, with the young Captain Fitzroy proving to be a hugely capable leader and seaman, and his travelling companion utterly tireless in his quest for knowledge. By the time the Galapagos hove into view, he could ride a horse like a gaucho, trek like a mountain goat, and shoot like a sniper. Darwin was ready – a man hardened by adventures on land and sea, armed with the knowledge gleaned in Cambridge and from countless mini-expeditions. He was in his prime, it was 15 September 1835, and history was about to be made.

Aliens in a Foreign Land

Akin to a great many gardens on the Galapagos, ours was a mess. I use the term advisedly – it was a mess in that it had piles of junk in it, but also in the fact that it had no idea of its own identity. Native species piled up on endemics, who were vigorously arguing with introduced plants, and all of whom were eyeing the invasives with genuine horror. Meanwhile, the invasives were doing what they do best – creeping, crawling, smothering and choking everything around them, always with one emerald eye on the next conquest.

After the initial heady rush of our arrival, life had settled into something approaching a routine in the tree house. After we had been there for about a week, I woke early one morning and quietly slipped out of bed to survey the garden in earnest. Tam slept blissfully beside me, the cool air of the highlands a deep anaesthetic that could only be dissipated by the dawn chorus – a series of chirps, clicks and whistles as the tree canopy around us came to life. This was the most glorious of alarm clocks, although it was sometimes preceded by Molly using one (or both) of us as a trampoline. Should this not be effective at rousing us from our slumber, she would occasionally use my face as an activity centre, with a particular favourite being seeing how far my lower lip would stretch before I woke up, dragging it out several inches before letting it go with a satisfying crack.

But this particular morning both Isla and Molly were still sleeping, and I looked forward to a rare moment of calm before the storm of approaching footsteps and demands for breakfast broke upon us. I padded downstairs, yawning and scratching, made myself a cup of coffee, and stepped out on to the balcony, leaning my elbows on to the rail as the forest around me muttered and twitched in the early dawn light. The green leaves shone and dripped, still slick with the fine mist of minute droplets suspended in the air, and the scene was redolent with the rich scents of loam and dark vegetation, the heavy essence of the life that surrounded me.

Our position high on the flanks of the volcano placed us in the heart of the forest, and even as I sipped the coffee – a potent local Galapagos bean, and the one introduced species I could grudgingly accept was crucial to civilised life – I began to see flickers of movement in the undergrowth around me. Foremost amongst these were the finches, nondescript small brown birds, the shape of whose beaks helped spark Darwin's world-tilting concept. He was, it has to be said, initially rather dismissive of them. Having eulogised and ruminated in his notes about iguanas and tortoises (which was fair enough), he summed up his collection of finches with a single line:

'Unfortunately most of the specimens of the finch tribe were mingled together.'

In other words, he and his shipmates had indiscriminately shot finches on the various islands, and then bundled the unfortunate creatures together in one feathery, blood-soaked mass. It was actually the mockingbirds that really fired his imagination. He noted that:

'My attention was thoroughly aroused by comparing the numerous specimens, shot by myself and several other parties on board, of the mocking thrushes.'

He observed that, 'to my astonishment', different species of mockingbirds lived on different islands, even when those same islands were in close proximity. This first thought was developed further when he returned to England, and confirmed that, if they were indeed different species from different islands, it 'would undermine the stability of Species'. And so it can be quite reasonably argued that it was actually the mockingbirds that inspired those first few magical thoughts of evolution – or species transmutation, as it was known at the time – in Darwin. This is perhaps the reason mockingbird scientists get rather twitchy when everyone gets so excited about the finches.

I watched one of these finches flit from branch to branch in the cedar tree that abutted the house, industrious and alert on its hunt for insects brought to life by the first touch of the sun. As it passed me, it paused for a moment, regarding me with curiosity before jumping straight into the air and landing facing in the opposite direction. This made me laugh out loud, causing it to vanish in a blur of wings, carving a low parabola through the garden to perch on the fence by the gate. I idly wondered, as one does during this first selfish hour of the day, whether it had any idea of its significance in the grand scheme of things.

When HMS *Beagle* returned to England, Darwin enlisted the help of the eminent ornithologist John Gould to examine his finch collection, and it was Gould who noted the differences in their beak structure. Darwin therefore concluded that much of that adaptation related to their diet, and to using their beak as a specialised tool to access food in order to survive.

Perhaps the most diplomatic conclusion, when dealing with irate modern ornithologists, still debating the importance of finches and mockingbirds in the birth of evolutionary theory, is that both families of birds were hugely important. For the girls there was no debate: the mockingbirds were far more interesting, as there was one particular specimen in the garden who was playing a starring role in their lives. Our particular mockingbird was a small, unremarkable-looking collection of russet, white and brown feathers who would perch on a branch overlooking our balcony and chatter away to us. There was nothing friendly about this exchange though – it seemed incandescent that we had the audacity to invade its personal patch. The mockingbird is fairly undramatic in appearance, lacking the buccaneering menace of the frigates, or the flamboyance of the blue-footed boobies, but nonetheless this particular mockingbird soon became a firm favourite. The girls would make me whistle a greeting every morning, although this seemed to be the equivalent to my making an obscene gesture, as the mockingbird (now christened 'Micky' by Isla and Molly) would hop from foot to foot and bob its head as it whistled back, giving every impression of being rather hacked off at this vulgar interloper.

As normal, Micky was out on his favourite perch that particular morning, bellowing insults at me. However, our customary exchange was interrupted by the arrival of Tam at my side, who smiled at me and kissed me on the cheek. She was holding a cup of tea, her hands wrapped round it to stave off the chill of the morning.

'Morning,' she said. 'You might like to pop upstairs. The girls have got a visitor.'

I raised my eyebrows at this, with visions of Molly wrestling a feral cat, or using a giant centipede as a feather boa.

'Oh, it's nothing to worry about,' said Tam. 'It's just one of our housemates has decided to make an appearance. It's sitting above the girls' beds.'

I had been curious as to why the girls weren't up and about already, and had an inkling that this might have something to do with it. Some charismatic member of the local fauna with whom they had inadvertently been sharing their room – a rice rat perhaps, or a vermilion fly-catcher. I walked quickly back into the house, took the stairs two at a time, and then slowed to walk quietly into their room.

Isla and Molly's beds were against each wall, almost fully occupying the small space that was their bedroom. There was a gap of about a metre between them, a gap that was being bridged – rather sweetly – by their outstretched arms, their hands clasped together.

Above their beds, set into the wall, was a long mesh window, which presumably was meant to act as a means of keeping nasty bugs out, and allowing refreshing highland air in. What it actually did was act as a fishing net, capturing all manner of delicious morsels, which in turn drew in larger, hairy scuttling beasts to browse on what was basically an insect smorgasbord.

The girls didn't look at me as I tiptoed in, which was unusual. They were both lying stock still in their beds, eyes swivelled upwards and covers pulled up under their chins.

'Morning Daddy,' said Isla, very quietly indeed, without averting her gaze from the ceiling. This was pretty civilised in the circumstances, because, perched directly over their heads like a hairy glove puppet, was a huge huntsman spider. Molly didn't say a word, she just looked solemnly upwards with those big blue eyes. When you're five and three, respectively, to wake up in what is still a strange house, surrounded by a strange forest, in a strange island, it is a positively life altering sensation to see what looks like a brown guinea pig with eight legs perched five feet from your nose.

Huntsman spiders are actually rather wonderful. They do not make webs, but are leapers, creeping up on their prey and jumping athletically to inflict a powerful bite with the gleaming pincers of their jaws. This one was a hefty specimen, about four inches across, and was eyeing the netting with its eight eyes, set like tiny jewels in its hairy forehead, periodically waving those long front legs. These are jointed at a different angle to the others so it can stretch forward, which also leads to its other name, deeply comforting if you're a little girl, of the 'giant crab spider'.

Huntsman are actually pretty good news, as they keep pests and troublesome insects at bay. They can bite people, but only if threatened, and even then, the bite results only in localised pain and swelling. That said, it might also result – in this case anyway – in deep psychological scarring, a powerful urge to immediately go home to Devon, and a lifelong simmering resentment against your dad for taking you somewhere so ridiculous in the first place.

'That, is, a, big, spider,' whispered Isla, not unreasonably. Molly nodded slowly in agreement, before removing the other hand from under the covers and reaching out in my direction.

'It's a big old friendly chap,' I trilled, with slightly unnecessary volume and energy. 'He's called Henry the Huntsman and his job is to look after you when you sleep.'

This was, as it turned out, very much an error of judgement. Both girls looked at me in horror, then looked straight back at Henry to make sure he hadn't edged any closer. It was a look that very much said 'We'd prefer a Pooh Bear night light and for you to check up on us every now and then, please.'

With some difficulty, I persuaded the girls to get out of bed, a process akin to talking someone down off a ledge after a stock market crash. They completed the entire process while looking straight upwards, followed by a short sprint out of the door on to the safety of the landing, their body language changing dramatically as they reached sanctuary. They looked at each other with wide eyes and big smiles, before hugging and then chattering excitedly like the tiny primates they were.

Over time Henry actually became a beloved member of the

household, hiding away by day and then emerging as the light faded and insects were drawn to the glow of the children's bedroom light. Occasionally we would see one of his feet poking out from under a skirting board during daylight hours, like a hairy trouser leg. But, strangely, we never saw him catch anything, although once or twice he crept towards a nearby moth or cricket, each leg rising and falling in that slow, uniquely sinister arachnid flow of limbs and intent. And yet, every time he pounced, he missed. Perhaps he just wasn't very good at it – in a way, this quality endeared him all the more to us as a family, a bit like owning a particularly clumsy red setter. For whatever reason, Henry soon lost his menace, and the girls would check each night just before the lights went out to make sure that great, bristly spread of jointed limbs and glinting eyes was sprawled on the wall above them.

Day-to-day life was proving just as full of surprises. About 80% of food produce on the island was brought in by sea, which is, incidentally, a major factor in the arrival of invasive species. The permanent population of the Galapagos has simply exceeded the capacity of the islands to feed them, and when the tourist trade is added, huge volumes of food and supplies have to be brought in from the mainland. This meant that the shelves of the shops would slowly empty over the course of a week, getting to the point where everyone was desperate for the arrival of the next merchant vessel.

'It's like a novelty cooking challenge on TV,' said Tam one evening, as she eyed some withered peppers, a bag of unidentified ochre-coloured sauce, and something that had used to be – possibly – broccoli. She looked up at me, twirling a knife on its point on the chopping board as she did so. 'It's no good. We're going to have to grow some of our own food.'

This was particularly necessary as the kids had quite specific tastes in food. This possibly shows lamentable parental skills, but dealing with them at meal times always reminded me of dining with incredibly fastidious five-star clients at a boutique restaurant. Or at least that was the case with one of them – Isla. She combined laser-like scrutiny of any plate of food that was put in front of her with a seemingly limitless ability to push it round the plate without doing anything with it. It was like dining with A. A. Gill on a bad day.

There was another element to throw in to this mix, just to really spice things up. Attending a restaurant with such a fastidious person as a companion would be trying enough, but picture, if you will, that for extra amusement they have brought a Viking along. That'd be Molly's input into the subsequent meal. Therefore, mealtimes were combative affairs, with a backing track of a certain quantity of belching and uproarious laughter. I would sit in the midst of this maelstrom, garlanded with stripes of sauce, and ponder the fact that I presumed that most kids were the same at this age. (That is a genuine question, by the way. Please say yes.)

But the one thing they did both love – a gift from the gods to us as parents – was good, fresh vegetables. And ice cream. As we couldn't grow the latter, we decided to grow the former.

The next day the entire family prepared to clear the ground immediately abutting the wall of the house. We approached this with military precision, eating a large breakfast, and drawing elaborate plans on a piece of paper in the middle of the table. We were in various states of undress, having come straight downstairs to eat. Or, to be 100% accurate, to feed, the term 'eat' not really doing justice to the scene before me as Molly palmed cereal into her face and Isla held up a piece of toast to the light suspiciously.

'Now, everyone,' Tam announced at the end of the meal, 'we're going out into the garden. So we need to wear something sensible.'

'Remember there are fire ants,' I said, as I drained the last of my coffee. 'So you need to be covered from head to toe. Come on, let's get you dressed, and go and start growing our own lovely, fresh veg.'

Forty-five minutes later we trooped downstairs. Tam was wearing long trousers, a sun hat, a long-sleeved top, and socks pulled up to her shins. I was wearing tatty jeans, a sweatshirt, and a baseball cap. Isla was wearing baggy cotton trousers, a flowery shirt, large gloves and a straw sun hat. Molly was wearing a faux-satin ball gown, modelled on her favourite Disney character. As a concession she was wearing longer socks than normal, each one of which I had managed to get on a wildly wiggling little pink foot after ten minutes of negotiation. It was 8am, I was sweating profusely, scarlet of hue, and was already feeling somewhat battle scarred.

The garden looked beautiful in the low light. Not manicured and landscaped, but wild, overgrown, and seething with life. The sun had yet to burn off the morning mist, giving the whole scene a sepia tinge, an evocative hint of untamed undergrowth straight from the pages of a Kipling book. The moisture in the air deadened all sounds and gave form to the sunlight streaming through the leaves and branches overhead. I looked round at the family with some pride, watching them tool up for the task ahead with trowels, forks, hoes and buckets. I hefted a large spade and, as one, we trooped round to the side of the tree house, shaded by the cedar beside our small patch of land.

'If we clear just along one edge,' said Tam, eyeing the tangled undergrowth and chewing her lip, as if suddenly aware of the immensity of the task ahead, 'then that should be enough to go on with. The key is exposing the soil to get something in the ground sooner rather than later I'd say.'

'Good plan,' I said, and glanced around to see Isla smiling up at me, brandishing her trowel and bucket, and Molly dragging a fork as big as she was into optimum position to get started. This, I thought, will be an absolute pleasure. How rare indeed to accomplish such an important task, to commune with the natural world with my family, to create a small patch of fecund ground as a brief homage to those settlers who had gone before, indeed to our own subsistence farming ancestors, tilling the soil in honest endeavour. The Halls family would toil, and mother earth would deliver.

I won't go into too much detail about the hour that followed, beyond saying that we soon had an appreciative gallery of finches, flycatchers and mockingbirds perched in the cedar tree, hopping from foot to foot and chattering excitedly to one another at the delicious anarchy of the scene before them. As opportunistic feeders – particularly the mockingbirds – they are drawn to bedlam and chaos, to the very fabric of an ecosystem being rent asunder to create a steady stream of small, bewildered food items scurrying for cover. They also (and I may be straying slightly into anthropomorphism here) possibly knew what was coming.

Our initial attempts at clearing the tangled matrix of low scrub went well. I hauled and heaved at the tough stalks of the various invasive and introduced species that stood before me, gradually clearing a small patch of dark earth. The family followed in my wake, tilling this new soil, turning it over, smoothing it out, and in the case of our rear gunner, tasting it.

There were surprisingly few insects in the midst of all this, a feature of the Galapagos that Darwin himself commented on, but I for one was pleased that we weren't doing battle with scuttling forms falling down our collars and creeping up our sleeves. It seemed to be a simple case of us against the plants, and we were unequivocally winning. Tam paused for a moment, puffing a stray strand of hair out of her face and wiping a sweaty brow. Isla and Molly scratched the earth in our wake, with Molls in particular intent on filling her bucket and, for reasons best known to herself, making a pile of dark volcanic soil back at the point where we had started digging. It was all going rather well, and I felt myself puffing up with the pride of the pioneer, surveying my family working the soil to make a new life. Or at least a modest vegetable patch, which is as good a start as any. But, as ever when it came to people settling on these islands, the Galapagos had a surprise or two up its craggy volcanic sleeve.

If the birds thought our efforts in the undergrowth an entertaining spectacle, the fire ants' nest towards which we were unwittingly ploughing a noisy furrow had taken a different view. They, as it turns out, were mobilising to ward off the clamorous and vulgar horde hoving into view.

'Ouch!' shouted Molly, 'ouch, ouch, ouch.'

I glanced around, precisely at the moment of feeling that familiar furious prickle on my own ankles, which caused me to spring upwards and backwards like Wayne Sleep. Isla, in the finest traditions of defending her family and her sister, legged it immediately back into the house, her final moment of retreat announced by the slamming of the screen door behind her.

'Oo, aha, ow,' said Tam, slapping her own legs. Fire ants are tiny, determined, venomous and – it turns out – very good at getting between the gaps in your clothes. I swept Molly up in my arms and we retreated to lick our wounds, heading inside to the loud and raucous catcalls of our avian gallery.

Our subsequent regrouping in the kitchen, somewhat shell-shocked at our abrupt transformation from pioneering farmers to large lumps of protein to be devoured, coincided with Roby turning up to find out what the plan was for the next few days. He politely knocked on the door, opening it slightly to peer round it. He seemed completely non-plussed by the scene that greeted him, as the Halls collectively rolled up their trousers and forlornly presented him with their red and speckled ankles and shins.

'Aha, you've met the fire ants then?' he said. 'Poor Molly! But don't worry, I have a solution.'

This alone was a reason to invite him in, let alone the fact that we had already decided en masse that he was a thoroughly lovely man.

A few minutes later he was sitting on the balcony with us, gesturing expansively towards the cedar tree, now devoid of cat-calling birds, doubtless having moved on to laugh at other hapless would-be settlers.

'Now, Isla and Molly, what do you think that tree is called?' he asked, crouching down so he was at their eye level.

'Trevor?' said Isla, after some thought.

At this, Roby smiled broadly.

'Ha, yes, a good name, but I meant what type of tree is it?' he said. He raised his eyebrows expectantly, looking from Isla to Molly, both of them transfixed by the buccaneer kneeling before them.

'A . . . cedar?' said Isla, showing that extraordinary recall children have for overheard conversations and muttered adult asides.

'Bravo!' shouted Roby, making them both jump. 'And do you know that fire ants never bite or nest in cedar. It's a natural pesticide!'

They both nodded solemnly at this important information, not having the first idea what a pesticide was, but both feeling it most important not to upset the pirate under any circumstances.

'And – this is the best bit – cedar is an invasive species! So, what must we do? Hmmm? Eh?'

There was a moment of silence, the theatrical pause that precedes the end of all good stories.

'Cut it down! It must be chopped down, and then chopped up!' He grinned wolfishly (the only way Roby knows how to grin, I suspected). He leaned closer to the two little girls. 'And when we cut up a tree, we get sawdust. But let's call it magic dust. Because if we sprinkle it all over the garden, the ants will pack their bags and leave!'

At this he triumphantly stood upright, looking down at the girls with palms outstretched, like a conjurer opening a cupboard with a flourish at the end of a trick.

This might have been somewhat lost on Isla and Molly, although they did look suitably impressed, it has to be said, but for us it was momentous news. And, of course, entirely logical – many trees have natural pesticides in their leaves, bark and wood, and cedar is particularly beloved of the homeopathic brigade as a natural insect repellent. There are even cedar wood shampoos available, presumably for those worried about shipworm burrowing into their scalp.

A few days later the cedar met its end. I would like to say that this caused me pause for thought, but it didn't. This was no storied, multi-layered green goddess. It was more of a sneaky interloper, lurking furtively in the corner of our garden having crept in without going through the correct customs checks. It was also, as far as I was concerned, a gigantic pillar of insect repellent that would mean our kids could go out into the garden to explore and to play.

The tree was duly cut up, and carted away to a local timber yard, returning several days later as ten huge bags of the most beautiful golden sawdust. This we sprinkled all over the garden, with the girls coating themselves in it like mini-schnitzels as they did so, throwing it into the air and running through it, joyous and free. It took a complete afternoon, and we gathered once again on the balcony at the end of the day, weary and triumphant, surveying the space beneath us – an emerald jungle dusted with golden snow.

'I wonder if the ants are already packing up?' said Tam, leaning forward on the railing to look more closely at the garden, as though expecting to see files of refugee insects carrying tiny suitcases.

'I'm sure they are,' I replied. I turned to look at the bare patch of soil we'd cleared, so dark and fertile amidst the rowdy green tangle surrounding it. 'It's nice to get a little bit of Galapagos back, I must say.'

'It is,' she said. 'It's said that you can put a walking stick in the ground here, and it'll sprout leaves. Can't wait to start growing that veg.'

Now we had beaten a small patch of the garden into submission, it felt right to consider what could be done to return the rest of our patch to its natural state. I was particularly keen to re-create growing conditions that would allow our scalasia to thrive. Scalasia are marvellous trees, and epitomise everything unique about the Galapagos. There are fifteen different species on the islands, all of which are endemic. They vary from low scrubs to towering monsters that reach ten metres in height, and form impressive forests. These are made doubly atmospheric by the presence of epiphyte mosses and lichens that hang from their branches, for all the world like a wizard's beard. This a rather clever arrangement, as the epiphytes harvest moisture from the air. The branches of the scalasia trees give the epiphytes the altitude they need to gather the mist that seems to be ever present in the humid zone. At the same time this water drips from their fronds, and waters the roots of the scalasia below. It also makes the forests look incredibly eerie, an otherworldly realm that really should be inhabited by trolls and goblins. As if to make up for the absence of such fantasy creatures, the scalasia have taken the thoughtful step of being from a genus normally associated with flowers, pro-viding a suitably jaw dropping moment when a visitor realises that they are walking – like Alice in Wonderland – through an immense field of daises.

The leaves of the fifteen different species are just as varied as the legendary beaks of the finches, and represent unique adaptations to their particular environment. What is pretty much a universal characteristic of all scalasia though is that the seeds are heavy enough to fall directly from the trees, and not be blown any distance by wind. To do so on an oceanic island would mean that the seeds ended up in the sea, where they would plainly be in deep trouble.

As I patted the trunk of our lone scalasia, I was touching a plant that is entirely unique to the islands, has shown tremendous adaptive radiation, and has developed all manner of interesting strategies to cope with life in the middle of nowhere. It made me rather fond of it, and I muttered under my breath that I would clear away its beastly neighbours at the next opportunity. First to go would be the immense balsa tree in the middle of the garden. This colossus is fast growing, spreads its branches wide to harvest the sun, and is very much an invasive species. Introduced to the islands to provide timber for buildings, balsa immediately started bullying all the other plants and hasn't stopped since.

This presented me with a neat dilemma that epitomised species eradication in the modern age. The tree was home to all manner of birds and insects, our mockingbird amongst them. If the latter was cheesed off that we'd moved into its territory, it was going to be incandescent that we were about to lop down its house.

These feelings were reflected by Isla and Molly, and, to a certain degree, Tam.

'Oh, what a shame,' she said, 'it seems such a lovely old tree.'

'You're going to WHAT?' said Isla. 'But that's where Micky lives.'

There was general chagrin and alarm at the prospect, but I was determined to return as much of the garden to its endemic state as possible before we left. And that meant hacking down the big old beast in its midst.

Roby had that great universal quality of always 'knowing a man', and in short order he arranged for someone to come and do the work – this was no simple hack and slash, it required industrial-scale equipment. And so the great day dawned, with the arrival of a very small man carrying a very big chainsaw.

'*Hola*,' he said, without ceremony, and waved the chainsaw in the direction of the balsa tree. He raised his eyebrows, and I nodded firmly in response.

'*Sí, estupendo.*' He strode purposefully towards the tree, putting on a helmet and pulling up a bandana to cover his mouth as he did so. This was going to be quick and brutal, it seemed. He reached the base of the tree, eyed it speculatively for a moment, then started the chainsaw with one brisk heave. It coughed into life, and was duly hefted into the approved position, dwarfing the operator entirely. He hit the trigger, Rambo style, and the rattle changed to a roar. Immediately he began, cutting two huge wedges into the trunk. The branches shivered in their death throes, and the leaves trembled high above. Birds took flight down the hill, racing over the leafy canopy to safety.

The family were all gathered on the refuge of the balcony, and by now were all glaring at me.

'It's got to go, girls,' I said weakly. 'It's an invasive.'

Such concepts are difficult enough to grasp as an adult, but when you're five and three and the tree just happens to be home to the only bird you've ever known that actually says good morning to you, then the arguments become even more opaque.

Or considerably simpler – Daddy was a vindictive git who didn't like Micky.

The balsa began to properly creak and sway, and then, with a crack like a gun shot, began to fall. The small man with the big saw stood back with pride, and, as we watched, the tree came crashing down, demolishing all before it. As a way of clearing a very large section of the garden, it was highly effective, although it did present us with the slight problem of what to do with several tonnes of newly acquired timber.

This was not a problem for our man with the chainsaw however, it was an opportunity. Once again the chainsaw roared into life, and what was once tree became – rather surreally – garden furniture. He slashed, he hacked, he trimmed, and he smoothed. With flashing blade and gimlet eye, he created a suite of chairs and a sturdy table that would have set me back several hundred quid at a garden centre.

His work complete, he slung his chainsaw over one shoulder, allowed me to press a few dollars into his hand, shrugged modestly as I tried to offer him praise and beer, and then left. As he did so I realised that I hadn't even got his name. All I knew was that he was a legend, and I very much wanted to be him, with his massive chainsaw, carving a mighty trail through the invasive species of the Galapagos Islands, one garden at a time.

Darwin was particularly interested in just how so many plants ended up on the Galapagos. His was an age where experimentation required as much imagination as it did scientific knowledge – indeed, many researchers of the day had huge amounts of the former, and very little of the latter. Darwin only collected 217 different plant species during his short stay in the islands (which is still pretty good going) and, over the next few years, discovered that at least 50% of them were endemic. This was a phenomenally high figure, and he knew he was on to something very special indeed with these findings. But how did the plants get there in the first place? One might instinctively think they were wind-borne, but it would have to be a moderately stiff breeze to blow a pineapple six hundred miles (not that they're endemic, I hasten to add). So, obviously, they floated there? But surely only a few very robust plants can stand immersion in salt water for weeks on end? And then how did they find their way inland? Being the sort of chap he was, Darwin decided to find out.

The answer was two-fold. By meticulously experimenting with different seeds in different mixtures of salt water for different periods, the great man was surprised and delighted to discover that the vast majority of them germinated. He therefore con-cluded – correctly, as it turns out – that many plant seeds can indeed survive the crossing immersed in salt water and success-fully germinate. The second part of the solution was birds. By scraping through bird droppings in his garden – Darwin was not averse to getting muddy knees and poo under his fingernails, even in his later years – he extracted seeds and duly watched them all successfully germinate. In this way he ascertained that the seeds may have washed up on shore in a state where they could germinate, but to be transported inland away from the barren coastline and into the fertile interior, they needed to be flown. This happened either in mud clinging to feet and feathers, or in an avian alimentary canal, before being launched over verdant soil as the bomb bays opened.

This might seem like a pretty basic concept for any modern botanist, but it was revolutionary stuff at the time. By careful experimentation, trial and error, and meticulous elimination of other possibilities, Darwin had found his answer – the seeds arrived by sea, and were distributed inland by birds. Such was the elegant simplicity of seeking scientific answers in the mid-nineteenth century, requiring, as it did, imagination, a large garden, and dogged persistence.

His collections of Galapagos plants, collected on the *Beagle* voyage, were to have a somewhat chequered time of it when he returned to England. When he got his specimens home, he was overwhelmed by the enormity of the task of classification. During the voyage he had sent some of them to his good friend and great mentor at Cambridge, John Henslow, and although Darwin hectored Henslow for his thoughts on their classification, he didn't receive a sufficiently speedy response. So the plants were sent to Joseph Hooker at Kew in 1843, who quickly realised that huge numbers of them were unique. Hooker and Darwin corresponded for many years, and, indeed, in January 1844, Hooker was one of the first people he confessed to about his growing conviction that different species 'are not . . . immutable', positively incendiary talk at the time. In fact, Darwin noted – famously – in the same letter that it felt a bit like 'confessing a murder'.

Fast forward a couple of hundred years and we were gradually getting to grips with our own garden, the vast majority of which Darwin would not have recognised from his own time in the islands. The cedar sawdust did seem to do the trick, and we were never again assaulted en masse by fire ants, although we did have an encounter or two with the few that had stayed behind, insect survivors in a post-apocalyptic landscape where their world had been strafed from above.

The vegetable patch did indeed prosper, although it would have taken a spectacularly ham-fisted gardener to cause it to fail. The rich volcanic soil combined with the gentle mists of the mornings and the equatorial sun of the afternoon, created a fool-proof environment for gardening. It was a neat representation for us as to the significance of the highlands for the early settlers, and indeed for the inhabitants of the Galapagos today.

But such ideal growing conditions also meant that every other plant in the garden continued to prosper, and it's fair to say that the Halls never quite defeated the undergrowth, and so the entire space was always more of a home to the birds and the geckos than it was to us. But we enjoyed many an afternoon pottering in the vegetable patch, eating at our newly fashioned garden table, and then, as the shadows lengthened, playing animal charades in the newly cleared patch of land around the fallen balsa. The mockingbirds would sit in the undergrowth around us, whistling and cackling, secure in the knowledge that our presence was temporary – just another invader in the ever-changing emerald world of the tangled patch of land below the tree house in the cloud forests outside the quiet village of Bella Vista.

Life in Cold Blood

One of the things that often strikes any visitor to the Galapagos Islands is the absence of noise from large animals. There is a smattering of bird song and, on the four inhabited islands, the occasional dog barking, the low of a cow or the late-night yowling of a cat. But there certainly aren't any noises emanating from large native land animals, no shrieks, barks, coughs or roars. Here is an ecosystem that, uniquely, has the majority of its larger terrestrial niches occupied by reptiles. This is a Jurassic world, with a backing track of hissing and gulping, accompanied by the occasional skitter of claws and slither of scales.

And why, might you ask, are there so few native mammals when elsewhere on earth they are the dominant order of animals? The reason for this is actually rather simple.

The Halls family encounter one of the Galapagos' most famous residents.

Snorkeling in Santa Cruz – Molls is not too sure about it.

A Galapagos sea lion basks in the sun at San Cristóbal.

The dive team return triumphant from the sea mount.
Salome, on the far left, looks suitably proud.

A blue footed booby (*left*). Isla and a baby sea lion, two young animals studying each other intently (*right*).

A Sally Lightfoot crab, a glowing ember on the dark lava rocks.

The perfect sea lion hang out point.

A mockingbird takes flight with the slopes of Sierra Negra in the background.

A green turtle sculls through the water of Isabela,
with the Halls family in tow.

Tam heads north of Isabela on the plastics survey.

Molls on one of her first ever snorkelling sessions.

Molly and Isla encounter a dinosaur on Santa Cruz.

Moments to savour, especially for dad.

A sleeping dragon.

Isla and Molly survey a wide horizon.

These are truly oceanic islands. This means that they have never been connected to the mainland of a larger continent. The Galapagos rose from a vast empty sea, roiling and seething from the depths, exploding in the midst of a blue desert (and what a moment that must have been . . .). That they happened to have done so six hundred miles away from the coast of Ecuador was a tad inconvenient for any mammals or plants that happened to be interested in exploring the new archipelago as a potential site to make their home. Six hundred miles, even bowling along on the Panama Current, represents a voyage of several weeks. With no freshwater available to any erstwhile mammalian settler, marooned on a log or mat of vegetation, death from dehydration is inevitable. In contrast, reptiles, with their much slower metabolism and their ability to go without fresh water for sustained periods, could withstand the brutal passage from east to west, and although probably not feeling entirely chipper when finally making it to the islands, could at least climb ashore and begin to forage. Over eons of time they evolved to become specialists in their particular niche, with iguanas diving deep into algae coated reefs, tortoises of an immense size, and lava lizards hunting insects over ancient fields of razor-sharp magma.

If there was one strong initial impression of the Galapagos for Darwin, it was probably the preponderance of reptiles and the lack of mammals.

He noted:

'We must admit that there is no other quarter of the world where this Order replaces the herbivorous mammal in so extraordinary a manner.'

If there is one such reptile that epitomises these islands, it is, of course, the giant tortoise. It is said that the name of the islands actually comes from the old Spanish word for saddle – *silla-galapago* – due to the shape of the tortoises' shells. This is a delightful theory, but (sadly) incorrect. It's actually the other way round. 'Galapago' is the old Spanish word for tortoise, and the saddle is named after the animal, not the animal after the saddle. This does however mean that the 'Galapagos Islands' can loosely be translated as 'Tortoise Islands', and as we drove the car up the track to El Chato Nature Reserve, we immediately saw why.

I had woken the children up that morning in a state of considerable excitement, dragging off the bedclothes with lavish promises that 'today we'll be seeing dinosaurs'.

This seemed to leave them relatively non-plussed, and even a brief description of mankind's turbulent relationship with the tortoise over the previous two hundred years, delivered over breakfast with much movement of cereal bowls and reptilian hissing, still failed to get them worked up. It was only as we drove into the highlands that they became animated, the simple reason being that we saw one. It was lumbering along the side of the road like a grey JCB, a wrinkled colossus ploughing its way along a timeless route towards some unknown destination.

I would suggest that the first sight of a giant tortoise is always an event in anyone's life. Any supersize animal draws an emotive reaction from those who see it, but for Isla and Molly this went beyond simple excitement. It was truly tectonic.

'A t-t-t-t-TORTOISE!!' bellowed Molly, extending a wobbly finger in the direction of her appalled gaze.

'Wow, oh wow,' replied Isla, trying to climb over her struggling sibling to get a better view. By now I had stopped the car, and Tam craned her neck to look. My erratic driving (one hand on the wheel, one fumbling my phone in to order to take a picture) had drawn an annoyed and richly deserved parp from the taxi behind us. It rounded us with a distinctly South American gesture from the driver, and then we were left alone, a clamouring family in a small car alongside a lumbering piece of living history.

It was a large tortoise, even by local standards, and was making regal progress along the strip of tarmac that abutted the main highway. The great dome of its shell was worn smooth with the passage of time, the same slow decades that had wrinkled and weathered the tortoise itself. It looked impossibly ancient, as though wind and weather had stripped away its features, leaving a stark reptilian head that turned on an arched neck to peer at us with interest, before sweeping back to look at the path ahead. Slowly, oh so slowly, it lifted an elephantine foot to continue its stately journey. Looking at it move I half expected to hear the hiss of reptilian hydraulics and see a burst of steam erupt from under its shell. Here was a Brunellian vision of an animal, a Victorian collection of iron and steam borne on cantilevered limbs.

By now the activity in the car had stilled somewhat, and both children had their faces pressed up against the window, with double exhalations of mist fogging the glass, jet streams of childish delight at the fantasy creature before them. I craned my neck to see them, and smiled at their expressions – both had their mouths open, and were entirely lost in the moment. I looked across at Tam, who shook her head in wonder, gripped my arm and looked back at the tortoise.

As I studied the tortoise before me, it struck me that here

was an animal uniquely ill-equipped to deal with the ravages of man. When people first set foot on the Galapagos, there were fifteen species of giant tortoise here, all perfectly attuned to their immediate environment. A mere hundred and fifty years later, three species have been completely eradicated, and the others are on the edge of oblivion. This tortoise was probably a centurion, and in its life had witnessed the very worst of our own species.

The first problem that faced giant tortoises when man hoved into view was that they are absolutely delicious. Even Darwin himself wasn't averse to tucking in, noting that 'the breast plate roasted . . . with the flesh on it, is very good'. The second problem is that they carry a bag of water with them wherever they go. At the base of the tortoise's neck is a store that can contain up to two gallons, an adaptation for the long periods between the rains in the more arid islands. In 1813, US whaler Captain David Porter noted 'on tasting this water we found it perfectly fresh and sweet.' And so here is an animal that contains several hundred kilograms of delicious meat, as well as drinking water.

And it doesn't end there. The oil of the tortoise was particularly fine, and could be used to make butter, to lubricate machinery, or to illuminate ship's lamps. And so, as a walking larder, water store and oil-production unit, it's fair to say that giant tortoises didn't have much going for them when people first set foot on the islands. The one thing they did have is time – the ability to endure hardships for great periods – but it was this more than anything that almost proved their undoing.

Here was a foodstuff that could be stacked in a ship's hold while still alive, and would remain alive – and therefore keep fresh – for months on end, and provide a means for crews to explore and exploit the wider oceans at their leisure. It was this factor above all others that rung the death knell for hundreds of thousands of these animals, and it is probably not an exaggeration to say that, for over a hundred years, the only reason pirates, buccaneers and whalers visited the Galapagos was to collect food. Darwin, once again, commented on the scale of the operation, showing perhaps a hint of his concern at the plunder of what was plainly a limited resource.

'It is said that formerly single vessels have taken away as many as seven hundred, and that the ships company of a frigate some years since brought down in one day two hundred tortoises to the beach.'

These numbers show that collecting tortoises was not a casual affair, but was more like a military operation, run with great planning and efficiency. It was fuelled not only by hunger, but also by greed, and accompanied by the sort of casual cruelty meted out by men hardened by the brutality of long journeys and intense proximity to one another. Darwin was not averse to a touch of tortoise-related sport, as he noted:

'I frequently got on their backs, and then giving them a few raps on the hinder part of the shells they would rise up and walk away; – but I found it very difficult to keep my balance.'

Going tortoise hunting, or 'terpening', as it was termed, involved expeditions on to the islands that could last over a week, with the men split into teams working round the clock. It was a debilitating task, with one sailor noting in his journal that he was 'intirely exhausted' [sic]. It was the immense size of the tortoises, combined with the inhospitable volcanic terrain, that ultimately saved them – some parts of the islands were too remote, and the tortoises too unwieldy, for them to be removed by anything other than a major expedition. But still the buccaneers, whalers, privateers and – perversely – naturalists collecting specimens from the more accessible islands, extracted a terrible toll that only today is being slowly redressed.

The total population of giant tortoises in the Galapagos before the arrival of man was in the region of 250,000. By 1980, only 15,000 were still alive, and of the fifteen identified species, only twelve remained (and one of those was a single individual – named Lonesome George – representing a species that was functionally extinct). Clearly a concerted effort would be required to bring the tortoise back from the brink, and the efforts over the subsequent forty years have been one of the truly great stories of conservation.

And so the animal before us represented so much more than a slow-moving relic from another age. It was a focal point, a vivid symbol of the battle for these islands, and a measure of our resolve to right the wrongs of previous generations.

The girls were now studying the tortoise in a more considered manner. Isla was the first to voice what they were both thinking.

'It doesn't do much, does it?'

As I looked at her, aghast, I was reminded that what might be miraculous for me – living history, a monument to the ability to endure, and the ultimate reminder of our solemn duty in these islands – is actually just a really, really big tortoise to a little girl. When you're five and three, ideally you need a bit of action to hold your interest. In this regard, the tortoise was letting them down rather badly, slowly lifting one elephantine foot, placing it down, before carefully lifting another. There then followed a moment's rest after such herculean endeavour, and then the cycle would be repeated. As a spectator sport, even I had to admit that it was somewhat limiting, and after watching the tortoise for a few more minutes, the mutterings of discontent in the back of a car grew to a cacophony of displeasure, and it was time to move on.

Happily, on the reptile front, there were also a fair few slightly more dynamic species around, several of whom were right under our noses in the tree house. Most beloved of these for the girls were the lava lizards. It was partly the name – although, as most visitors to the islands will tell you, point at any animal or plant and put the word 'lava' in front of it and you've got a reasonable chance of being right. This is not unreasonable when one considers that the entire archipelago is made of the stuff. But the lava lizards were absolute rock stars as far as Molly was concerned. This was partly because they were such accomplished predators – they would take pretty much anything on, and were not averse to eating each other when really peckish. The females also had a blaze of red on their throat, like lavishly applied blusher. The males were larger and definitely a bit more drab, but the females looked properly feisty – an easy parallel when you're a little redhead. Lava lizards also changed colour when in a bad mood, so the parallels with her were positively spooky.

And finally, they indulged in vigorous head nodding when threatened and, best of all, started doing large numbers of press ups when in the presence of a competitor. This made me like them as well, as I frequently did the same thing.

Geckos were another favourite, mainly because of their nocturnal hunting behaviour. We would sit on the sofa of the tree house and watch them creep around the windows, their adhesive feet miraculously keeping them plastered to the glass. The hunt would develop before our very eyes, with small insects and moths drawn to the light, and the geckos lurking in ambush. They would move imperceptibly slowly, then flow like a falling droplet towards their prey. We would shout in triumph when they were successful, luxuriating in our front row seats – avid viewers of Jurassic Park in miniature.

If Molly loved the lava lizards, it's fair to say that she was also a huge fan of the geckos. Perhaps it was their minute size, their magical ability to climb any surface, or the strange combination of kinetic activity – particularly when another gecko hove into their patch, which they seemed to take great exception to – and complete reptilian stillness. When looking for their next victim, the only thing that would move would be their eyes, great green orbs like soapstone marbles, flicking from side to side as they surveyed the hunting grounds on the shining glass around them.

Molly liked to creep up to the window, padding on silent feet, drawing ever closer, and then study the gecko's underside. Here was a tiny, perfectly formed little dragon, sitting near the tip of her nose, separated only by a couple of millimetres of glass. She would press her palms to the window on either side, and lean even further forward, her nose turned into a pale, splayed button on the window. It was a momentous moment when she saw her first gecko capture a small moth, and quite simply off the scale when she saw it lick its own eyeballs at the end of this fluffy feast. This was a feat that – for her – secured the gecko's status as the ultimate Galapagos creature, and from then on I would periodically see her sticking her tongue out of the corner of her mouth and peering optimistically down at it.

But the reptilian stars of the show for the girls, and indeed the vast majority of visitors to the islands, were undoubtedly the marine iguanas.

One of our favourite haunts was the small elliptical curve of sand next to the Charles Darwin Research Station. Here the girls would splash in the shallows, jump the waves, and sit contentedly in the shade as the inhabitants of the foreshore went about their business. The iguanas would appear from the depths like black wraiths, a sinuous ripple driving a dark head through the water, the animal making its way determinedly to shore. One huge iguana swam directly at them, passing within a few feet as they stood breathlessly in knee deep water, glancing at each other in wonder at the proximity of a swimming dragon. But although the kids enjoyed the iguanas, it's fair to say that no one had more fun with them than Darwin.

That's not to imply that he liked them. In fact, his description on encountering them for the first time could not have been more scathing: 'It is a hideous looking creature, of a dirty black colour, stupid, and sluggish in its movements.' A seaman onboard the *Beagle* decided to test their amphibious credentials by tying one to a rock and hurling the unfortunate beast over the side. Such was the relationship with the natural world in 1835, with man lording it over the animals by divine proclamation. When it came to this particular marine iguana, on the wrong end of a brutal experiment by a bored sailor brutalised by many years at sea, Darwin noted: 'but when, an hour afterwards, he drew up the line, it was quite active.'

He didn't add ' . . . and unbelievably annoyed', which would have made perfect sense in the circumstances, but perhaps that is a manifestation of the benign tolerance that all Galapagos animals seem to have for man's excesses and ham-fisted ministrations. This was never more apparent as Darwin explored the iguana's persistence in coming ashore at the same location. He devised a devastatingly simple test for this, by hurling one iguana again and again into the sea.

'I threw one several times as far as I could, into a deep rock pool left by the retiring tide, but it invariably returned to the same spot where I stood.'

From an entirely anthropomorphic point of view, this might be viewed as pretty dense behaviour on behalf of the iguanas (and reinforced Darwin's initial impression that these were singularly un-intelligent creatures), but, actually, it was doing nothing more than trying to survive. The fact that it had recently exited the water indicated that it was trying to warm up – marine iguanas will only swim for a maximum of an hour a day for this reason. Getting out of the water was infinitely more important than any possible hazard on land. Even if that hazard happened to be the greatest natural scientist who has ever lived using you as a fleshy frisbee.

But marine iguanas face a host of other issues. Foremost amongst them is El Niño. This phenomenon, which translates as 'The Infant Jesus', is essentially a weakening of upwelling ocean currents and trade winds around the islands. It takes place every three to six years, and depending on the severity of the El Niño, this can have two effects. It can increase rainfall in the Highlands, which is beneficial for the interior, as crops grow and water abounds, but it can also cause the shallow coastal waters to dramatically heat up, which can be devastating for the animals that rely on the shallow seas surrounding the islands for food. A particularly powerful El Niño in 1983 saw 77% of the penguin population die due to their food source – small fish – moving too far off shore for them to hunt. Similar figures were recorded for some populations of marine iguanas, as the green algae that made up their diet simply died off.

But this is the home of evolution in fast forward, of finding ingenious solutions to environmental hazards, and the marine iguanas have come up with an absolute belter. As Molly and I lay on our stomachs on the beach by the Charles Darwin Research Centre, it was thought provoking to know that walking right past our noses was the only animal on earth that can shrink its own skeleton. Marine iguanas have been known to decrease in size by as much as 20% during severe periods of environmental stress. That's the equivalent of a six-foot-tall man becoming five feet tall during times when food is in short supply. It was no surprise that the iguana we were looking at walked with a distinct strut – I would too if I knew I could become the size of Ernie Wise when I was hungry.

In so many ways, the reptiles of the Galapagos, in all their cold-blooded, hissing and scaled glory, represent the essence of the conservation dilemma here. The larger species of reptile are all unique, and have a rare physiological fortitude that has allowed them to not just survive, but to prosper on these remote islands. But their very timelessness, that prehistoric ability to slow down and sit it out when times are tough, has become a point of weakness in this new world of change that is anything but languid. The adults fall prey to invasive species, their eggs are devoured by pigs and ants, and climate change impacts the temperature of the nests that in turn define the sex of their offspring. Captive breeding programmes, the restoration of long-lost habitats and the eradication of invasive species have all helped, but their grip on the land remains tenuous to say the least. They sit, somewhat bewildered, on the cusp of a new world – an ancient family of animals that define the Galapagos, and yet face the most uncertain of futures with the bewildering changes that now beset their island home.

All that Scuttles and Crawls

When one considers that man's historic impact on these islands has involved the enthusiastic and systematic slaughter of various native species, it is remarkable that trust still exists between people and animals on the Galapagos. But exist it does, and nowhere does it loom larger than in the fish market at Pelican Bay.

Whenever we visited Puerto Ayora, we always made it our business as a family to pass by the market where daily the fleet would land their kaleidoscopic boxes of fish, shimmering and glinting in the afternoon sun. This was something of an event not just for the local people, waiting patiently with baskets and bags, but also the local sea lions, pelicans, frigate birds and anything with feathers and flippers that happened to be passing. The first fish box that clunked noisily on to the concrete counter was the cue for scavenging bedlam, as everyone, and everything, clamoured for optimum position.

The market is small, about the size of a squash court, and yet it encapsulates so much about the archipelago itself, and indeed the tensions that surround it. The relationship between the fishermen of the Galapagos and the National Park has generally been a turbulent one, representing something of a front line in the conservation battle. The two sides have been diametrically opposed for decades, but an uneasy peace has now been brokered, mainly due to the discovery of a rich lobster fishery in the shallows, and the sensible application of quotas and catch limits. As such, the market operates in something approaching a sustainable manner, allowing for the purchase of fish and lobsters with a relatively clear conscience. That alone is reason enough to visit, but an added attraction is that one gets to witness an entire ecosystem in action, all in 3D and surround sound – all the more impressive if you're only four feet tall.

Having stopped at the market on one particularly boisterous morning, I glanced down to see Molly and Isla dumbstruck by the spectacle before them. As I watched, Molly slipped a small pink trembling hand into her big sister's palm, and Isla squeezed hard in return. Before them was a wheeling, wild cacophony, all flashing beaks and bristling whiskers. Directly overhead were the biggest birds they'd ever seen, flying and fighting over the top of sea lions that coughed, barked and barged each other aside. And in the midst of it all the knives flashed, deals were struck, and boggle-eyed fish were rapidly disassembled into their fleshy constituent parts.

Leading the aerial charge were squadrons of frigate birds. These beautiful, powerful animals are a personal favourite of mine, partly due to their acrobatic ability, but also because they are (and there really is no other way to put this) complete villains. There are two separate species in the Galapagos – the great and the magnificent frigate – but in terms of their morals, there's nothing to separate them. They are aerial sociopaths, stealing food from other honest and decent working-class birds. They bully, steal, intimidate, bite, twist and tear, and they do it all in mid air at terrific speed. The frigate has the largest wingspan of any bird relative to its body size, and can fly at up to 100mph. To see them hurtling directly towards us, then abruptly stall and turn ninety degrees and plunge to earth, was like watching a black satin cape rippling in the wind. They are satanic, bewitching, piratical and invincible.

Beneath them, squat and comical on the fish-market floor, were several brown pelicans. They rolled like drunken sailors as they walked, and peered at the world from over the top of a colossal bill. They seemed to view it with an air of faint surprise, as if someone had superglued a giant prosthetic to their face while they were sleeping. Periodically another pelican would join them, soaring in from the bay in a wide, elegant arc. They were quite beautiful in flight, with a grace and poise that instantly evaporated the moment they landed. The moments before impact – and it was an impact, bordering in several cases on a full-scale crash – saw their wide feet splayed out before them, a frantic stall, and a wide-eyed scattering of any contemporaries that happened to be on the flight deck. Once they had skidded to a halt, they would fold their wings, draw back their head, gulp in satisfaction, and survey the scene. They would then plunge into the mêlée, squabbling and scrapping over the pieces of fish on the floor, extending their necks and turning their heads at lightning speed. The membrane at the base of the bill would distend to an extraordinary degree to accommodate the larger pieces of fish, and while it remained in the pouch it was fair game for the other pelicans, who would pursue the frantically gulping, waddling winner in a noisy lynch mob.

Beside each of the local ladies cutting and preparing the fish lay morbidly obese sea lions. This – plainly – was the best seat in the house, and they would periodically nudge a welly-booted foot, a signal that a piece of fish was to be dropped. This tended to happen every third or fourth request, and the result would duly be consumed with a sigh of contentment. One colossal sea lion had a huge pile of fish scraps in front of him, and was noisily working his way through it, nose to the trough, with his colossal backside rolling from side to side as he did so.

Picking her way delicately through the throng was a lava gull, looking impossibly fragile and delicate within the surrounding vulgar mob, her feathers the colour of brushed slate, her watchful eye as dark as quartzite, ringed with a perfect snow-white circle. But appearances can be deceptive, as she too is a scavenger and nest robber, preying on young nestlings as well as newly hatched iguanas and turtles. She had every right to look haughty, as she was an uncommon creature, one of only a thousand of her kind, a bird that chooses to associate itself with the easy pickings from men. She and her kin are therefore frequently seen, although paradoxically they are also largely ignored by the tourists with their camera phones, blissfully unaware that parading before them was one of the rarest birds on earth.

At the very front of the fish market are the lobsters, lined up in clicking, squirming, armoured ranks in overcrowded fish boxes.

Molly, having finally realised that she was not going to be carried off and consumed by the gigantic birds overhead, glanced down to reveal what looked to her like giant bugs, crawling over the top of one another, with their long antennae twitching and probing, seeking any avenue of escape. This put her slightly on edge, and she shuffled closer to my legs, all the while eyeing the lobsters with considerable suspicion.

One of the fishermen noticed Molly's interest, and ambled over to pick up one of the larger lobsters, an armoured monster wearing a chain mail of white barnacles, its body a living reef. The fisherman smiled, clutched it in one brown hand, and lifted it up to give her a closer look. The lobster – not unreasonably – protested vigorously at the indignity of it all, and flapped its splayed tail in a staccato machine-gun display of outrage. For Molls this proved the final straw. Letting out a wail, she clambered athletically up my leg, a small pink primate in full retreat, throwing her arms round my neck in order to bury her face in my shoulder.

We stood for some time looking at the market, all the links of the food chain before us clamouring in all of their ribald, boisterous glory. The islands had shown us a great deal during our time here, but there was never a better demonstration of how the animals and the people of the Galapagos are so inextricably bound together. The market is a microcosm of the unique nature of these islands, a vivid representation of the fact that survival – on both sides – depends on an unwritten charter of trust.

The lobster fishery is a source of great pride for both the fishermen and local conservationists on the Galapagos. It is – or certainly appears to be – sustainable, heavily monitored, lucrative and produces a product in high demand by the tourist trade. This, in turn, ensures that local restaurants can offer a food item considered a global delicacy, and there isn't a café or cruising yacht that doesn't have it on the menu.

But there is, as ever, a more complex story behind this fishery, and indeed fishing in the Galapagos generally. If there is one area that has truly represented the front line of the conflict between conservation and population, between the park and the people, it is here. Never was this more apparent than during the boom days of the sea cucumber fishery in the early 90s.

The fishery in the Galapagos came to prominence due to the sea cucumber having been fished out in the coastal regions of the Ecuadorian mainland. This unprepossessing little animal – essentially a tube of intestine with knobbly skin and limited aspirations in life beyond feeding and reproducing – is a delicacy in the Far East. Hugo Idrovo's superb book *Footsteps in Paradise* tracks the period when this fishery was at its height. He quotes one local fisherman as saying: 'It was an incomparable source of income. Everyone on the island was dedicated to sea cucumbers.'

In a model that would be repeated around the world whenever a new artisanal fishery was discovered, Asian backers began to inject money into the market to enable more and more local people to conduct fishing operations. Another local fisherman, breathless with excitement, noted: 'The Chinaman who bought cucumbers loaned my cousin and me 13 million sucres to buy a boat and start the business. With the first catch we paid back the money and made 11 million on top of it.'

And so a feedback loop began, with big finance creating high yields from a mobilised local population. The crash in sea cucumber stocks was inevitable, with the critical depletion of their numbers resulting in a complete ban on fishing by executive decree on 6 August 1992. To say this was handled badly by the authorities is an understatement, with very little empathy shown to an island population that had until then been experiencing unprecedented prosperity.

The result was revolution. These were tough men working in a deeply hostile environment who had – without consultation – had their livelihoods taken away from them by a stroke of a bureaucrat's pen. Even the introduction of a limited season didn't assuage their anger, and for a period the Galapagos teetered on the brink of all-out revolt. A dozen giant tortoises were found dead after a fire on Isabela – almost certainly started deliberately – and the Charles Darwin Research Station was also set ablaze. The fishermen seized the airport at San Cristóbal, and blocked roads leading to the National Park on both Santa Cruz and Isabela. It took until 1998, with the publication of the Law of Special Regime for Conservation and Sustainable Development in the Province of Galapagos, before tensions finally eased. Even today the relationship remains fragile, an uneasy truce brokered because both sides knew the ultimate price of failure.

Although the sea cucumber fishery crashed beyond recovery, and it remains illegal to catch them, today there are 1,200 fishing licences granted for small boats to catch fin-fish and lobsters. Of these licenses, only 400 are in use for lobster fishing, and cover a fleet of small open boats that can venture only so far into the open ocean. Lobster pots are illegal in the islands, due to their impact on the seafloor and indiscriminate haul of other species, and so there is only one way to catch them – by hand.

And so the lobster today come at a price. And that price is the danger of venturing out to sea to dive and catch them by hand, a role undertaken by a select band of individuals, who work in an environment of medieval intensity. It is at night that the lobsters emerge from their rocky hideouts, to robotically scuttle over the shallow reefs, foraging for food and patrolling dark and tumbling undersea terrain. And as they emerge, so men are there to meet them. Diving for lobster is no underwater amble through crystal visibility, no gentle drift over white sand; it is a diving experience of brutal intensity, over sharp lava rocks, in pounding ocean swells, in pitch darkness, cold water, and surrounded by night-time predators. It is not a place for those with a vivid imagination or anyone averse to burrowing head-first into the craggy maw of a lava cave in pursuit of a fleeing crustacean. Roby was keen that I experience a night-time shift with one of the fishermen. I was considerably less keen, but he persisted.

'Monty, how will you know what it takes to make this fishery sustainable? How will you know the challenges that face the divers unless you do it yourself?' He looked at me quizzically, head on one side. A challenge, unless I was much mistaken. 'I think you should do it.' This last sentence was stated with great conviction, and a half smile. Roby was playing me like a cheap violin.

If there's one thing that makes my sap rise, it's a pointless challenge wrapped in an insinuation that I might not be up for it (more the fool me, of course). When someone knows how to push the appropriate buttons, as Roby undeniably did, it means they can get me to do pretty much anything.

'You're on,' I said, bristling.

Roby smiled again, this time slightly more triumphantly.

'Bravo, Monty! Be at the dock tomorrow night at 7 o'clock and I'll get you on a lobster boat.' He excused himself, and walked away with a spring in his step, his work done for the day.

The following night I found myself restlessly pacing the quay next to the fish market. By contrast to the cacophony of the day, the market was now dark and almost silent, the only sounds the gentle slap of waves on the painted hulls that lined up next to the harbour wall, and the occasional creak of a rope looped round a bollard. The boats themselves heaved and swayed on their mooring lines, sleek and predatory shapes in the gathering gloom of the night, restless at the prospect of the hunt.

Just when I was beginning to think (hope) that Roby had forgotten, I heard the low rumble of an approaching car, and saw the flare of headlights against the concrete of the dock. As a pick-up drew to a halt beside me, I could see three shadowy shapes within. One was Roby, who gave me a cheery thumbs up as he stilled the engine. The two figures with him climbed out and walked towards me, unmistakably father and son, my hosts for the evening ahead.

The elder man held out a calloused hand and introduced himself with a broad smile.

'*Hola*, Monty,' he said simply. '*Me llamo* Enrique.'

As I shook his hand, his palm rasped on mine, a lifetime of labour in a single touch.

'And I am Boris,' said the younger man, in heavily accented English.

Boris looked like a prize fighter, a compact barrel of muscle whose training ground was the uncompromising world of the seafloor. The power of oceanic surge and current, the need to twist and writhe in the cloying darkness for hours on end, the constant demands on heart and lungs, and the ever-present dangers of his workplace, had created, in essence, an aquatic athlete. I had seen the other lobster divers at the market, and they all shared this same elemental hardness, a type of confident stillness by day that belied their turbulent existence at night.

Introductions over, I picked up my bag and followed Enrique and Boris to the closest boat. They both stepped easily onboard, and immediately turned to assist me, reaching up to take my hands and ease me down from the dock. It made me feel grateful and reassured, but also a little bit like the Queen Mother. I hoped that, over the course of the evening, we would operate on a slightly more level footing, but, then again, being watched over by two teak-hard locals might have its advantages in the maelstrom of the turbulent shallows.

Enrique indicated my place on the boat by simply lifting his chin in the vague direction of the stern. I duly scuttled into position. Meanwhile, Boris cast off, and within moments we were turning away from the comforting glow of the waterfront, and pointing the bow towards the forbidding darkness of the horizon.

There is something magical about being in a small boat, in a big sea, in the dead of night. Puerto Ayora quickly receded around the headland, and soon we were moving entirely alone along a track as black as molasses. The presence of the coast itself was marked by a white and hissing line of surf, heaving and falling against the rocks. This was the realm of the lobsters: alive, seething, kinetic, eternally churning air into the shallows in an endless spin cycle, creating a blurred boundary between the land and the sea, where the air became water, and the water became air. This creates a rich seam of life, shallow enough in daytime to receive sunlight, and yet also saturated with oxygen and nutrients – no wonder that the lobsters moved up from deeper water at night to graze, forage and hunt here. And tonight we would be the predators that awaited them.

My reverie was interrupted by the engine tone dropping, becoming less strident as Enrique eased off the throttle and the bow lowered from the plane. Enrique and Boris – father and son – communicated without words, busying themselves with equipment, net bags, coiled lines and a small grapple anchor. It seemed to me that, out here, their relationship was perhaps more binary than on land – two fishermen at work, one of whom was about to enter a dangerous world, and the other undertaking the sacred role of keeping him alive as he did so.

Boris would be diving on a hookah – essentially an air-line connected to a compressor on the boat at all times. This is notionally safer, as there's no way to run out of air. I say notionally because, as Enrique duly threw back a stained tarpaulin, it revealed a compressor that might charitably be described as being past its best, and slightly less charitably as a collection of loosely connected parts. Central to its function was a flywheel, which resolutely refused to turn despite Enrique's increasingly vigorous ministrations. He tweaked a few valves, applied a touch of oil, and then braced himself on stout legs against the roll of the deck. He pulled the starter cord with a grunt, at which the compressor merely coughed in protest. Muttering under his breath, he tried again, with identical results. Standing for a moment, he pushed his hands into the small of his back, stretched, directed a well-aimed kick at the compressor with a single welly-booted foot, then braced himself for the big one. Using both hands this time, legs bent, like an Olympic hammer thrower in the circle, he glared at the compressor and, with a mighty explosive 'Gaachaaaa!', violently spun and threw both hands into the air. This time it roared into life, before settling into a rheumatic, shuddering death rattle. It sounded much like a biscuit tin full of nuts and bolts being rolled down a hill.

I would no more have dived using that compressor than I would have eaten my own Speedos, but Boris seemed perfectly at ease. By now he had his wetsuit on, and was checking the mouthpiece of his regulator. I too hastily kitted up, pulling on my wetsuit, throwing on my cylinder, and checking my torch (a new one, which emitted a beam of lobotomising intensity, which I thought might come in handy for what lay ahead).

Boris sat on the side of the boat and without ceremony rolled into the water, swallowed by the darkness in an instant like some aquatic conjuring trick. I too sat on the side of the rail and looked behind me into the gloom. I could see Boris's torch disappearing into the depths below the boat, its glow illuminating a patch of the surface that writhed and heaved directly beneath me. I happened to know that two large tiger sharks had been spotted a little way up the coast the night before, and also knew that, for the next few hours, I would be making my own way along the reef in the midst of the darkness. As I rolled backwards to follow

Boris, it dawned on me what a pity it was that diving gear didn't have rear view mirrors as standard.

After righting myself at the water's surface, I bent my head forward to scan the depths. There was Boris's torch, a patch of light making its way across a lunar landscape far beneath me. Head down, with a few strong kicks to break the hold of the surface, I descended into the gloom to join him on this most hazardous of night shifts.

I kicked strongly towards the reassuring pool of light cast by Boris's torch, a haven in the darkness that pressed in on me from all sides. Although daunting, it was also thrilling, a three-dimensional flight towards an unknown destination. Such romantic notions were, I'm sure, lost on Boris as he began another long shift, but for me a night dive in this remote site in this most isolated of archipelagos was exciting beyond measure. Nonetheless, I was anxious to be alongside Boris on the seafloor, to have the elemental comfort of the proximity of another person.

I touched down like some lunar module, and it became immediately apparent as to why the lobster divers required a certain level of athleticism, dogged determination and physical resilience. The combination of current and swell immediately picked me up and moved me several metres sideways, before tossing me back to my original position. I leaned down and grasped a rock, which meant that my body and legs pivoted above me, an undignified bicycling of fins restoring order before the next swell came along to spin me around once again. I glanced over at Boris and could see that he was already hugging the seafloor, working his way along the reef in the lee of the immense boulders that littered his path. He was essentially tucking himself into small pockets of still water, stepping stones through an undersea torrent. As I did the same, in an undignified scramble between the rocks, it dawned on me that the lobsters had spikes for toes, and indeed armour for skin, for more than simply defensive reasons. This was their world, where the ability to hang on to a rock in the midst of powerful currents, and the resilience to take a battering when you couldn't, were essential survival skills.

I became aware of a commotion ahead of me, and saw Boris vanish into the darkness underneath one of the larger boulders, a wetsuit-clad pitbull. Within a few seconds, all I could see were his legs, pistoning wildly to drive that wedge-shaped body deeper and deeper under the overhang. At least I assumed that was what was happening – given the range of movement as his body thrashed from side to side, he might actually have been seized by some immense troglodyte and was now being messily devoured. Either way, I was quite interested to see the end result, so I hopscotched my way over and settled beside his shins, as that was all that I could see of him by this stage. These stilled for a moment – either the troglodyte had by now completely eaten his head, or he had his hands on something interesting – and then began to spiral and twitch as he reversed out of the hole. He emerged in a cloud of silt, out of which he thrust a gauntleted fist. In it was held an unfortunate lobster.

If ever there was an illustration of just how hard-earned the food on our plate can be, then this was it. As Boris had charged into that deep, dark cavern, alerted by the twitch of a crustacean antennae, he had no idea what else might have awaited him within. There are numerous tales of lobster divers being attacked by moray eels, of them being lacerated by razor-sharp rocks, pierced by urchin spines, and stung by scorpion fish. The conservationists among us might instinctively applaud this – a marauding raider of the undersea world being repelled by a reef community simply defending itself – but we are the same folk who were doubtless very happy to see the removal of spear fishing from the islands in favour of more sustainable techniques. As ever, it is all about balance, and acknowledging the bigger picture.

And the bigger picture was very much applicable when it came to the unfortunate crustacean in Boris's fist. Ever since the Galapagos Marine Reserve was first established in 1998, no large-scale commercial fishing has been permitted within its borders. However, that left the 1,000 or so artisanal fishermen based on the islands to go about their business relatively unchecked, and – as netting was banned at an early stage – it was perfectly logical that they would go for the high value catch. Wherever the fishermen were also able to dive, that meant lobsters. The traditional method of catching them was the spear, which meant that by the time the fisherman realised that the lobster in question was too small, he was very disappointed and the lobster was very dead. No catch and return system existed here, no returning 'berried' lobster hens – females carrying eggs – back to the water, and no chance for populations to regenerate and recover. This, as it turns out, has an impact way beyond the menus in Puerto Ayora.

Lobsters eat sea urchins, which in turn graze on marine algae. Fewer lobsters means more urchins, which means less algae as the urchins proliferate like antelope sweeping across the Serengeti. Another animal that relies entirely on the algae is one of the Galapagos Islands' most iconic species, the marine iguana. Tourists travel from across the world to see them and, as tourism employs a large portion of the total population on the islands, fewer and fewer iguanas could be deemed highly significant in terms of the long term island economy.

Thankfully, this did not escape the attention of Conservation International who, over many months and years, worked with fishing focus groups and the Galapagos Park Authorities. They slowly built support for a regulated lobster fishery, with a clear set of rules (including no spear fishing, a size limit, and the return of any lobster carrying eggs). They even brought in lobster fishermen from mainland Ecuador and Mexico to provide absolute proof that these measures worked.

For the last twenty years, therefore, lobster numbers have steadily recovered. Due to this abundance, the catch now accounts for approximately $2 million (US) of the total catch in the Galapagos annually, and as is so often the case for any really effective fishery, the fishing grounds are policed by the fishermen themselves. It is a particularly fine example of disparate groups, initially diametrically opposed, pulling together to work out a solution that benefits the wider ecosystem. 'We can say that more lobsters means more marine iguanas,' explained a very satisfied Jerson Moreno, the fisheries specialist on Conservation International's Galapagos team. 'And that's good news for tourism.'

My musings were rudely interrupted by the fact that Boris was now attempting to stuff the wriggling lobster into a large net sack. My attention was also diverted by the fact that there were no bubbles coming from his regulator.

This was, surely, fairly significant. Even with my fundamental knowledge of physiology, I was aware that breathing in when underwater (and indeed on land) requires you to breath out first, and Boris seemed to be doing neither. I finned closer to him and noted that he wore a rather preoccupied expression, and was tapping the hose that led to his mouthpiece.

Unbeknownst to both of us, the compressor on the boat had wheezed its last feeble hiss of air a couple of minutes previously, finally expiring in a consumptive rattle of defeat. As he did battle with the lobster, Boris had been breathing the remaining air in the hose, and was now sucking on empty.

Considering the situation – forty feet underwater, in pitch darkness, a giant swell, holding a furious lobster – he was preternaturally calm. He gestured that we should ascend by waving the lobster vaguely towards the surface, and set off trailing vapour trails of silt. We both arrived at the surface by the boat simultaneously, to be met by an explosion of invective as Enrique attacked the compressor. He was trying to get the belt back on the flywheel, which would have been fine except for one slight issue. During our ascent he'd managed to get the compressor going again, and as such was leaping back and forth on the deck trying to fix the belt to the wildly spinning metal wheel. The scene reminded me of those skipping games little kids play, with the difference being that if you get your timing wrong in this case you lose three fingers. As we watched, he miraculously managed it, standing back with a look of triumph and rubbing his hands on his shorts.

'Papa,' shouted Boris, causing Enrique to look round in surprise.

'Ah, Boris,' he said, looking faintly guilty, 'it's nothing, nothing.' He gave a dismissive wave of his hand and – perhaps just my imagination – edged sideways so we couldn't see the compressor. His body language clearly said: 'All under control here son, back down you go.' Boris, being a stout-hearted sort of fellow, did just that, with me trailing once again in his wake.

The remainder of the shift passed relatively uneventfully. I watched Boris as he hurled himself into caves and crevices again and again, frequently with startled (and irate) resident eels and parrot fish erupting out past him as he did so. After an hour of searching, I was cold, tired and somewhat battered by wave and current. A normal shift for Boris would be in the region of eight to ten hours – an unimaginable period for me in this gloomy, turbulent world. It was with real relief that I noted my air gauge was creeping into the red, and tapped him on the shoulder to indicate that I had to surface. He waved a friendly farewell and returned to work, leaving me to rise slowly through the dark water to the boat.

Although intense efforts have been made by all parties involved in the lobster fishery to ensure it remains sustainable, there are nonetheless warnings hidden in the past. Perhaps the most poignant comes from the testimony of an old fisherman called Don Gustavo Jaramillo Delgado, who enjoyed the now distant boom times of the very first days of the fishery:

'We would catch 500 to 700 pounds of lobster tail in two days, almost 40 or 50 thousand pounds in two months . . . There was all the lobster you could want.'

As I ascended, I looked down and I saw the pool of light cast by Boris's torch still tracking a path over the ocean floor, as it would do for many hours to come. He moved steadfastly behind it, a predatory silhouette working every inch of the reef with deadly resolve. An hour's intense work had caught two lobsters, a distant echo of the halcyon days gone by, but perhaps a measure of just how hard this method of fishing really is. Maybe therein lies the salvation of the fishery itself, as a few special men risk everything to work the sea floor in search of their increasingly elusive quarry.

There is a rather lovely postscript to this tale. Or a slightly absurd one, depending on which side of sentimentality you happen to fall.

Reassured by the provenance of the lobsters at the market, I returned with Tam, Isla and Molly a week later, determined to eat a traditional lobster feast with them on the beach that evening. It would be a culinary, and indeed sensory, extravaganza. We would devour the product of deep, cold clear water, caught sustainably through an initiative between local fishermen and a suite of conservation agencies. All the while we would be assailed by the roar of the surf, the sweet caress of an ocean breeze, and feel our toes wriggling into white Galapagos sand. It would be something we would remember for ever.

I picked out a great, hefty specimen, paid a considerable chunk of cash, then left carrying my booty with some pride back towards the car.

We all clambered in, and I set out for the short drive towards Bella Vista, where I would dispatch the lobster, cook it up, and then return to the beach. I placed it between the seats, resting it on a bag, and turned the key in the ignition. As I did so, I noticed that a silence had descended on the family, who were all now looking at me. I glanced down at the lobster, who was also looking at me.

'We don't want to eat Lenny,' piped up a tiny voice from the back seat. The mere fact that our previously anonymous crustacean had now been given a name by Isla augured badly for the feast ahead.

'It's where our food comes from, sweetheart,' I said, 'and it's important that we all understand that.'

'But Lenny wants to go back in the sea to his family,' said Isla. Lenny waggled his antennae in agreement. I glanced down at him in annoyance.

'Look, I'm not paying $50 for a lobster just to chuck it straight back in the sea,' I said, my voice rising shrilly, aware at some basic level that the argument was already lost.

'It would be a bit odd, though, wouldn't it, to eat him?' said Tam. 'Shall we just let Lenny go?'

'It's not bloody Lenny,' I said, now sounding petulant. 'It's dinner, and it cost $50. I'm not putting the damn thing back.'

Ten minutes later, we'd found a suitable spot by the harbour wall which was, distressingly, within the perfect eyeline of the market where I'd bought Lenny an hour previously. He in turn was being lowered reverentially back into the water by me, with all three girls cooing in admiration as I did so (not at me, I hasten to add, but at Lenny). I was fervently praying that the bloke who was probably even now folding my $50 into his wallet wasn't watching with his mates.

'Good luck Lenny,' said Tam.

'Bye Lenny. We love you,' said Isla. Molls reached down and patted him on the shell.

I released my hold on the carapace, and Lenny gave a triumphant flick of his tail, and vanished into the gloom. He'd shared our company for just over fifteen minutes, which breaks down to about $3 a minute. The kids were delighted, Tam gave me a quick kiss on the cheek, and Lenny – I imagined – was over the moon. The only player in this little drama who was deeply hacked off was me.

That evening we ate pasta, at home, in silence.

Floreana – The Mystic Isle

Sitting quietly at the southernmost edge of the archipelago, with a total area of only one hundred and seventy square kilometres, there wouldn't seem to be enough of Floreana to raise much of a scandal. But the island has one key characteristic that made it irresistible to the early pioneers. The middle of the island is 650 metres above sea level, and with altitude in the Galapagos comes rain, fertile soil, freshwater, and the ability to survive through the cycles of the year, and so people were drawn here from the very first days of settlers arriving in the Galapagos. Where there are people, there will inevitably be drama, and Floreana certainly didn't disappoint in that regard.

If the Galapagos could be said to be a microcosm of our entire relationship with the natural world, then Floreana is a neat representation of our entire relationship with the Galapagos. For such a small piece of real estate that has only been colonised in any meaningful way for two centuries, it really has seen the lot — murder, revolution, environmental pillage, romantic subterfuge, a (briefly) Utopian society, and economic boom and bust on an epic scale. It is the burial ground of many a dream, a diabolical melting pot of the very dregs of society, and yet also an example of what can be achieved by individuals with the highest motives who treat those under their charge with humanity and dignity.

Things actually started rather well, as, at the head of the first colonisation effort, was a remarkable man, whose qualities of decency and resolve so nearly created the Eden that everyone craved.

In the middle of 1831, one General Jose Villamil formed the Galapagos Settlement Company, and approached the president of Ecuador, Juan Jose Flores, to suggest that the islands be permanently inhabited, and incorporated as part of the Ecuadorian nation. Flores was receptive to the idea and, on 12 February 1832, a delegation arrived on the deserted island of Floreana to conduct the appropriate ceremony. The first settlers to arrive were Ecuadorian soldiers who had been condemned to death and had their sentences commuted if they agreed to join Villamil as the first permanent Galapagos residents. They could also bring their families, so the choice wasn't exactly a tricky one.

Villamil was, if nothing else, an optimist, so having been appointed Governor of the Galapagos in October 1832, he duly gathered together his band of 'settlers' (or, if you prefer to be completely accurate, recently pardoned swindlers, murderers, rebels and thieves), and created a colony in the highlands, which he called 'Haven of Peace'.

And he damn nearly pulled it off. He created a viable little settlement – numbering about 120 people – imported fruit trees and livestock, and started trading with passing whaling ships. Most significantly, he treated everyone with dignity and decency, and by all accounts the tiny settlement was indeed a peaceful retreat, a promising harbinger of things to come. His vice-governor, a Norwegian called Nicholas Lawson, even hosted a certain young biologist called Charles Darwin. This resulted in a seminal moment, for as they walked up the hill towards the highlands, Lawson casually mentioned that he could recognise where any tortoise came from in the Galapagos just by glancing at the shape of its shell. Darwin acknowledges this conversation in his journal:

> '. . . by far the most remarkable feature in the natural history of this archipelago . . . is that the different islands to a considerable extent are inhabited by different sets of beings. My attention was first called to this fact by the Vice-Governor, Mr Lawson, declaring that the tortoises differed from the different islands.'

This turned out to be a truly momentous observation, and plainly lodged in Darwin's mind, although the true Eureka moment was many years in coming. It was only when he published *On the Origin of Species* in 1859 that he acknowledged just how significant this comment was, planting a seed that took two decades to truly germinate.

But by the time Darwin's visit was taking place, the rot had already begun to set in. In March 1833 the Ecuadorian

Government had decided that Floreana should become a penal colony. Costs spiralled, trouble brewed, and faced with imminent bankruptcy, Villamil resigned as governor in 1837. This signalled the death knell for his Haven of Peace, as a series of despotic and/or incompetent leaders followed, resulting in a mutinous and bloody uprising in 1841. This caused most of the original settlers to return to the mainland, and it seemed that Villamil's dream had gone with them. He returned to the island in 1842, and made a valiant attempt to rebuild, but it was all for naught. In 1848, finally admitting what must have been a most bitter personal defeat, he took up a permanent post as a consul in America. Symbolically, this date coincided with the last tortoise being killed on the islands.

And so Floreana was abandoned, an erstwhile paradise now ravaged and denuded by man, with livestock roaming free to destroy what little remained of the original ecosystem. A mere seventeen years had elapsed since Villamil's bold vision, and now it seemed all hope had gone.

And yet today, here in the first part of the twenty-first century, a mere 160 years later, a scheme had emerged, so bold and so visionary, that it had the eyes of the world upon it. The people of Floreana, the modern settlers, had decided to 're-wild' their island, to try to introduce a new tortoise species, to restore vanished landscapes and species on the brink, and to eradicate the island completely of rats. It was an ambition on an epic scale, and if successful would be the largest inhabited island of its kind anywhere on earth to become rat free.

And so, as we landed on Floreana for the first time, I was excited. The level of this excitement was only heightened by an encounter in the harbour as we hove to at the steps. This was actually the work of Isla, who as a five-year-old obsessed with the sea was permanently scanning the water alongside any boat in which we happened to be travelling. This would continue long after us grown-ups had lapsed into that mumbling, semi-comatose state induced by heat, the growl of an outboard, and the rhythm of the swell.

'Penguin!' she shouted, leaping up and lunging forward. I caught her by the waist band as she cannoned past, holding her wriggling in what rapidly became a painful-looking wedgie. This was another, less desirable, characteristic of hers when it came to observing marine life – the urge to join it in the water. It showed commendable enthusiasm, but questionable judgement.

Sure enough, in the clear water of the harbour I saw a living bullet, the air held in its feathers shining like mercury, vapour trails of tiny bubbles tracking its progress as it hurtled past in pursuit of groups of silver fish. These shoals shattered and splintered before it, the light catching their tiny bodies as each desperately twisted and turned to avoid capture. It made me shout in delight, and Isla laughed, pointed, and wriggled even more vigorously at the sheer energy and exuberance of the hunt.

It seemed entirely incongruous, this penguin. A small visitor from another world. The equatorial sun beat down on the back of my neck, the heat shimmered on the concrete of the dock, and yet we were looking at the perfect form of a tiny polar creature in the clear harbour waters. The exact origins of the Galapagos penguin remain a mystery, but they almost certainly arrived with the cool Humboldt Current, and took up residence as the shallows of the Galapagos are (just) cold enough to ensure their survival. They are the northernmost penguin on earth, at 50cm tall amongst the smallest of their kind, and walk a tightrope of continued survival with less than 2,000 remaining. I was delighted to see one. And hunting as well – what a welcome to Floreana.

Buoyed up, we bade farewell to the penguin, now almost out of sight as it pursued the shoals deeper and deeper, and loaded our bags on to the harbour side. This was the second reason I was excited, as I was hoping to meet something of a local legend. In fact, I was hoping to meet a brace of them.

The first man I was hoping to meet was Claudio Cruz. Claudio's father had originally settled on Floreana in 1939, and had created a small farm in the highlands. Being a resolute sort of chap, after four years on his own he decided he needed some companionship, and duly set sail to find Mrs Cruz. Dashing good looks being a family trait, this did not take long, and he duly returned to the islands to make his house their home. They went on to have twelve children. I'll say that again: they went on to have twelve children, in Floreana, scratching a living in the Highlands, in the 1940s. This shows either commendable multi-tasking and survival skills, or a lack of an ability to think of ways to occupy yourself on the colder nights at altitude. Either way, the Cruz name went swiftly from settler, to family, to dynasty. Claudio was child number eight, and he and his brothers would go on to have a seminal impact on the island's conservation efforts.

I walked up the steps on the quayside, and shook hands with the driver of the small bus that had turned up to meet us. After exchanging hellos (much nodding, smiling and gesturing to surmount the language barrier), I helped him throw a few of the bags into the back, then left him so I could round up Isla and Molly.

They were by this stage leaning over the quayside, peering at an exposed lava reef five metres below, counting Sally Lightfoot crabs while jostling each other for position.

'Wow, look at that,' said Isla, defying several laws of physics as she cantilevered her body out over the (potentially lethal) drop. 'I can see a massive iguana. And it's bright red!'

Molly found this very interesting indeed, and climbed on her sister's back to get a closer look, causing Isla's arms to buckle somewhat. I arrived on the scene moments before my own family legacy was about to be messily terminated, and hauled them both protesting noisily away from the quayside and towards the bus. The driver smiled at them, and helped them aboard. Tam finished loading the last bags – who says the age of chivalry is dead? – and climbed aboard herself.

'The Wittmer Hotel, *si?*' said the driver over one shoulder.

'Yep, great,' I said somewhat distractedly, as I was still wrangling the kids. The bus had open sides with wooden benches for seats, and as such I was anticipating an exhilarating journey of sharp corners and sliding bottoms. I finally got Isla and Molly within arms' reach, by which stage the bus had started, a guttural roar of the engine and a crunch of the gears signalling the start of our journey. We sped over the dark gravel of the harbour entrance and on to the main road, with a cluster of houses appearing on either side and the highway stretching ahead of us. And then, with a squeal of brakes and a hiss of hydraulics, we stopped.

The driver jumped out, and moved to the side of the bus to gesture at me – clearly he was making a 'you need to get off my bus' motion. Had I offended him in some way? Was this customs and immigration? I climbed down wearily, and was surprised to see a large pair of wooden gates, and a sign welcoming us to the Wittmer Hotel. This was particularly interesting, as we were about a hundred metres from the harbour.

This gave me the first indication of the quirkiness of island life here on Floreana. There are only 120 people who live here, and everyone needed a role, a job, a profession. Clearly our bus driver was responsible for delivering tourists to the hotels. If the hotel happened to be within a stone's throw of the arrival point, then so what?

He helped the children out of the bus, and lifted out our bags. I thanked him, and indicated with an elaborate mime involving my watch, and waving my arms around (one slightly crooked at the elbow was the hour hand, one at full stretch the minute hand) that I'd see him the next morning to travel to our next destination. I was hoping to take a ride into the verdant hills of the interior to visit Claudio's farm, ground zero for the rat eradication programme that was going to be so central to the island's future. The driver looked at me, utterly baffled, then smiled warmly, shook my hand, climbed into the cab, and drove away in a cloud of dust. It struck me that there was every chance that I'd never see him, or his bus, ever again.

Tam and the kids had gone on ahead, and I picked up what remained of the luggage and followed. The gates led to a white concrete walkway, which in turn led to a row of rooms facing a black sand beach. By the time I arrived, Isla and Molly had already kicked off their shoes and were sitting on the sand a few metres away from a young sea lion pup, who was regarding them with genuine curiosity. This was signified by the fact that its head was upside down, having used that ludicrously flexible neck to bend over backwards like a living question mark.

'Look, Daddy – black sand,' said Isla, picking some up and letting it trickle through her fingers.

'And an upside-down seal,' added Molls, herself bending over backwards to see if her head could touch her toes (it could – oh to be young again). As far as they were concerned, Floreana was already living up to its mysterious billing.

And that billing is worthy of note. The mere fact that an online article was written in 2015 about the settlers on Floreana, entitled 'Nietzsche-Fueled Homesteader Death Showdown', says pretty much all you need to know about the dramas that had taken place here, and so it was particularly exciting that the hotel we were staying in was very much part of that turbulent past. Or at least the owners were.

Floreana lay abandoned for many years, and then experienced a series of settlement attempts that would grace any dime novel (and indeed briefly held the attention of the world in deliciously scandalised thrall). It had the lot – eccentricity, sex, murder, poisoning, neighbourly disputes, and mysteries that have not been solved even today.

I will paraphrase here, as to go into any detail would require vast amounts of time, would reveal all manner of unanswered questions, and would leave us all feeling rather under-done and dissatisfied. But I'll leave in the juicy bits, rest assured about that.

The first people to recolonise Floreana were a German couple – Dr Friedrich Ritter and his lover, Dore Strauch. They arrived on 15 September 1929, and immediately established a small farm they called 'Firedo'. Theirs was an experiment in nihilism; indeed they had been drawn together by a mutual love of Nietzsche, but they were nothing if not hard working and capable (though I'm not sure they would have been terrific company – in every image that survives of Ritter he is unsmiling, almost as though the camera is a gross intrusion). He also insisted that Dore have all her teeth removed before they moved to the island, just as he had done. They had one set of metal false teeth, which they shared. This would have made a dinner party with the Ritters an intriguing affair, although the menu would have been limited, as they were both vegetarians (that may seem an inconsequential fact, but it is worth remembering, as it ultimately had some significance in Friedrich's grisly fate).

In August 1932, they were joined by another German family, the Wittmers, who had also decided they wanted to relocate to paradise. 'Joined' is a generous term, as Ritter saw this as nothing more than an invasion of his privacy. Although not openly hostile to the Wittmers, he certainly wasn't up for family outings together and long evenings playing charades. He made it perfectly clear that he didn't want them anywhere near him, so the new arrivals moved into a cave that had been previously used by pirates. This is particularly notable as the Wittmers consisted of Heinz (dad), Margret (mum) and Harry (grumpy teenager), and they weren't exactly in ideal condition physically for reverting to stone-age living. Heinz had rheumatic heart disease, and Margret was four months pregnant when they arrived. She duly gave birth to another son, Rolf, in the cave at the end of that year.

This German enclave could have worked out quite nicely – these new settlers were after all practical, hard working, and hugely resourceful. But hoving into view was trouble, real trouble.

Floreana was about to receive the landed gentry, in the form of Baroness Eloise Wagner de Bousquet. She was accompanied by three lovers, which seems a tad excessive, although this was quickly whittled down to two, as one of them – Felipe Valdivieso – soon scurried back to the community on San Cristóbal, noting with some vigour on his arrival: 'That woman is totally crazy'.

And she was. The title was made up, the vision of a luxury hotel for millionaires a fantasy, and her beleaguered lovers doomed. The two of them – Rudolph Lorenz and Robert Philippson – set about building the hotel, the result of which was a pile of lava rocks called 'Hacienda Paradiso'. This was faithful to the long tradition in the islands of creating something terrible, then giving it a really nice name so other people will come to join in the collective misery.

Eloise declared herself the 'Empress of Galapagos', and became the darling of the gossip columns back home in Germany. Ritter – scratching away at the earth, gumming at a coconut husk, and attempting to reach a higher spiritual plane – was horrified. For two years chaos, bedlam, random snogging and general anarchy seem to have been the order of the day. And then, on one steamy night in March 1934, the baroness and her favoured lover, Philippson, vanished. They were never seen again, and their bodies never found. There were stories of screams and gunshots, but none were ever verified. Someone had taken the adage of 'what goes on tour, stays on tour' to its absolute limit.

The baroness's other less favoured lover, Lorenz, was also no use in revealing the truth, due to his 'shortly to be dead' status. He decided to flee the island by using a vessel skippered by a Norwegian sailor called Trygyve Nuggerud. They made it to

Puerto Ayora, where Lorenz persuaded him that they should continue to San Cristóbal. Setting sail on Friday, 13 July (plainly not one for superstitions, our friend Lorenz), they were lost at sea. Their desiccated bodies were discovered on 17 November on a beach on Marchena Island.

Now that the baroness and her chaps had been shot/drowned/eaten by seagulls/buried under lava rocks/hidden away/turned into biltong on a beach, it seemed that order could be restored on Floreana. That same year however, on 21 November 1934 – only a few days after the bodies of Lorenz and Nuggerud had been found – Ritter died from food poisoning. This was utterly bizarre for a number of reasons. The first was that he was a survival expert, who by this stage knew every plant and berry on the island. The second was that he died from eating undercooked chicken. An evangelical vegetarian, a man who advocated (humourless) pure living, died from not cooking a bit of meat properly.

Only two weeks later his companion, Dore, left Floreana on a passing yacht, leaving the remaining family – the Wittmers – to quietly get on with building a legacy on Floreana that now extends to four generations. I'm no detective, but I think there was a bit of skulduggery afoot there. And this next statement might get me in a bit of trouble legally, but I'm going to go out on a limb and say that Dore did it. She killed the baroness and Philippson for imposing on her personal paradise, and then she killed Ritter because (and I'm speculating a bit here) he must have been bloody annoying to live with. Then she left with a dashing Californian sailor – G. Allan Hancock, owner of the aforementioned yacht – and went home to Germany to write her memoirs.

The Wittmers – truly remarkable in their fortitude and ability to take the vagaries of fate in their stride – continued to live happily on Floreana, and still do. Rolf, the baby born in the cave, became a highly significant figure in conservation and ecotourism in the islands, and his bust is one of the first things you see when you land at the dock.

And so, as I strolled on the beach in front of the hotel, I was rather hoping to meet the current proprietor – a certain Inge Wittmer, the daughter of the original settlers. Her full name of Floreana Inge Borg Wittmer shows that she really is about as steeped in this island's history as it is possible to be. She now runs the lodge with her own daughter, Erika.

Tam was sitting on the veranda of the main hotel, talking to a middle-aged lady, so I wandered up the beach to introduce myself. As I did so, a silver-haired, much older lady emerged from the main entrance, and began to amble towards the rooms. As I saw her, I quickened my pace – this could only be Erika and Inge.

I intercepted the older lady, and stood on the path in front of her, smiling broadly with a hand extended. She graciously extended her own, and shook mine while giving me a curious half smile. She then politely edged her way around me, and went on her way. If you grew up in such uncompromising circumstances, I'm guessing that you have little time for grinning buffoons who don't even introduce themselves properly (I had been somewhat struck dumb).

Erika proved a little more chatty, and showed me to the small museum where they had collected their possessions from those first few extraordinary years on the island. There were typewriters and chessboards, binoculars and rifles, all carefully maintained from all those years before. You don't tend to think of fastidiousness being a key survival skill, but of course it is. A slip-shod approach to the administration of life means you might, for example, inadvertently murder one of your lovers, or eat a bit of dodgy chicken.

I didn't really have time to explore the exhibits, as I was joined by Isla and Molly, now dusted in dark sand and demanding their dinner.

'I'm really hungry,' said Isla.

'Me too,' said Molls, with considerable emphasis.

'Don't worry, little ones,' said Tam, walking up behind us, 'my new friend Erika has told me that there's a really lovely little place just a short stroll down the beach. Let's go.'

Without further ado, we began to walk down the path that ran parallel to the shore, very soon entering an area of white sand and low scrub, with the waves chuckling and rustling on the shoreline only a few feet away.

'Wow, look,' said Isla, stopping abruptly, 'a turtle.'

And sure enough, in the shallows just offshore, a turtle had broken the surface to breathe. We looked at it appreciatively, Molls hoisted high on to my shoulders for a better view, and were delighted when another appeared, and then another. The shallows were alive with them, stepping stones of glistening reptilian heads enjoying the sanctuary of the proximity of shoreline and seabed.

We continued our amble in the golden glow of the evening sun, and soon a series of huts appeared before us. At the far end was a larger, sheltered area, and waiting for us there was, randomly, our bus driver. He smiled warmly, and waved us to the table nearest the beach, where we dined on local produce he cooked in a small kitchen a few yards away. It was delicious food, made all the more so by the mood music of the waves, and a cabaret of passing turtles. By the time we were done it was dark, and we trailed back to the Wittmer Hotel, Molly snoring and dribbling on one of my shoulders, and Isla holding her mum's hand in that special darkness one only seems to get on small islands in the middle of a great ocean.

Despite my misgivings about the part-time bus driver/chef, he turned up exactly on time the next morning as we stood outside the gates of the hotel. The air was still cool, with finches jumping about our feet as we stirred up the dust at the road side. They scattered at the squeal of brakes, and our driver leapt down from his cab to expansively welcome us.

'*Buenos días, buenos días,*' he said briskly, all industry and movement as he lifted Isla and Molly to their seats and helped us put our bags in the back. He was plainly an energetic chap, and I began to feel bad about my post-journey snap judgement yesterday. Here was a man who could not only take you where you wanted to go, but could also cook you a damn good meal when you got there. Virtually marriage material, now I thought about it.

The ride into the highlands was wonderful, particularly in our open-sided bus. The kids leaned out of the sides, waved their fingers in the wind, breathed deep and closed their eyes, and all the while the bus roared and rattled its way to our final destination – a farm in, and of, the clouds. At last, the track beneath us levelled, and the roar of the engine lowered to an exhausted grumble. Around us were animal pens, with the unmistakable silhouettes of cattle and the occasional donkey moving within them. A large metal gate barred our way, held in place by twine (good to see some farming traditions are truly universal).

I leapt out of the bus, lifted down Isla and Molly, and helped Tam down by one hand, rather like welcoming a visiting dignitary. We were both anxious to meet Claudio, this man who had positioned himself on the front line of the fight to restore this island. His farm was famous within the islands – successful, verdant, sympathetic to the landscape around it, and established by his dad on that first visit in 1939. Claudio had placed it at the heart of the rewilding effort, choosing to lead by example, and by reputation he was a progressive, intelligent visionary who was engineering great change.

The bus driver kindly opened the gate for us. I made a mental note to tip him a few pesos before we left, perhaps to assuage my guilt about my ill-judged assumption the day before. I gestured to the collection of fences, pens and farm buildings ahead of us.

'Claudio Cruz?' I asked the driver. 'Where is ermmm . . . ¿dónde está . . . ? Claudio Cruz?'

I was pretty confident he'd know the great man, it was a small island after all.

He liked this question a lot. He smiled, then he grinned, then he laughed, showing perfect white teeth. He took his glasses off, and peered at me, then laughed again, before shaking his head, and pointing to his own chest.

'Me llamo Claudio Cruz,' he said. '¡Hola!' He gripped my upper arm in delight, shook my hand, and then turned away, still chuckling at the quaint absurdity of outsiders. 'Come, come.'

I followed, chastened and mute. I'd had a rather quaint – entirely clichéd, western, first world – vision that Claudio spent most of his time surveying his land, crushing delicate leaves between his thumb and forefinger to sniff their essence, and ruminating on his veranda about how to bring about change. But, of course, this was miles out. This was Floreana, and he was going to damn well drive the bus, cook the food, till the land, run a lovely little resort (the Lava Lodge, where we'd eaten our exquisite meal), and, what's more, he was going to do it all himself. Change was indeed going to come to Floreana, even if he had to personally create it. Such was the island way.

Claudio waved us over to a low pen, and when we arrived, he crouched down to Isla and Molly's level. He reached out, and with the warmest of smiles, put his arms around them to give them a hug. It was a lovely gesture, a welcome to his ancestral land. Then he looked at them closely, from one to the other, put his fingers to his lips in a conspiratorial gesture, winked, and then vaulted into the concrete pen behind him. There was a terrific commotion from within, and then he emerged triumphantly, clutching two tiny piglets. He duly gave one of these to Isla – a black-and-white spotted one – and the other to Molly – a perfect pink one. They wriggled and squealed (that applies to both the pigs and the little girls) and then settled. Isla and Molly both looked up at Claudio with wide eyes – hero, legend, provider of piglets.

What followed was a tour of his land, and a brief introduction to the devastation created by rats. He showed us his maize crop, with almost every ear of corn nibbled, and every stalk scratched and shredded. This was the fruits of months of brutal labour and yet had been decimated to the point where it could not be harvested. He showed us a vast avocado tree, orange groves, guava plantations, and banana plants – a Utopian vision realised by Dickensian labour.

'How do you feel, Claudio? As you look at this?' I gestured to one of the maize plants, ravaged and shredded beyond repair, the optimism of harvest a distant memory.

My gesture, and my question, effortlessly bridged the language barrier – Claudio shrugged, gave a philosophical smile, then clasped his hands together in prayer and cast his eyes skywards. Then he looked back at me, flashed that invincible smile, and clapped me on the shoulder.

But this philosophical approach hid a core of steel – it was no coincidence that his family had survived three generations of farming here, surmounting challenges that were not just agricultural but sometimes meant the difference between life and death itself. Claudio was actually a major force in the attempts to completely eradicate rats from Floreana, and indeed the slow re-birth of something approaching the original environment of the island.

The problem here, of course, is that you only need to leave two rats – one male, one female – and you haven't eradicated them at all. Rats have a gestation period of twenty-one days, and can have litters of up to fourteen pups. They also reach sexual maturity after only nine weeks, so those young then start producing their own offspring.

In perfect breeding conditions (and a highland farm in Floreana is pretty damn close to perfect breeding conditions), those two rats can produce 1,248 offspring in twelve months, with their young starting to have their own young from only three months into that year. But then the law of exponential growth kicks in, and we have the truly terrifying figure of those same two rats – after three years – having created, wait for it, 482 million offspring. Yep, that's half a billion rats from a founding population of two.

So the scheme to rewild Floreana and eradicate the rats is hugely ambitious, involving helicopters, drones, several cooperating scientific and conservation bodies, and all of the local people. The last part of that sentence is very important indeed – without complete local cooperation, the scheme will inevitably fail.

We sat underneath the spreading branches of the huge avocado tree, hanging heavy with the bulbous green shapes of the ripening fruit. They looked immense to me, like a crop of ripening rugby balls. Claudio sat with me, as the children leapt and shrieked, chasing the chickens around the green base of the old tree, and he smiled once again.

'My papa,' he said, pointing at the great trunk, and then himself. It was quite a thought – in 1939 a young man had thrashed and cut his way through the undergrowth here, and planted a sapling to mark the centre of his new farm. And now, in the cool morning air of the mountains, I shared a drink with his son to mark the start of another epic undertaking – this time to save the long-lost soul of their home. We sat at the epicentre of an island that had been ravaged by man like no other in the Galapagos, with one species gone for ever (the tortoise), twelve locally extinct, and fifty-five listed as threatened.

The rewilding would start the following year and would happen in three phases. The project essentially involved strafing every environment, every nook and every cranny, with poison, so the first stage is ensuring that the poison will not kill native species as well as the rats. This means a series of controlled tests and cautious, limited applications of it in small areas – a phase known as mitigation. Then follows the eradication process itself, when the entire island will be systematically covered in poison – in itself an extraordinary concept of course, but such is the scale of the problem, and the ambition of the solution. Livestock will be rounded up and placed in specially built pens, domestic animals kept indoors, and many prayers directed towards the heavens as the drones whirr overhead, the helicopters clatter, and the deadly pellets rain from the sky.

And then, many months later, comes the reintroduction. Locally vanished species, such as the Floreana mockingbird and the Galapagos racer, will be returned to their ancestral home. This will be an emotionally charged moment, a hugely symbolic gesture of recapturing a piece of the past, and will require a monumental international effort, multi-agency expertise, and a great deal of money. All of this will happen over the next three years – a truly epic undertaking – but, if it works, if mankind can indeed turn the clock back in a place such as Floreana, then maybe there is hope for us all.

Looking across at Claudio, I raised my glass in salute. He lifted his drink in return, an indefatigable, indestructible symbol of a new type of islander, doing his best to make amends for those who had gone before.

Isla had always been fearless around water, to a positively alarming degree at times (an incident involving a large wave, an ill-timed attempt to pick up a pebble, and a subsequent rescue by grandma being a stand-out moment among many). But our progress to date had been in the form of much anarchic splashing, with a little bit of snorkelling tuition thrown in. I hadn't really done a proper exploration of a shallow bay with her, and as there was such a beautiful area of shallow water just down the coast from the Wittmer Hotel, one that seemed to be perpetually dotted with turtles, this seemed the perfect opportunity.

My theory relating to water safety with Isla was a fairly simple one. It involved putting her in a ludicrously thick wetsuit, making her instantly the most buoyant object in the Pacific Ocean. She tended to treat me as a mothership, clinging on to me and even climbing on to my back, periodically making brief forays out into the blue to return with exciting news/a mouthful of water, depending on how that particular mini-expedition had gone.

As we kitted up on the beach, I asked her if she was nervous.

'Not really,' she said, adding entirely unselfconsciously, 'because everything in my head, and everything in my heart, I learned from you.'

I spent the next five minutes attempting to remove something from my eyes. Whatever it was, it was plainly a powerful irritant as suddenly they had started to water quite badly.

Having pulled myself together, I managed to get Isla into her wetsuit using the tried and trusted method of dads the world over. This involved wedging her feet into the neoprene of the legs, then picking up the entire ensemble and waving it around. By the time I stopped, the wetsuit was on the outside of Isla, and Isla was on the inside of the wetsuit, so all seemed to be in order.

We pushed off into the shallow water, as clear as Evian, chuckling restlessly around us as we finned out towards the fringing reef. This barrier of lava rocks had created a natural lagoon only a few metres deep, with lazy, small waves that allowed us to make easy progress. All of these things made it an excellent place to snorkel, and indeed an excellent place to be a turtle. As air-breathing reptiles, they essentially snorkel all their lives, albeit to a rather better standard than we do.

Isla settled on my back for the short journey out to the centre of the lagoon, a natural platform of lava rocks covered in a scrubby film of green algae. I could immediately see why there were so many turtles here – it wasn't just the sheltered environment and the shallow water; the algae also provided a colossal buffet. We were essentially drifting over a service station for any passing turtle. Rest, eat, and then head back out to sea.

One of the rocks detached itself from the seabed and drifted up towards us, propelled by elegant sweeps of wide flippers. An ancient head swept from side to side, the eyes surveying us with what can only be described as polite curiosity. This was not an emotion that was reflected on our side. Isla gave a falsetto squeak through her snorkel, and leapt off the mothership, only to immediately lose her nerve and climb back on board. She decided on a compromise and wrapped her arms tightly round my neck, which allowed her to lower her face into the water while still firmly attached. It also somewhat restricted my own ability to breathe, but that, for now, could be regarded as acceptable collateral damage. This was an encounter for the ages, one that I would rewind endlessly, even if it meant that I was periodically losing consciousness throughout. Before her was an ancient, a Bedouin, a traveller following routes invisible to us but held deep in her ancestral memory: it was a female green turtle.

Green turtles are the most common of the five turtle species found in the Galapagos, and this bay was alive with them. Only the females come ashore to breed – the males spend their entire lives at sea – but they are all drawn to the same sites, with shallow water, abundant food and gentle waves. It is a rest from the currents and the chaos of the open sea, a moment to drop their guard, and even to meet curious little girls encountering their first ever underwater dinosaur.

Green turtles are, of course, endangered. Historically, this has been through hunting activity – indeed, their name comes from the fact that the soup they create is green. To show how recent this threat was, it was actually Winston Churchill's favourite food. But now it is by-catch – when they are caught by accident in fishing nets – predation on their eggs, destruction of their nesting grounds, and ocean plastics that are wreaking a terrible toll. Captive breeding programmes are having a positive impact, as are education initiatives and more vigorous policing of nesting sites globally, but, nonetheless, these remain perilous times for this prehistoric animal.

But just for this brief moment, none of that mattered. This was an encounter on the turtle's terms, and it sculled towards us with genuine curiosity. Isla lay stock still, not even breathing, as this great old beast, an antique, a scarred relic of a thousand oceanic journeys, edged ever closer to study this small interloper into its watery world.

Soon they were virtually nose to nose. Isla gave another tiny squeak through her snorkel, and gave a small wave of her hand. The turtle looked non-plussed – one of the drawbacks of reptilian living being that you always look non-plussed – but gave a vague twitch of one flipper, which was quite enough for Isla. It then turned elegantly on the spot, revolving in place like a vinyl disc on a turntable, and headed off into the limitless, turbulent blue of the Galapagos shallows, leaving behind two breathless mammals and a memory to last their lifetimes.

Dancing with Isabela

Floreana might have provided us with food for thought and moments to savour, but it also delivered one of the worst journeys we made during our entire residence on the islands. For reasons best known to myself, I had decided that the best way back to Santa Cruz was via a water-taxi, as opposed to the larger ferry we had used to arrive.

'It's a bit small,' Tam said, shading her eyes as she stood on the edge of the dock. 'That can't be it, surely?'

I had a very strong inkling that it was indeed 'it', and sifted rapidly through a few excuses to try to rationalise the decision.

'Smaller is more agile, Tam,' I said. 'This type of boat cuts through the waves, not over the top of them. We'll be in the harbour in Puerto Ayora before you know it.'

The bulk of that sentence was made up. The only bit of it that had a semblance of truth was that we'd ultimately be in the harbour at Puerto Ayora, and even that should have had 'eventually' as a substitute for 'before you know it'.

Tam seemed convinced though, and we climbed aboard as the crew (well, the man) helped us with our bags. The boat really was quite small, about the size and shape of a pointy Transit van. Lots of other people were climbing aboard too. Evidently this was going to be a cosy two hours or so. Isla and Molly, who were by now philosophical beyond their tender years, settled themselves on to the deck at our feet, while we wedged ourselves on to a narrow bench at the stern.

The final touch was the lowering of a polythene cover around the area where we passengers were crowded together. The idea seemed to be that it would keep us dry, but what with the searing equatorial heat, and the stench that was immediately released from the decking, it was exactly like spending a decent amount of time in a greenhouse where someone was trying to grow tomatoes using vomit. The added touch was that the greenhouse was soon rocking from side to side, with the occasional oceanic heave. As such, very, very soon a large number of the passengers were following suit with a few oceanic heaves of their own.

I won't go into too much detail about that forty-mile crossing back to Santa Cruz, but suffice to say that most of the population of Puerto Ayora smelled the boat before they saw it, and the triumphant unveiling of the occupants by the crew/man revealed a group of hollow-eyed cadavers covered in each other's partially digested lunch. The gust of humid air that emerged as we were uncovered would have felled a passing frigate bird, and even the hardened roustabouts on the dockside were breathing through their mouths.

The upshot of this was a resolution as a family never to travel by boat between the islands again. This was actually a fairly simple proposition, as our time in the Galapagos was coming to a close anyway. We had one last visit in the two weeks that remained, to the newest, shiniest, volcano-iest island of them all – Isabela.

'No problem, Monty,' said Roby, when I broached the delicate subject of how we were going to get there. 'It's really easy to fly, and there's a decent airstrip on Isabela that takes commercial planes. I'll set it all up for you.'

Good old Roby. I had spent the majority of our time on the islands making my problems his problems, and he had always remained the epitome of good grace and logistical poise.

'Thanks, chap,' I said, sorely tempted to take him home with me to England. This makes perfect sense, by the way, as everyone needs a Roby.

A week passed, and we were very much ready to go to Isabela. I had heard only good things about the island – the largest in the Galapagos with a surface area the same as Yorkshire, yet with a population of only 1,700. It seemed to epitomise the days of yore, when the islands were newly colonised and full of promise.

Roby kindly drove us to the harbour at the northern end of Santa Cruz, where we caught the ferry across to Baltra (only 200 metres away, so that doesn't count as a boat trip). We jumped on to the bus, and rattled our way to the airport.

Everyone else disembarked first, taking with them expensive suitcases and ergonomically designed carry-on bags. We left the bus last, checking in at a small kiosk in the main terminal before going through security with everyone else. We then had a short wait – this always strikes me as a dangerous period of modern travel, confined as you are with time to spare and money to burn, in a vast colosseum of tat. Somehow we negotiated this witching hour, with only three or four punch-ups with Isla and Molly, and then we heard our names being called.

'*Hola*,' said a charming young lady, who had walked around the departure lounge trying to find us, 'you flying to Isabela, yes?'

I said we were, and handed over our boarding passes. This was becoming very exciting indeed – personal service leading to a gleaming jet that would whisk us between the islands.

We were led out on to the hard standing, shimmering and pulsing in the heat, and walked towards the edge of the main terminal. We then walked around the side, to the equivalent of a parking lot, and there waiting for us was our plane.

If the boat that had taken us from Floreana was the size of a Transit van, then spookily enough so was this. It had wings on the sides, which was good, a tail at the back, and propellers at the edges. All of this was reassuring, but it was the bit in the middle that worried me. Or rather, how little there was of the bit in the middle.

Molls had a tantrum as we tried to lift her in, which showed more of an instinct of self-preservation than anything else. Tam simply looked at me with wide eyes. I shrugged helplessly, not knowing quite what to say, and so we wedged ourselves into the cabin, put the large, bright-red ear defenders on (which proved a handy noise-excluding device for Molly's bellows of disapproval, if nothing else), and waited for events to unfold.

The pilot, suitably dashing in gleaming white shirt with golden epaulettes glinting in the sun, looked over his shoulder and gave us a cheery wave. He seemed a competent enough fellow, although his safety brief involved nothing more than a casual wave at the emergency exit (or 'the door', as I would have more commonly termed it), and waggling the emergency card in our vague direction.

He pushed a few buttons, toggled a lever or two, and then the engine coughed into life. The propellers began to spin in the approved manner, and with a lurch we were away.

I actually quite like small planes, but not as a rule when I am flying with my entire family. And when that fact means that they are full up. This particular aircraft, having taxied to the main runway (looking rather pleased with itself to be among the big boys), accelerated swiftly and then took flight. It seemed to do so with a distinct sideways tilt, a kind of crabbing ascent beloved of black-and-white films involving Sopwith Pups over Ypres. I glanced at the pilot, who could not have looked more relaxed if he tried, which was reassuring. He even took a selfie on his phone as we ascended, which was less reassuring, and a new one on me in the world of commercial aviation.

The subsequent flight was what a veteran pilot might describe as 'sporting'. It was a hot day, with some brisk winds, and the combination of both of those things resulted in some exciting vertical and horizontal movements. For myself and Tam it was a relentless rollercoaster ride of sickening drops and euphoric ascents. In many ways it was a neat metaphor for married life, now I come to think of it. Throughout the pilot seemed entirely content, although if I squinted hard, I was sure I could see tiny beads of sweat appearing on the back of his neck. The transitions between the land and sea and then back again were particularly exhilarating, with the pitch of the engine changing and the super-structure groaning around us. This was due to the sudden changes in air temperature, as the warm air from the land below billowed upwards in a series of booming thermals as we travelled through them from the cold air over the sea.

We were, of course, completely safe, but such rational thoughts tend to elude you when you're being shaken hard enough to make your fillings fall out. Glancing out of the window, the terrain below hardly looked like an inviting landing area, all folded lava rocks and spiky cactus. In fact, I could think of no piece of ground on earth that was less appropriate for an aircraft to touch down, even with a pilot who would doubtless be rattling off a selfie or two as we spiralled to our fiery demise.

I glanced across at Tam, who looked terrified, and then across at the kids. Isla was looking with interest out of the window, and Molly was fast asleep. I had to admire their chutzpah, if nothing else.

When you land in a small plane, you really land, and this aircraft was no exception. Forty minutes later the engine pitch changed dramatically, and the pilot stopped daydreaming to actu-ally start pulling levers in earnest, heaving away on the steering as, with a bit of sideways, a touch of forwards, and another bit of sideways, we made our final approach. I was staring at the landing gear, which was about six inches from my nose, and to my intense relief saw the runway rise to meet it with a tiny volcanic puff of smoke, as if to announce our arrival on the glorious, magical, mysterious island of Isabela.

*   *   *

Isabela is the largest island in the Galapagos archipelago, and very much a new arrival on the scene. To understand its current status as one of the most volcanically active inhabited islands on earth, one must first understand how the archipelago as a whole was formed. This is simply explained through the use of a large piece of pizza dough, and a Bunsen burner.

For a long time it was thought that the Galapagos was formed via volcanic eruptions between the cracks of tectonic plates – the islands lie on the junction between the Nazca and Cocos continental plates, after all – but the truth is that all of their formation are due to a combination of the Nazca plate moving slowly east, and a stationary hot spot beneath it all. This is where our pizza dough and Bunsen burner come in. If one were to hold said dough over the blue flame of a Bunsen burner, then edge ever so slowly sideways (about 3cm a year is the current estimate) while the Bunsen burner stayed still, then you'd end up with a series of eruptions in the dough. The result is a group of oceanic islands, popping up in the middle of nowhere, having never been connected to another land mass of any sort. This is where the Galapagos come from – a tectonic plate moving slowly over the top of a static point belching magma upwards. And young Isabela, sitting on the western edge of the island chain, very much still has that fire in her belly.

The western islands are perpetually blowing their tops in a series of dramatic geological events. There have been at least fourteen episodes of intense tectonic activity or volcanic eruptions since 1801, with the latest coming in June 2018, when Sierra Negra began to belch smoke and haemorrhage lava. All of these major events have taken place in Fernandina and Isabela while the rest of the archipelago sails serenely away in contented middle age, having cooled their adolescent ardour.

Isabela is only a million years old, and even though it is only 100 kilometres long, it is made up of a string of six volcanos running from south to north. Five of them remain active. As such a turbulent and restless piece of the planet, it seems entirely fitting (and not remotely surprising) that it also has a dramatic, and rather dark, human history. It is one that is only now switching to a more sedate, Calypso-style existence built around white-sand beaches and strolling tourists.

The entire island, with an area of 4,588 square kilometres, only has a population of 1,700 people, most of whom are centred in the capital, Puerto Villamil – named after the visionary first governor of the islands. That is a density of 0.47 of a person per square kilometre of the island, by the way – this really is a vast, empty landscape.

Puerto Villamil was established in 1893, and by 1905 its population had swelled to 200 people. At its front is Bahaia de la Tortuga, which translates as Turtle Bay. There seem to be rather a lot of Turtle Bays in the Galapagos, for obvious reasons, although one can't help thinking the early pioneers could have tried a little harder on the naming front. But then again, they did have other things on their minds, which, in the case of this particular Turtle Bay, was burying their treasure. This was a regular haunt of pirates, with the latest find of buried booty being made as recently as 1974.

Such a villainous theme continued with the opening of a prison in 1944. Here 200 inmates, shipped in from mainland Ecuador, were housed in famously brutal conditions – if you were a criminal on the mainland, Isabela acted as the ultimate deterrent. The prisoners lived like animals, without even basic comforts in a place that was called, without a trace of irony, '*El Porvener*', The Future. Perhaps the most telling monument to the horror of their confinement remains in the form of the '*Muro de las Lagrimas*' – the Wall of Tears. It takes a particularly twisted mind to come up with a scheme that requires men to toil in the merciless heat shifting large basalt rocks, to create a huge barrier that starts and ends nowhere. The wall remains, and today is a popular tourist attraction, perhaps causing visitors a moment's pause in paradise, to reflect on the diabolical conditions under which men toiled and died here. The prison was closed in 1949 after a mutiny, but the wall is their monument: a headstone fifty metres long, five metres high, and eight metres wide, sitting squat and silent in the equatorial sun.

But Isabela has moved on, a fact that our guide, Pablo Valladares, was extremely keen to point out as we drove the short distance from the air strip to the jetty to pick up our bags, which had arrived by boat.

'Ah, you have come to the most beautiful place in the whole of Galapagos,' he said proudly. He smiled, the lines etched deep into his face a testimony to a life spent squinting into the sun. He was whip-cord thin, compact and elegant in his movements, with bright eyes and a quick smile.

'I have watched this island change in the twenty years I have been here,' he said. 'Now, when boats leave the harbour, they take people to see the animals, not to kill them. It makes me grateful for who we have become.'

After the flight, Tam was simply grateful to be alive, and Isla and Molly were, as ever, peering out of the windows. Before them passed a blurred collage of sand, sea, surf and gently waving palm trees.

'How about breakfast?' said Pablo, as we stopped behind a building on the edge of town.

I suddenly realised that we hadn't eaten that morning, as the threat of imminent death had made it seem rather futile. This realisation saw the doors of the car fly open, and the kids dash in a harum-scarum sprint to a table that was laid out at the head of the beach waiting for us. I was rather warming to Pablo.

We feasted on local bread, porridge, fresh fruit and scrambled eggs heaped in steaming, flaxen piles on wooden plates. I felt the tension of the journey seep away as Isabela worked her magic. I had only been on the island an hour, and already I could feel this was a fundamentally different place to the rest of the inhabited islands in the Galapagos. I looked happily around the table at the family, beaming in contentment as I did so.

The tension so recently departed made its vigorous return, however, with the buttock-clenching realisation that Molly had gone. Not 'playing in the sand nearby' gone, but 'I literally cannot see her anywhere' gone. This is a very exciting moment indeed for any parent, but is doubly so when one is next to pounding Pacific surf, no matter how azure and picturesque it happens to be. Our three-year-old had ambled off to who knows where, and even now might be eyeing the waves speculatively before bimbling in for a dip.

I jumped up and ran to the edge of the beach, shielding my eyes with one hand, scanning frantically from left to right. Tam was beside me in a moment, her hand on my arm. And there was our little girl, gloriously lost in a world all of her own.

The roar of the waves, the rustle off the palms, and the soft brush of a traveller's wind had proved too much for her, and she was dancing. This tiny young animal, entirely alone, was twisting and whirling on the sand, with the surf as her percussion, and the horizon as her backdrop. She looked completely transported, red hair flying, arms waving, fingers twisting, and feet skipping. One of my favourite poems by Atticus sprang to my mind unbidden as we watched our Molly dance, hand-in-hand with Isabela.

> 'This desert flame, this pixie in the sand,
> with dusty feet and painted skin, burning to the moon.
> With fire dancing from her wings, she dares the stars to fade,
> until the jealous sun will rise again, to cool the heat she's made.'

Our visit to Isabela – more of a brief holiday than anything else, a mini break at the end of a long three months of work – was also to be our swan song on the islands. Our residency was up, and aside from this single week, we would be heading back to Santa Cruz for a matter of a few days before returning to England. During our brief stay Pablo proudly showed us around Puerto Villamil, his home for the last twenty years, although it has to be said the tour didn't require a huge amount of time. The town was tiny, a sprawl of houses along the seafront, with a further two or three layers of dwellings behind them. The bay itself stretched away into the distance, shrouded in mist that looked like gun smoke from each resonating impact as wave after wave exploded on to the beach. Two jet-black lava reefs jutted out into the bay, shining like quartz as the seawater washed over them. They were alive with marine iguanas, who would make their way up the sand in solemn processions at the end of each day. From one of the reefs their destination was a pile of dark rocks next to a garish pink house, now converted into a bar. Plainly this had been their ancestral resting place, and the presence of flashing lights and two-for-one drinks offers was not going to drive them away.

One fine day Pablo took us up a winding track that led to the heart of the great volcano that dominated the south of the island, Sierra Negra. We walked the last couple of miles, huffing and puffing along a cinder-red path that snaked through dense scrub. Sierra Negra is a shield volcano – so called because, with its gentle slopes and deep caldera, it looks like a warrior's shield laid flat on the ground. The walk was long, hot and disagreeable, particularly for Molly. Possessing a wilful streak, she decided quite early on that this was an unacceptable state of affairs, and tramped on stout legs to a point just ahead of me on the path, turned on her heel to face me, and raised her arms in the universal 'you can carry me now' gesture. This wasn't a request; it was an instruction. Ten minutes of distinctly one-sided negotiations followed, after which we continued, with Molls tucked into the crook of my arm looking rather pleased with herself. The path became steeper, and she decided the best way she could assist was by steering me by my ears. This in turn made me become a tad emotional, a development she countered by whispering into one (now very red) ear, 'You're my best friend.' This showed unusual emotional intelligence for a three-year-old, in that the immediate result was me beaming in delight, and continuing on my way like the obedient pack animal I had just become.

After an hour of this biblical toil, we arrived at the edge of the main crater. It looked infinite, like a Conan Doyle landscape that was of such a scale it defied comprehension. The base of the caldera was a gigantic disc, dark grey, criss-crossed with lines and furrows. This stretched away from us in a prodigious curve, with the remnants of the morning mist still shrouding the smaller valleys and ridges along its length.

The volcano floor beneath us measured nine by seven kilometres, but such figures didn't even begin to do it justice. Encircled by a ridge one hundred metres high, it looked like a colosseum where celestial gladiators might do battle, wreathed in smoke, with their efforts echoing from the slopes that surrounded them.

Even Molly was struck dumb by the spectacle, and as a family we instinctively huddled together. Here was the great engine that had fuelled the creation of the Galapagos, with the hotspot only two kilometres beneath our feet – closer than the car park from which we had begun our journey. This immense, dark, muttering mountain showed that these islands are a work in progress, a thought that possessed me as we made our way back to the car and into Puerto Villamil.

The next morning we discovered a large rock pool in front of our accommodation, a lava structure frozen in time, and one that proved to be absolutely the ideal size for two little girls to splash and play. It was just deep enough that they could stand, and yet of a scale that it could harbour its own population of fish, flashing like silver confetti against the white sand of the floor. These fish would nibble our toes as we sat in the pool, our very own lava jacuzzi, making the girls squirm and shriek. Next to the pool was a broad glade of mangroves, with a perfect arch through which iguanas would make their stately progress from sea to shore. We watched them pass, our elbows resting on the edge of the pool and legs floating in the water behind us.

One evening, as Isla and Molly played, I saw a young sea lion emerge from the surf about a hundred metres away. It gave itself a brief shake, stretched, then lifted its head as it heard their voices, scanning back and forth to seek the source.

What happened next epitomised the Galapagos Islands, a neat encapsulation of why this archipelago is like no other on earth. The young sea lion identified the source of the noise – two young animals playing in the water – and immediately broke into what could only be described as a gallop. Its rear flippers seemed to almost overtake the front ones, such was its frantic haste. But it was not running away from the bedlam of these two noisy inter-lopers, it was running towards them, desperate to join them in the pool.

'Isla, Molly, look!' I shouted. 'Someone wants to come and play.'

By now the sea lion was nearly upon us, head held high and bounding along the sand. Without pause or ceremony, it reached the edge of the rock pool and plunged in, immediately beginning to twist and turn in its depths.

Isla and Molly shrieked and clapped, scanning the water around them to catch a glimpse of the quicksilver presence in their midst. To be in close proximity to such agility was mesmeric, a celebra-tion of life itself. The young sea lion would speed directly towards them, before changing direction at the very last moment in a turn that left a glittering scimitar of effervescent water in its wake. Then, in a rare moment of stillness, it hung upside down at the surface, twisting its head one way then the other before blowing a stream of bubbles at the girls. It then gyrated away once again, turning tight circles on its own body length in a corkscrew of energy and acceleration.

The girls played with the young sea lion for over an hour, until at last the sun slowly began to dip towards the horizon behind them. Finally they were spent, and stood in the pool shivering and pale. Tam and I stood waiting for them, having watched the entire performance. The young sea lion seemed to take great exception to their departure, and hauled itself on to a lava shelf to peer at its playmates, mystified as to why the game should be over so soon. Isla stood up to her shoulders in the water, the two of them looking directly at one another in their moment of final farewell as the sun set on another day on the mystical volcanic island of Isabela.

Wolf and Darwin

Although the main islands of the Galapagos hold immeasurable riches, there are many who say that the real gems, the true jewels in the crown, lie in the far-flung reaches of the archipelago. These rocky outposts, of only passing interest to privateers, traders and merchant vessels, remain citadels of life. They give a glimpse of another time, with shrieking hordes overhead and teeming shoals beneath. Nowadays their inaccessibility gives them a special allure, making them a beacon for adventurers and well-heeled eco-tourists, keen to push beyond the margins of conventional travel. There are a great many of these isolated islands, varying from what can only be described as rocks emerging from the surface of the sea, through to larger outcrops hosting every level of the ecosystem in glorious, clamouring isolation. The collective term is islets, or (charmingly) rocklets, and their number is somewhat debated. The reason for this is the simple question of what actually defines a viable islet/rocklet – just how big do they need to be to count – allied to the fact that some only emerge at low tide. What we do know is that there are a great many of them, with many thousands of rocklets sprinkled hither and thither.

There are no isolated islands within the archipelago that grip the imagination quite like the two islands of Wolf and Darwin. Both of them have a surface area of just over a square kilometre, and are situated about one hundred miles north of Isabela, twenty-five miles apart from each other. They rise a couple of hundred metres from the sea surface (253 metres in the case of Wolf and 168 metres in the case of Darwin), and as such have become a permanent home to nazca and red-footed boobies, frigate birds, sea lions, and hordes of endemic Galapagos species. One of these is the vampire finch – a species that on occasion drinks the blood of larger birds. This behaviour is thought to have come from when the finches pecked the parasites off frigate birds and boobies, and, curiously, the larger birds seem to show very little reaction to the finches as they open up a vein and help themselves. If this doesn't seize the imagination then I'm not quite sure what will – two outcrops of volcanic rock, born of fire and fury, that are the unique realm of a tiny, scurrilous, blood-sucking bird. It's wonderful stuff, and typifies the mystique and evolutionary magic of this mysterious world at the edge of the wider Galapagos.

But regardless of how stirring the sights and sounds are above the waves, it is the wonders beneath the surface that have made Wolf and Darwin a place of global significance for scientists, photographers and divers. It is here that the legendary schools of hammerheads gather – made famous by many a photographer and film-maker – stacked from seabed to surface, grey wraiths ghosting along timeless migratory routes known only to them. The whale shark – at any other location around the world a pulse-raising encounter for a diver, something to recall fondly for ever – can be so numerous here that at certain times of the year they are seen on every dive. So too mobulas, sunfish, Galapagos sharks, manta rays, turtles and huge shoals of fish, dizzying sciroccos of life in the blue water off precipitous undersea cliffs that vanish to abyssal depths.

It was only in 2016 that a 40,000 square kilometres marine sanctuary was established around Wolf and Darwin, granting it full 'no-take' status. There is no fishing allowed here of any kind, with very heavy penalties imposed on anyone caught doing so. Combine this with the fact that it's 200 miles to the nearest harbour, and the vast majority of fishing boats in the Galapagos are single-engine skiffs no more than seven metres long, and one might assume that the islands are at last completely safe. But there remains the sinister threat of larger scale international boats, and the thing that draws them here is sharks, as was so vividly illustrated by the incursion of the *Fu Yuan Yu Leng 999*. If one imagines a single terrestrial wildlife reserve with thousands upon thousands of rhino corralled into two areas about the size of Wembley Stadium, then that is a fair impression of just how valuable this location, and the resource it holds, has become. The reality is that, although fishing is banned here, it unequivocally still takes place, generally in small boats dispatched from larger ones that sit outside the margins of the marine reserve. These small skiffs do not show up on radar, and transport their catch back swiftly to their motherships – or 'reefers', as they are known – to be processed. They then return again and again to reap their harvest, each one, on each trip, leaving every school of hammerheads slightly denuded, and a few less shadows gliding along deep reefs. This is a multi-billion-dollar industry, well resourced and superbly equipped, closing in on the final bastion of a species, one that is defended by a poorly funded, over-stretched policing operation. This same pattern on land has seen too many species eradicated and too many habitats stripped bare for there to be anything other than desperate concern for Wolf and Darwin in the decades ahead.

Wolf and Darwin were places that I had heard of throughout my life. Ever since I had started diving in 1984, it had been spoken of as the promised land, a fantasy world where giants roam in such numbers that they blot out the sun. And in thirty-five years of diving, I had never visited – it was just too remote, too expensive, and too unrealistic.

As such, when Roby breathlessly told me out of the blue that the National Park was planning a research trip there, and what's more there might be a berth onboard the evocatively named *The Queen Mabel*, I could have kissed him. In fact, I could have taken him out for a romantic dinner at the most expensive restaurant in town, then kissed him. And then stayed fastidiously in touch afterwards, shortly before making a clumsy proposal.

'You have to turn up to the HQ of the National Park tomorrow,' he said, as we sipped coffee in a waterfront café that afternoon. 'It's by no means certain, but if we can convince the Park Officials that you might be useful, then there's a chance. It's 9am tomorrow. Don't be late.'

Don't be late? Don't be late? I was a fifty-year-old man who had waited pretty much his entire adult life to visit this one site, in this one archipelago. I would be on time, or – as it turned out – two hours early.

By early morning I was sitting nervously on a low wall outside the National Park headquarters building. I had been up very early indeed, fretting about what I should wear. I wanted to look responsible, but rugged, precisely the sort of chap that you'd want with you if an irate Galapagos shark attempted to bite your bum, but also the sort of fellow who would be good company over a game of canasta in the boat's saloon. First impressions count, and I was leaving nothing to chance.

Roby duly turned up, and without ceremony ushered me into an austere office where he spoke passionately in Spanish to the man behind the desk. Behind the man behind the desk was a huge poster of different shark species, which said all that needed to be said as far as I was concerned. To this day I'm not quite sure what Roby said, but I think it was along the lines of assuring the official that I could hold my breath for an hour, made a fantastic cup of morning coffee, and would if required sleep with any crew member to assure my berth. All of which were true apart from the first one. Whatever he said was enough to convince the official that I was worthy of a place on the trip. The official stood, smiled, shook Roby's hand, gave me a curt nod, and swept magisterially out of the room. I was going to Wolf and Darwin.

This trip would mark the end of our time in the islands, and coincided with the date that we were due to be leaving. A few hasty phone calls and some re-jigging of flights allowed me to delay my departure, but the arrangements for Tam and the kids proved too complex to alter. As such, a few days later, we said a tearful goodbye on the dock at the northern edge of Santa Cruz, as the ferry waited alongside to take them to Baltra and the flight home.

'You will be careful, won't you?' said Tam.

'Of course,' I replied, none too convincingly. 'It's a piece of cake. I think your journey is going to be a lot harder than mine. I'll see you at home in a couple of weeks.'

'A couple of weeks!' said Isla, outraged that I was off to see sharks and she wasn't. 'But that's ages.'

I hugged them all, a mass of limbs, giggles and kisses – my girls – and then found myself standing forlornly on the quayside waving them off. If ever there was a vivid reminder that the upcoming trip required me to be cautious not cavalier, then there it was in the form of my departing family.

The next day I met Roby at the main harbour in Puerto Ayora and we loaded a water-taxi with bags and hard cases full of diving gear, then sat atop the entire wobbly pile for the short journey out to where *The Queen Mabel* was rolling gently in the harbour. This was to be a two-week sampling trip out into the wilds of the Pacific, so plenty of kit was the order of the day. I couldn't actually see the vessel from the jetty, as her mooring was slightly further out than the pleasure boats and larger tourist ships that occupied the inner harbour. In fact, I had never clapped eyes on her before, although I had a clear mental image. This was an oceanic research vessel after all, about to set out on a voyage into the wilds of the Pacific – I envisaged clean white lines, a vast sweeping bow, generous deck space, an aquiline profile, and possibly even a helicopter landing pad. As we motored further and further away from the jetty, I craned my neck for the first glimpse. I thought perhaps I might see the slow turn of her radar atop of her towering mast, or the proud pennant that doubtless fluttered from her stern. But I still couldn't see her, my vision being somewhat obscured by a very small, rather tatty old fishing boat. One which had the unmistakable words *The Queen Mabel* written on its hull.

Wolf and Darwin are a very, very long way from anywhere. More precisely, they're 230 miles away from Puerto Ayora. My initial impression was that our water-taxi would have a slightly better chance of making it there than *The Queen Mabel*, a view reinforced as we hove to alongside her.

One notable characteristic that immediately became apparent was that there was not a lot of her, lengthwise, but this was more than compensated for by how much had been crammed on to her superstructure. It seemed her boat builders had started creating a wheelhouse, and then just kept going upwards in a frenzy of creativity. Perhaps they were offered an altitude incentive scheme, or her first skipper had been nine feet tall. Either way, *The Queen Mabel* had neatly reversed the iceberg principle, with very little of her in the water, and vast amounts out of it. This top-heavy design meant that she rocked merrily at her mooring, despite the fact that there was barely a ripple in the harbour.

'The Unstable Queen Mabel,' I muttered aloud, before I could stop myself. Roby looked across at me and grinned wolfishly. He had been on *The Queen Mabel* several times before, and was still alive. This I took as a positive development.

Her superstructure – that which wasn't obscured by clouds anyway – looked well maintained, which was also reassuring. Our water-taxi did a neat handbrake turn at the stern platform, and

Roby and I threw cases and bags on to the bits of the deck we could see, and clambered aboard. There, standing ready to meet us, was our skipper.

'*Hola*,' he said, with a beaming smile, 'welcome, welcome. This is *The Queen Mabel*, and I am Vico, your skipper.'

In much the same way that owners can look like their dogs, I also feel that skippers can frequently look like their boats. Vito was all superstructure, with a large chest, big shoulders, a generous girth and short legs. He looked friendly and competent, which are pretty much the only two things you really want from any skipper. The polar opposite – grumpy and a blithering idiot – are not unknown characteristics for boat captains in my experience, so we were off to a good start with Vico. His crew by now were bustling about the deck, grabbing our bags and hefting them into cubby-holes and recesses at the back of the wheelhouse. Not an inch of it went spare – if you had magically snapped your fingers and the whole of the superstructure of the vessel had disappeared, you would have been left with a precise outline of it in the shape of luggage and stores.

'Come,' said Vico, placing his hand on my shoulder. 'Come and see your cabin.'

We moved along a hilariously narrow companionway from the stern towards the wheelhouse, slipping through a doorway into the quiet of the saloon. Immediately facing me was a wooden bar, with a serving area behind it that was about the size of a bread board. Chopping some vegetables on this board was a short man of undefinable age who looked absolutely livid about something. In fact, he looked more than livid, he looked utterly incandescent, and he was taking it out on the veg.

'This is cook,' said Vico. The cook glanced up, gave me the sort of furious stare that would be enough to start a gun fight in most places in South America, then went back to eviscerating an onion. This was to be the most we communicated during the entire ten days of the trip.

Vico duly led me through the saloon, which already had a group of people gathered around the central table, tinkering with an impressive array of gadgets, tags and spearguns. It looked intoxicating to me, a heady mix of science, adventure and conservation, and I smiled across at them as I moved past. They raised their hands in return, and then bent their heads back to their various tasks. The group consisted of two men and a young woman. The men sported the distinctive khaki National Park shirts, with the logo of a tortoise and a hammerhead shark on the breast pocket. As I descended the gangway into the passage that led to my cabin, I reflected on the fact that I had waited to be on this boat, with these people, pretty much all my life. The adventure ahead was Boys' Own stuff, something that, as a ten-year-old, I had imagined night after night.

Vico pushed open my cabin door and waved me in. He stayed outside in the passageway for the simple reason that two normal sized human beings wouldn't have fitted in there at the same time, and I was surprised not to see monogrammed towels with 'Frodo' and 'Bilbo' written on them on each of the bunks. It was compact and bijou, to the point of being slightly too narrow for my pelvis, causing me to shuffle sideways between the bunk and the wall. But it did command good views of the water through the narrow slit that passed as a window, meaning I would approach Wolf and Darwin peering at them like a tank commander at El

Alamein. I threw my bag on the bed and hastily made my way back to the saloon.

The group were still in place, and politely shuffled aside to make space for me on the end of one of the benches. They introduced themselves as Jacquie Alvarez from St Francis University in Quito, and Harry Macliff and Jeff Herrera from the Galapagos National Park. Jacquie had a broad smile, dark hair tied up in a rapidly disintegrating bun, and eyes that sparkled with excitement.

'*Hola*, Monty,' she said, 'we are very pleased you are joining us on this trip. Do you know much about the research we've got planned?'

I said that I didn't, so Jacquie poured me a cup of coffee from the pot in the centre of the table, and then sat back, looked at Harry and Jeff for her cue, then began to speak.

'Well, although this is predominantly a trip to tag sharks to monitor their movements – that's Harry and Jeff's role – I am just as excited as you to be here, as it is my chance to get some samples from what I think is the most amazing animal in the Galapagos, the *mola ramsayi* or southern sunfish. We feel fairly confident that the mola around the islands are a separate sub-species, so we need to take some samples to prove that.'

'And how do you do it?' I asked, sipping from the cup.

'We jump in, grab one, bring it to the side of the boat, and snip out a bit of skin. Easy!' She clapped her hands, and laughed at my expression and the fact that my cup had paused in mid air, halfway back to the saloon table.

The reason for all this merriment is that a sunfish can weigh up to two tonnes, measures four metres from fin tip to fin tip, and don't take kindly to a couple of wriggling snorkelers dragging it back to a boat to be sampled.

The Latin name for a sunfish – *mola* – means millstone, and that is as good a description of it as any. It is an immense disc of muscle, fat and skin that is up to 8cm thick. Essentially, its life strategy can be summed up in the simple expression 'I'm not going to bother you, so I suggest you don't bother me', and they spend the bulk of their existence drifting on the great ocean currents (hence their kite-like outline), eating jellyfish, and watching the world go by with great benign eyes the size of tennis balls. Not being an animal to do anything on a small scale, they lay about 300 million eggs – more than any other vertebrate on earth – and if each larvae grows to the full-size sunfish, it's the equivalent to a human baby growing to the size of five Titanics. Therein lies their defence: they are simply too big and too tough for anything to eat. This podgy pacifism works just fine. Overall, they are benign, rather aimable (and undeniably colossal) discs of flesh drifting through the oceans of the world.

'Have you . . . ermm . . . done this before?' I asked.

'Yes,' said Jacquie, slightly too quickly for my liking. The fact that she didn't follow up with any meaningful details, and turned to Harry and Jeff to change the subject, I excused as the actions of a person with a great deal on their mind.

The conversation was interrupted by the unmistakable clatter of the anchor being lifted, and *The Queen Mabel*, plump, overloaded, and already out of breath, beginning to wheeze her way asthmatically out of the main harbour. I stepped out on to the deck and watched Puerto Ayora disappear from view, a moment that brought with it mixed feelings. I was undeniably excited to be embarking on a journey that I had anticipated for so long, but was somewhat unsettled that it could result in certain death either in the ample and rapidly descending innards of the boat, or by being bludgeoned to death by a furious sunfish. As we hit the open sea, *The Queen Mabel* gave an inebriated roll to port, miraculously righted herself, then leaned drunkenly to starboard. I was standing on several tubs of diesel at the time, lined up along the side of the wheel-house, which added an exciting level of lubrication to the soles of my sandals. But glancing around me I could see the scientists still working away, completely unphased, in the main saloon. And when I stood on my tiptoes, I could look into the wheel-house to see Vico slouching in his skipper's seat. He looked across and gave me a cheerful wave, one I returned. This was a mistake, as it required me to release my vice-like grip on the superstructure, which in turn caused me to vanish wide-eyed out of his view to duly land cat-like on the deck. The cat in question being one of those really old ones that doesn't leave the house much.

I decided this was quite enough excitement for one day, and picking myself up headed back down to my cabin. Slipping sideways into my bunk, which would have just about passed as a CD shelf at home, I found I could remain reasonably stable by bracing my elbows and knees against the side walls, and the top of my head against the bulkhead. As my feet were also pressed against the cabin wall at the base of the bunk, this gave me surprising rigidity even during *Mabel*'s more exuberant rolls. It was also strangely reassuring, entombed as I was in a fug of warmth and darkness, with cold Pacific water hissing and gurgling against the timber an inch from my ear. And so I drifted off into a deep sleep, with dreams of wombs and tombs, of crypts and cocoons.

The Queen Mabel was steaming west, towards the southern coast of Isabela, where she would turn north for the long haul to Wolf and Darwin. But before doing so we would pause within the sickle shaped caldera of Tortuga Island, and go on the hunt for sunfish to tag.

Tortuga is a perfect crescent that breaks the surface of the ocean like a quarter moon, with uncanny geometry creating a geological feature of great beauty. The tips of the island narrow into points, and the central lagoon fades from turquoise to a deep sapphire in a seamless gradient of colour. It is an entirely fitting home for a giant sunfish, something out of a Tolkein-esque fantasy.

After several hours of the deepest sleep, I was woken early the next morning by the rattle of the anchor dropping and the shouts of the crew. Extracting myself from my bunk – a sideways lunge, with mid-air pike and half roll to execute a neat two-footed landing – I made my way up on deck, feeling refreshed and ready to rumble with a gigantic slab of sunfish. The Zodiac was already being brought up to the stern, and Jacquie was readying her sampling gear. She glanced up and gave me a broad smile, beckoning me over.

'Ah, *hola*, Monty. Hope you had a good sleep. Quick, get your wetsuit on and get ready to tag a giant.' She looked delighted, emanating a palpable air of excitement at the day ahead.

As I kitted up, she told me the rules.

'Okay, as you may know, the sunfish has some of the thickest skin of any animal – at least four inches deep for the big ones – and the skin is also very abrasive. As such you need to wear these . . .'

she handed me a pair of bright red woollen gloves. 'You'll need them, as it'll be your job to get to the sunfish first and grab it. Don't grab the fins, make sure you grip the body.'

I nodded. As a sunfish is 95% body, at least that part should be easy enough.

'Once you've grabbed it, I'll be there by then, so between us we should be able to drag it alongside the boat . . . '

'And you've definitely done this before?' I said.

'Yes, yes,' she said, giving a wave of her hand and not looking me in the eye, 'lots of times. Anyway, once we've got it to the side of the boat, one of the other scientists will lean over and take a skin sample. Then we let it go. Okay?'

'Ummm, okay,' I said.

'Good, good. Right, let's go.'

I decided I liked Jacquie a great deal, even if I was not entirely convinced about her sunfish-wrestling credentials. There was only one way to find out, though, and that was to head out in a small dinghy, do a belly flop on to one of the largest fish in the ocean, grab it with my red woolly gloves, and see what happened after that.

A few minutes later we were cruising along the coast of Tortuga, with Jacquie standing tall in the bow of the Zodiac scanning the waters around her. Roby was manning the small outboard motor. The small boat jumped and skipped in the waves, and Jacquie shielded her eyes with one hand while hanging on to a rope for security with the other.

'Just out of interest,' she shouted over one shoulder, still scanning the sea's surface, 'very often when we do this killer whales turn up to see what's going on. They hunt here, and I've seen them lots of times when we've been sampling.'

'Oh, okay, great, righto,' I said, glancing down at my blood-red woolly gloves and uncannily seal-like wetsuit.

'Yes,' said Jacquie, 'we're so lucky, we really are.' She sighed contentedly, and went back to her work – head up, cheeks glowing and eyes sparkling.

Our search continued through the morning, the Zodiac motoring back and forth parallel to the jagged rocks of the shore, the looming volcanic ridge of the island towering above us. The sun slowly tracked across the sky, and frigate birds wheeled overhead under a cloak of dark wings. There was real alchemy in this moment, a realisation that despite this archipelago being the most studied on earth – to date there have been 7,500 separate research projects on the Galapagos – there is still so much pioneering science to be done here. It wasn't too much of a leap of imagination to picture Darwin on this Zodiac, eyes glinting in anticipation, collecting bottles clinking before him and red gloves at the ready.

'There!' shouted Jacquie, her arm shooting out, a trembling finger pointing to the middle distance. 'I see one, I see a fin.'

And there, breaking the water's surface a hundred metres away, was the unmistakable dorsal fin of a sunfish. It was waving slowly from side to side, as the great animal beneath it cruised the sunlit uplands of its world seeking out food.

'Okay, okay, here we go,' said Jacquie. 'Monty, to the front of the Zodiac. When we get close, I will give you the signal and you jump. Roby, please get us closer then ease off the throttle so we drift over the top of it and don't harm it with the prop.'

I glanced back at Roby, who gave me a delighted grin and a thumbs up. He was enjoying himself immensely, particularly relishing the prospect of me wrestling something that had an

800kg weight advantage. He twisted the throttle, and the outboard went from a low mutter to a high-pitched roar, accelerating us forward with a comet's tail of white water spreading in our wake. We skipped and danced across the waves, on the hunt and closing in on our prey. At the last moment Roby turned off the power, and we drifted silently the final few metres until that great dark shadow was just ahead of us, beneath the glinting sail of that gigantic fin. I could clearly see its mottled flanks through the surface, and the lower fin sculling from side to side, driving it gently through the water. It plainly had no idea we were there and – like many large ocean creatures – was placidly confident in its size, secure in the knowledge that only the most foolhardy would take it on.

Coincidentally, there was a boat-load of the foolhardy only a few metres away, the foremost of whom was just checking gloves, fins, and trying to recall if he had made a will of any sort. I braced myself against the tube of the bow, and looked aghast at the vast dark shadow, which was now directly beneath me.

'Okay, Monty,' shouted Jacquie gleefully, 'go, go, go!'

And go, go, go I did. Leaping none too elegantly off the bow, I landed face-first in the water and kicked hard towards the sunfish. By now it had figured out that something was afoot, and accelerated with a pulse of energy, causing a wave of water to hit me as I swam. But by then it was too late, and I was upon it. I triumphantly reached out with both hands and clamped them to the behemoth's flanks. By now the sap had risen, an ancient hunter-gatherer strand of DNA within me had come alive, and I gave a shout of triumph through my snorkel. I would wrestle the beast back to the Zodiac single-handed, a brave Nimrod of science, to return to the main vessel and have Vico clasp my hand in his, shaking his head in admiration as the crew looked on agog.

Unfortunately there was a flaw in my plan. The gloves – being made of wool – adhered immediately to the coarse skin of the sunfish. This was a very good thing, as it created terrific traction. What was not such a good thing was that the gloves were a couple of sizes too large for me, and as the sunfish accelerated away, so did the gloves. This left me treading water, peering into the gloom as I watched the sunfish swim off with two perfectly splayed red hands on each side of its body. As the gloves were wool, and were biodegradable, I didn't feel too bad about this, although I did feel for the poor creature who would have every marine animal it passed for several weeks looking at it in a slightly odd way.

I climbed wordlessly back aboard the Zodiac, to find a delighted Roby and thoughtful looking Jacquie.

'Have you definitely, definitely done this before?' I asked again.

'Yes, yes, lots of times' she said, this time with slightly less conviction. 'Okay, let's . . . ummmm . . . go again. This time Monty you grab the main part of the body, and I'll steer it towards the boat.'

Another half hour of searching revealed another fin sculling innocently along, and this time we made no mistake. Jacquie and I jumped together, and to my great surprise, once we had grabbed the sunfish, and turned it on its side, it allowed itself to be gently led back to the Zodiac. This seemed miraculous to me, and although one shouldn't anthropomorphise, it appeared for all the world to display that Galapagoan characteristic of being entirely placid and trusting in the hands of man. Roby reached over, and snipped a segment of skin to be placed in a plastic vial – a piece of DNA that would reveal so much about population and lineage, a hard drive of stored information that represented a treasure trove for Jacquie in the weeks of laboratory work to come.

As we motored back to *The Queen Mabel*, I reflected on Jacquie and the work she was undertaking. The water was cold that day off Isabela – perhaps 12 to 14 degrees Celsius. Her wetsuit was too big, and would have allowed huge amounts of this water to flush through the suit next to her skin, chilling her to the bone. She sat trembling with the cold, being bounced on the side of a small Zodiac in a big sea, her hair awry and her teeth chattering, beaming from ear to ear as she clutched her precious skin sample. Without the Jacquies of this world – driven, enthusiastic, focused – there would be no increase in our knowledge of this remarkable place. She was cavalier in the best possible meaning of the word, taking on anything and everything to hunt down the data. She trod in the steps of Darwin, of Beebe, and of the many pioneers who had come before, and seemed entirely worthy of that path, doing whatever it took to research and ultimately protect her beloved sunfish.

And so *The Queen Mabel* waddled north, up the east coast of Isabela, her plump haunches sluicing through cool seas, her bow rearing and plunging, her engine thumping away below decks. I enjoyed a series of delicious meals that miraculously emerged from the galley, served with a scowl but tasting like manna from heaven. As we passed the northern tip of Isabela, we were looking at fifty miles of open sea, with immense muscular rollers passing before and beneath us, seething with thousands of miles of elemental energy. *The Queen Mabel* went into her version of overdrive, lifting her skirts and dipping her hips in the water, first one side then the other, wake spreading behind her like a white pinny. Meals consisted of tracking your plate across the table, taking one forkful, then waiting patiently to take the next as the food passed beneath you on the return journey. The air of relaxed bonhomie aboard changed into one of restless expectation – within a day Wolf island would appear on the horizon, the lair of giants, a sentinel in the ocean guarding one of the final bastions of the shark in our seas.

It became my habit to sit at the stern of the *Mabel* as she travelled, watching the track of our journey revealed in the white waters of the wake. It also gave me the opportunity to watch, for me, one of the most miraculous birds in all of the oceans, as it danced and dipped between the waves that followed us.

The storm petrel is my favourite bird of the open sea, mainly due to its absurd delicacy in the midst of the chaotic forces that surround it. It is a tiny scrap of nothing, a will o' the wisp collection of feathers tap-dancing on the water's surface in search of food. Their ability to skip and weave between the larger waves – any one of which could inundate them – was hypnotic, and they would often follow the *Mabel* carving elegant arcs through the valleys of the great oceanic swell. Watching them was a wonderful way to pass the time, and I could immediately see why mariners of old had viewed them as mystical creatures. The name they gave them – Mother Carey's Chickens – persists to this day, and refers to the fact that they were thought to be the souls of lost sailors. Mother Carey was a mythical figure, representing the menace and latent violence of the sea, portrayed as an old woman bringing with her storms and death. The petrels – birds that live their lives on the ocean, coming ashore only to breed – were seen as her companions, the troubled spirits of sailors she had claimed who were now doomed never to return to land. It is a compelling image, and watching these tiny birds' restless movements over the waves, one can immediately see why the legend emerged. I found them a hypnotic spectacle, a triumph of agility and poise in the diabolical bedlam of the world that surrounded them.

Early the next morning, I was sitting on the deck. It was dawn on the momentous day when we were due to arrive at Wolf. My kit was prepared – the camera having been slipped into its underwater housing by hands rendered clumsy with anticipation – and all I had to do now was be patient. Fifty years down, only ten hours to go. After several days on board, I had grown rather fond of the *Mabel*, a redoubtable old soul with the hydrodynamics of a skip but the buoyancy of a duck. We were in the middle of that vast stretch of wild water between islands, with no trace of land on any horizon, and yet I felt sheltered and secure.

'Man overboard!!!' came a shout, the voice hoarse with horror and fear, snapping me instantly out of my reverie. There was the sound of running footsteps on the deck above me, and I quickly jumped to my feet and sprinted to the stern.

I joined three other crew members who were peering frantically beyond the spreading wake, looking into the swell beyond, seeking a glimpse of a waving arm or a dark head in the immensity of the sea. This was a very, very dangerous place to fall off the back of a boat, plunging your body into an environment of rolling mountains and strong currents, one that is deeply hostile in every sense of the word.

'I see him, I see him!' shouted one of the crew, pointing to the middle distance. I strained to see, scanning the peaks and valleys of distant waves, and there . . . a glimpse of a head and raised arm, a pale face stricken in a dark, heaving landscape.

The *Mabel* began to turn, her engines hammering at full throttle, the reptilian hiss of the sea on her flanks creating a gloating backing track as the boat raced to pick up one of her own.

One of the crew readied a Zodiac as we drew closer, the real-isation dawning that we were now in a race against time. The crewman was plainly struggling – like so many Galapagos res-idents, he was a surprisingly weak swimmer, (an amazing 70% of the islanders either cannot swim at all, or can only do so at a basic level). He had been treading water with thousands of metres of darkness beneath him for fifteen minutes now, and was visibly weakening. As we drew ever closer, I noticed some-thing else – distinct signs of movement in the water, with a glistening grey back and sickle shaped fin breaking the waves within a few feet of his flailing arms and upturned face. This struck me as particularly cruel, with salvation so close at hand, that he was now being circled by something with teeth and bad intentions.

It was only when we got within a hundred metres that I could make out what was actually happening. The dark bodies around him were dolphins – whether drawn to him through curiosity or through an urge to assist I would never know, but the romantic in me liked to think that out here, in the immensity of the open sea, a group of mammals was watching over one of their own.

By now we had closed to within twenty metres of the stricken crewman, who I recognised as a portly and friendly young man who had quietly gone about his business throughout the voyage.

As he was hauled into the Zodiac, I exhaled in relief, an explosive release of tension. It had been genuinely close, a few more moments and he would have disappeared into the silent expanse beneath him, lost for ever.

I moved to the stern platform to assist, and helped him aboard as the cook bustled out of the galley with a hot drink. I saw him glance up to take it, and his eyes looked stricken. It is every mariner's nightmare – he had slipped off the stern of a boat, and watched helplessly as it receded into the distance. Any warmth, security, companionship and survival became more remote with every turn of the propeller. He had stared into the abyss, a harrowing glimpse of mortality, and his expression reflected that moment.

It was a subdued group that ate lunch that day, quietly reflective, and distracted by thoughts of what might have been. It was a relief to hear an enthusiastic shout from deck, and I rushed out of the saloon to see – rising from the ocean, as if reliving its volcanic birth – the great dark mass of Wolf. We had arrived.

Wolf Island is named after the geologist Theodor Wolf. This energetic German arrived in the Galapagos Islands in 1875, and borrowed a schooner from a particularly forward-thinking and humanitarian man named Don Jose Valdizan, a Spaniard who had established a colony on Floreana built around livestock and agriculture. In a splendid example of international cooperation, the German scientist explored the Ecuadorian islands in a Spaniard's boat for three years, meticulously sampling water temperature, mapping the islands, and taking precise meteorological measurements. He produced a comprehensive report that surmised

– correctly – that the climatic conditions and flora and fauna of the Galapagos owed a great deal to the unique way the currents converged on the archipelago. He even suggested ways the Ecuadorian Government could exploit these conditions to maximum economic effect. A grateful nation granted him the title Illustrious Citizen of Ecuador, and named a volcano on Isabela after him, and a small and seemingly insignificant island north of the Galapagos. How wonderful then that the island has now become a focal point for scientific endeavour and conservation research.

There are two theories about the formation of Wolf. One postulates that it emerged as an off-shoot of the main island group – essentially a channelling of energy and magma from the main plume responsible for the Galapagos itself. The other theory is that it is from an entirely separate upwelling between the cracks in the Nazca and Cocos tectonic plates. Either way, its origins are volcanic, and as I looked at the island for the first time, it seemed entirely appropriate that its birth had been so elemental. Perhaps it was the isolation – there were no other islands to be seen around the entire wide horizon – but it also seemed particularly severe to me, as though ready to sink back below the waves and rejoin the seething earth's crust at any moment.

Although it is easy to look at an island such as Wolf in isolation, it is of course only one section of a vast ecosystem. I was observing the summit of a mountain, one that stretched away for two kilometres beneath our keel. At every layer of undersea altitude beneath us, on every dark ridge and misted gully, there lurked a multitude of animals either living upon the rocks or gliding overhead on the currents. This extended through the surface, where the shadows cast by the clamorous avian hordes of nearly fifty different bird species created a mosaic on the water's surface.

'Hey, Monty, watch this,' said one of the crew, who had been mopping the deck as the engine stilled beneath our feet. He walked to the stern platform, and slapped the mop on the waves again and again. I was not sure what I was supposed to be looking at, and smiled uncertainly, thinking that this might be some surreal ceremony to celebrate arrival at the islands. And then I saw two shapes materialise beneath the stern platform, drawn by the thrashing of the mop overhead. This close to the surface their backs were a deep, rusted brown, their tails shaped like scythes, their presence driven by curiosity, but masking predatory intent. Two large Galapagos sharks, drawn in by percussive waves of sound that resonated through the water column, sounding for all the world like an animal in distress. I made a mental note not to fall in, and particularly not to sound like a mop if I did so.

'Come on, Monty,' said Roby, who had also appeared on the stern platform beside me, 'let's get started.' The crew member chuckled, gave a thumbs up, and went back to swabbing the decks, his party trick complete.

I shouldn't have been surprised at the abrupt appearance of the sharks. We rocked on a mooring over the greatest biomass of large predators anywhere on earth. An extensive study conducted over two years in 2013 and 2014, over seven separate sites in both Darwin and Wolf, concluded that the abundance of marine life was a staggering 17.5 tonnes per hectare. The report, published in *The Journal of Life and Environment Sciences*, also went on to note that: 'At Darwin and Wolf, top predators account for an astonishing 75% of the fish biomass.'

In essence, the scientists who conducted the survey were confirming, with a hint of hysteria that pierced even the dry lexicon of scientific writing, that this was indeed the shark capital of the world. I was about to step into a body of water alive with the dark shadows that had coursed through my dreams since childhood.

The sampling was going to work on a simple principle. Harry and Jeff would be tagging sharks, creeping up on them and attaching a beeping plastic cylinder just below the dorsal fin. This would be done by using a Hawaiian sling – essentially a hand-held spear – which required the user to be exhilaratingly close to the shark he or she was tagging. At one end of this operation you have a mammal encased in rubber, holding its breath and squinting along one arm, and then six feet away you have the result of 400 million years of predatory evolution. One sticks a pin in the other, and basically hopes for the best. It was a process I was looking forward to witnessing, in the way other people watch motor racing for the crashes.

I would be taking photographs. This isn't quite as prosaic as it might sound. Much of the data gathered in the 2013/14 research was done using photography, albeit of a much more methodical and sophisticated kind. Nonetheless, my own images would prove vital should we encounter any whale sharks, as each has a unique set of markings – a fingerprint of dapples and dots – and, as such, any photographs can be used to identify individual animals. Roby would act as my safety diver, making sure that nothing untoward happened as I snapped away.

Minutes later we were leaving the side of the *The Queen Mabel*, crammed into a Zodiac and armed to the teeth. Harry and Jeff had their spears, I had my camera in its underwater housing, looking rather like a sinister explosive device, and Roby was in full piratical mode with a bandana on his head and a glint in his eye. We were marauding scientific buccaneers, a raiding party sent to save the world, the commandos of conservation embarking on a covert raid.

An hour later we were back, looking crestfallen. We had seen nothing – not even a hint of a shark. Sure, we had seen plenty of sea lions, but I could see them outside the supermarket in Puerto Ayora without dicing with death on the *Mabel* first. Jose and Jorge's spears looked distinctly unemployed, and I had taken two pictures, one of which was Roby and the other was of my own foot by accident. I glanced across at Roby, who now looked a bit like a pirate who had forgotten where he'd buried his treasure.

'It's the currents,' he said, as we climbed out of our kit on deck. 'When there's a sudden switch in temperature, the sharks go deep – they're there, but well below us. Sorry, Monty.'

He smiled and clapped me on the shoulder.

'Next time. For sure, next time.'

But there weren't any the next time. Or the time after that. I tried grabbing the mop and thrashing it around before I jumped in – a slightly desperate measure, I had to admit – but it seemed that even our two Galapagos sharks had been driven off by the sudden drop in temperature.

Morale on the *The Queen Mabel* slumped, and meals became rather desultory affairs, with us pushing our food round our plates and not talking a great deal. When we did talk, the conversation revolved around the location of the sharks, with serviettes and pepper pots called into action to recreate undersea ridges and skulking predators. But still, after several days and on dive after dive, the sea around us remained entirely devoid of sharks – a great, endless, empty, echoing space mocking us with unfulfilled promise.

As I slept one night, I was woken by the rattle of the anchor chain and the rumble of the engines. *The Queen Mabel* was on the move, with Vico at the helm guiding us to Darwin, the northern-most of the two islands. This was still a voyage of some distance – twenty-five miles over open ocean – but represented the last few miles of our passage north. We would travel entirely in the hours of darkness, arriving at first light. Beyond Darwin there was nothing more of the Galapagos Islands. This final push was our last chance, and if the chill of the currents had also spread further north, then the bulk of our voyage would have been for naught.

I was out on the deck early the next morning. This is always one of my favourite times on any voyage by boat – there is something about the sea at dawn, the air cool and crisp, the breaking day alive with promise. In this case it was doubly so, as before me was perhaps the most famous natural feature in all of the Galapagos.

It seems entirely appropriate that here, of all places, guarding the island that bears his name, is a huge rocky bridge – Darwin's Arch. It stands as a sentinel over the seething activity beneath, a monument at the centre of an unparalleled convergence of life. As I looked at it in the soft morning light, it occurred to me that it was only the efforts of my companions on the *The Queen Mabel*, and others like them, that would prevent it turning into a headstone. This was important work, at a key time, in one of the last places in the world where sharks still abound.

We anchored in the lee of the main island, several hundred metres beyond the arch, and without ceremony immediately began to kit up. There was real urgency in our movements, with Roby hastily draining the last of his breakfast coffee as he hopped on one foot into his wetsuit. Harry and Jeff would be free diving, snorkelling on the top of us, hoping to dive down on a passing shark like a Spitfire coming out of the sun. They looked entirely focused, acknowledging my presence with only a faint smile as they walked past me towards the stern platform. I walked quickly after them, and commenced my own checks on camera and dive gear. Time was now against us, our futile attempts of see, let alone tag, a shark near Wolf meaning that we would only have two days at Darwin. A fleeting moment in our trip as a whole, but representing forty-eight hours that would define its success.

Roby, as ever, was upbeat and entirely ready for what the day and the dive would bring.

'Hey, Monty,' he said, as we climbed once again into the Zodiac, 'this is it! This is the day – I can tell.' He nodded conspiratorially, and gave me a theatrical wink. It dawned on me that some travel through life creating a bow wave of positivity, and drag you along in their wake – an entirely appropriate metaphor considering our current situation. I smiled and gave him a quick nod of thanks.

Within moments we were rolling in the swells just a few metres away from the arch. It looked even more impressive close up, and far from losing a sense of scale, seemed to actually have increased in size. Darwin's Arch sits on a large rocky platform, so shallow that the sea writhes and twists over the top of it, its energy condensed by the sudden proximity of surface and seabed. At the edge of the platform, undersea cliffs drop away vertiginously, and it is here that the sharks cruise. The edges of these cliffs are a border, patrolled by any animal seeking nutrient-rich upwellings and easy pickings.

'Okay,' said Roby, 'are we all good?'

He looked round the group, and received brisk thumbs up from everyone, masks on and regulators in place. The Zodiac jumped and twisted beneath us, with wavelets slapping against the underside of the tubes. The thunder of oceanic swell striking the rock shelf resonated through my bones, a sound punctuated only by the shrieks of the frigate birds and boobies atop the arch. I glanced over my shoulder and saw the reef beneath us, a mosaic of different hues and textures. The plan was to swim down as quickly as possible, to crouch in the lee of the great current that swept up and over the lip of the cliff, and then wait to see what came along.

'Good,' said Roby. 'Okay, three, two, one – go!'

As one we rolled backwards into the sea, and immediately turned turtle to kick furiously downwards towards the sanctuary of the reef below. Pause for too long, fiddle with a bit of gear, miss a fin stroke or two, and the current would take you out into the blue water beyond the rock shelf. This in itself is more of an inconvenience than a danger, but with time against us we all wanted to get in position to complete the job in hand.

I followed the stream of bubbles made by Roby as he hurtled downwards, and soon settled in a pocket of calm water at the top of the reef. Immediately overhead millions of tonnes of water barrelled along, an undersea river in which vast schools of jack and trevally hung, facing into the current and moving as one vast pulsing entity. I inched forward, and looked over the edge of the drop-off, only to find myself in the grip of the current, resulting in an immediate and undignified retreat back to the sanctuary of the reef crest. Plainly the best thing to do was hunker down and wait. I rolled over on to my back and watched my bubbles heading for the surface, initially ascending directly upwards in a tumbling silver mass, before abruptly being shattered and whisked away by the current.

Over our heads, silhouetted against the sun and the surface, there was mischief afoot. Harry and Jeff were drifting along the edge of the cliff, and were tracking two silky sharks out in the blue, gliding along the invisible contour line where the current struck the rocks. This represented something of a border between calm and chaos, so the two scientists had stayed over the reef crest, moving laterally to follow the languid silhouettes before them. The silky is a wonderful shark, so named because of the texture of its skin, which is so smooth it almost seems to shine as the sunlight hits it in shallow water. Here is an animal that also looks precisely how a shark should look – lean, streamlined, and perpetually up to no good. Its foraging technique is to follow large schools of fish – tuna in particular – and then accelerate through their midst, snapping and twisting in a moment of kinetic preda-tory action. It is not the most subtle means of acquiring food, but is certainly spectacular. It has also meant trouble for the silky, as these are precisely the same shoals that are targeted by commercial fishing fleets, with the sharks getting caught as by-catch. As such, the silky is now classified as vulnerable by the International Union of Nature Conservation. To tag one would be a real coup – and

Harry and Jeff edged their way along the cliff edge, spears ready, eyes wide and knuckles white.

I had by now lapsed into what was becoming a standard routine of scanning the great blue spaces before me, willing something to appear. The motivation for this was partly scientific – it would, of course, be immensely satisfying to contribute to the conservation of the sharks here – but also ran deeper. I had dreamt of this location my entire life, and really didn't want the small boy within me to be crushed by the disappointment of being pretty much the only person ever to visit Wolf and Darwin and not see a single whale shark.

Such gloomy thoughts were interrupted by a distinctive squeak from alongside me, the noise of an excited man trying to express himself through a diving regulator. I glanced sideways at Roby, to see him gesturing frantically overhead, eyes wide behind his mask. I followed the direction of his gesticulating arm, and there – hanging in mid water – was a giant.

It looked wrong somehow, this massive female whale shark, as it drifted like a storm cloud through the blue water. It looked as though it should be towed by tugs, that there should be clamour and ceremony around it, a great monarch of the sea making an arrival on the scene. And yet it simply made its regal passage through the water above us, impassive and vast. Such an immense object seemed to be less of a result of biology processes, and more of a result of simple laws of physics – momentum, mass, velocity. As it grew closer, I waited to hear a noise like a low rumble or a deep boom, as surely nothing this immense could appear completely silently.

We sculled up as one from the reef, like acolytes ascending

towards a passing deity, each of us trailing a stream of bubbles, driving upwards in an attempt to take station alongside the whale shark. As a filter feeder, its mouth was a wide, broad oval, within which remoras hung, each as long as my forearm. The head was broad and flat, with a great broad back leading to a sail-like dorsal fin – a feature that may ultimately prove to be the sharks' undoing, as it represents $20,000 on its shoulders – and behind that a series of ridges that narrowed towards the tail. The tail gently sculled from side to side, barely perceptible movements that drove it through the water at a speed that we had to fin furiously to match.

We were swimming towards the largest non-mammalian creature on earth. Everything about the whale shark is big (except, one could argue, its personality. A life spent generally alone, focused entirely on swimming, feeding and mating, does not require the development of dazzling social skills). Their skin is the thickest of any animal at up to 16cm, part of their fairly straightforward survival strategy of being very large indeed with a virtually impenetrable outer layer, much like sunfish but on an altogether more massive scale. This limits their predators to orcas and the larger sharks, such as tigers and great whites, although even these would not take on an adult whale shark. Their back and flanks are covered with an exquisite pattern of spots, a palomino dappling that replicates the light streaming through the water's surface. This is a realm in which they spend a great deal of their time, feeding on plankton that is drawn upwards to warmth and sunlight. Each shark has a pattern of spots that is entirely unique, a polka-dot fingerprint that allows an individual animal to be clearly identified. This was my role on this particular trip, to swim alongside a single vast flank and record a clear image of the markings. This is easier said than done, something that was at the forefront of my mind as I accelerated upwards from the reef. The shark might look as though it was barely moving, but it was actually swimming effortlessly through an undersea gale. In a few moments I would be battling to stay in position alongside, and I tightly gripped the handles of my camera in anticipation.

In the modern world, all whale sharks are significant due to their dwindling numbers and the paucity of our knowledge about them. But those at Wolf and Darwin are particularly valuable for two remarkable reasons. The first is that the vast majority of them are large females, and, most significantly of all, it is thought that they are all likely to be heavily pregnant.

This is something of a holy grail for shark scientists, and has only recently been discovered. Before 2014, only one pregnant whale shark had ever been definitively identified, and that was a dead one off the coast of Taiwan that was subsequently found to have 300 embryos inside it at varying stages of development.

It took a sustained effort by scientists, led by Dr Alex Hearn and Jonathan Green, to visually confirm that most of the sharks they were encountering at Wolf and Darwin were pregnant. They then had the challenge – and, like the shark, it's a big one – of confirming that this is the case. Attempts to ultrasound underwater were accompanied by efforts to draw a blood sample as the shark swam by. This was precisely the sort of heroic and slightly mad science that defined Darwin, so is entirely appropriate for this study in this location.

Neither attempts were particularly successful, encountering the same issue that has thwarted most creatures that encounter the whale shark. The most powerful setting on an ultrasound scanner can penetrate 8 centimetres of skin, so the 16-centimetre abdominal wall of a whale shark presented an – if you'll pardon the pun – impregnable barrier. Attempts to draw blood were thwarted by an inability to find a vein in a speeding shark in a big current (although I would have paid good money to see the attempts).

But the defining characteristic of a great scientist is a mule-like refusal to let something go, and the team continue to devise means to confirm their suspicions – that this might be one of the most significant whale shark locations ever discovered. You don't have to be a dry academic to appreciate this. To find the place where the largest fish in the sea gives birth, and thus secure the future of the species by ensuring that site is protected, is an epitaph any of us would be proud of.

For me, it was now or never, the end of a very long journey indeed. As I drew level with the shark, I furiously kicked my fins to keep up. A geyser of bubbles rose to the surface as my breath heaved and sawed, and a glance at my pressure gauge saw the needle dipping like the dial on a burst boiler. I drew level beside the gills of the shark, each the length of my outstretched arm, and allowed myself to stop finning for a moment. The current immediately took me, and as the shark passed alongside like a liner at sea, I raised the camera and took shot after shot. The database of whale shark identification photos numbers approximately 8,000 specimens globally, but none of the sharks photographed in Galapagos have been seen anywhere else. I was taking a unique image, of a unique animal, in a truly unique place.

As I hung in mid water, I glanced up to see something of a

commotion above me. Harry and Jeff were just off the edge of the reef, high-fiving and gesticulating. Jeff pointed in triumph at the end of his spear, which clearly had no satellite tag attached. This could mean only one thing, but if I was in any doubt it was soon dispelled as they finned down to me with wide eyes and big smiles. A silky shark had been tagged, and was even now creating data through the tag, a constant scientist beeping away on its dorsal fin, that added to our scant knowledge of these animals.

In the middle distance I could still make out that great, gently undulating tail, driving the whale shark onwards to an unknown destination. It struck me that if anyone doubts the importance of the work being undertaken here, and of the significance of protecting this site, then there could be no more poignant image. A colossus of the sea, swimming off an island named after our greatest scientist, vanishing from our view towards an unknown future.

Here at the outer reaches of the Galapagos archipelago, in the home of the shark, one lingering impression seemed more poignant and powerful than ever. It was that the islands were on the cusp of success or failure, of salvation or environmental disaster. Our residence in the Galapagos had vividly illustrated the depth and richness of the story here. As I turned for the surface one last time, a symbolic moment that signaled the start of my long journey home to England, I resolved that, at some point soon, I would return to try to truly understand how that story might end.

Two

'One is astonished at the amount of creative force, if such an expression may be used, displayed on these small, barren, and rocky islands.'

Charles Darwin, on departing the Galapagos, 1835

The Isabela Beach House

The beach at Isabela stretched away from me in an elegant curve, a snow-white parabola narrowing to a distant green headland. Two pelicans flew low over the sea, their wing tips brushing the waves, and they banked in perfect unison to head towards the horizon. At the end of the beach rose the dark mass of the interior, with the pastel hues of volcanic ridges vanishing into the mists of the highlands. This had always been one of my favourite spots on Isabela, with serried ranks of Pacific breakers charging the shoreline, detonating on arrival with an impact so percussive I could feel it through the soles of my feet. It was a scene unchanged in millennia, deeply comforting in its endless rhythm.

And yet, as I stood on this beach after two years' absence with an unchanged scene to the fore, behind me the diggers roared, the hammers pounded and the buildings rose. I was back in the Galapagos Islands for another residency; however this time the family and I were to be based on Isabela throughout. There would be the occasional sojourn to other islands, but in the main we would live here, just a few miles from the volcanic hotspot that had spawned the entire archipelago, and in the midst of a seminal moment in its development and its future.

Although only a couple of years had passed, the change in Isla and Molly had been profound. As any parent will note, there is a huge gulf between being five and being seven. Isla had developed into a thoughtful, deeply compassionate little girl, completely absorbed by the natural world – the seeds sown during our first sojourn in the islands having blossomed into genuine interest and passion. By the same measure, Molly had progressed from a three-year-old who just wanted to run around hitting things with a squeaky hammer into a funny, energetic, gloriously wilful five-year-old (although she still had a penchant for hitting things with a squeaky hammer if the opportunity presented itself). I was thoroughly looking forward to seeing how these two extra years would shape their interactions with the islands, particularly as we would be living in an altogether wilder, more elemental location than on our first visit.

We had been met a few days before by a beaming Pablo at the small pier just outside the town. This was exciting for a couple of reasons. The first was that it was such a pleasure to see him again, his enthusiasm unwavering, and his passion for the island undimmed.

'Monty! So good to see you and your family. Hey, girls, you remember me?' He grinned, and leaned forward with a conspiratorial wink. 'Welcome back to the number one place in the Galapagos!'

He grasped my hand and slapped me on the back.

'I am so pleased that you are here for a while so you can really get to know the island. You must meet my wife Laura and my boy Kian – they are so happy that you are here. Come, let's get your bags into the car and take you to your home.'

As we walked towards the car, the second reason for being rather excited made its appearance. The pier at Puerto Villamil protrudes from a landscape that might have been cut out of the centre spread from a Galapagos guide book. Dense green mangroves crowd in from either side, creating a network of clear channels and quiet pools. To the right of the pier is a small beach, against which small waves flop lazily before sliding back down the sand into the shallows. Just offshore in the calm waters of the lagoon, lava reefs break the surface, as dark and shining as polished quartz.

Spread throughout this scene are the animals beloved of any visitor to the islands. Sea lions snore on every walkway, requiring passers-by to gingerly tiptoe round them, or even step directly over them, as they carry their bags inland. In response, the sea lions simply open one eye, yawn, and, if you're particularly lucky, scratch their belly. Iguanas are everywhere, spread-eagled on the pavement, flat out on the road, and stalking the sand. They are huge, the largest of any in the Galapagos at up to 11kg. Molly eyed them warily as we walked towards the car, which is not entirely unreasonable, as they were the size of small crocodiles. Two penguins swam in the shadow of the main pier, with bright orange Sally Lightfoot crabs dotting the lava walls above them like living embers, and blue-footed boobies hunted just offshore.

This is a bird that is synonymous with the islands, with the bright blue feet a sign of good health and a means of attracting a mate. They display these in a slightly ludicrous, high stepping dance, like a child showing off a new pair of shoes. Despite their somewhat comical appearance on land, in the air and on the hunt, they are a magnificent spectacle, going from effortless flight to a sleek predatory dart in an instant, to knife through the water's surface with barely a ripple.

I could quite happily have spent our entire time in Isabela on this very pier, as it all seemed to be happening right there. Isla and Molly were also rapt, once again back in their magical fairytale kingdom, and once again dicing with death as they stared over the rail at the clear water between the mangroves, shouting out the names of the animals beneath them as they did so. This caused both of them to teeter on the edge of the railing in a distressingly familiar manner, the line between triumph and disaster a small patch of their stomachs balanced on the top, and a few millimetres of flip flop, scuffing and scraping on the concrete path beneath. This all proved a bit much for Tam, who jogged briskly over and bustled them protesting into the back of the cab.

The road we travelled from the dock had changed in one key respect in the last two years – it now had a hard surface of basalt rocks, pitted and honeycombed from their fiery birth but now smoothed by the passage of time and tyre. This made the ride into town less romantic, with no clouds of billowing white sand in our wake, Lawrence of Arabia-style, but must have been a blessed relief to the locals. Nonetheless, as we turned on to the main street, I was delighted to see that it remained a corralled expanse of beach, along which a few cars progressed at a sedate pace. There was even a man on a bicycle towing a small trailer of coconuts, riding in the middle of the road without a care in the world. He gave us a friendly wave as we drove past, making me feel rather pleased that we'd already hit 'peak Calypso', even though we'd only been on the island half an hour.

The street was lined with restaurants and cafés, clustered around a smart new town square. Here, in the cool shade of newly planted trees, stood a shiny playground, which drew admiring noises from Isla and Molly on the back seat. In the park there were three statues – two of which I didn't recognise, but one of whom was entirely distinctive. The beetling brows, and Santa beard, the vast acreage of domed forehead: Charles Darwin. Every time I saw a statue of him in the islands – and there were a great many – it always made me ponder how very incongruous it is that a fellow from Shrewsbury who lived in the nineteenth century should now be the predominant figure in a group of islands off the coast of Ecuador two hundred years later. It is a constant reminder of the momentous nature of his five weeks here, both for the Galapagos and for the way we all think about the world around us.

We were renting a small house on the main street, and as this had once again been done remotely through the good words and honest efforts of Pablo, I had absolutely no idea what it would be like. I had seen a photo or two but due to their poor resolution these images seemed to encompass the full spectrum of accommodation, from opulent luxury to corrugated lean-to. If I squinted and used my imagination, the house looked perfectly acceptable, which was good enough for me. Whether it would be good enough for Tam and the girls would be revealed very shortly indeed.

We drew up outside a white, single-storey building that looked out directly on to the road. It seemed nice enough, and soon the girls were tumbling out of the taxi to explore. This was partly out of curiosity, but was driven mainly by the urge to bag the best bed. This was a sacred ritual whenever we turned up somewhere new, and was a legally binding obligation based on the words 'This is my bed', combined with actually sitting on it at the time. There was frequently considerable violence leading up to this point, and I hurried from the car to act as mediator.

I entered the house with Tam following close behind me and the girls scuttling ahead. The main living area was small but neat, with a couple of battered sofas in the corner and a simple table and chairs next to a barred window that looked out on to the main street. Two small bedrooms led off from this main space, with one of them already the venue for some fisticuffs as the girls debated sleeping arrangements. The kitchen was tiny, and notably had a large blue-plastic water dispenser instead of a tap for drinking water – potable water on Isabela in particular, and the Galapagos generally, being one of the main challenges facing the burgeoning population. If the Galapagos is a microcosm of global challenges, then water shortages and the hygiene issues associated with it represent one of the most pertinent facing humanity. Indeed, it may end up being the factor that curtails what appears, at present anyway, to be unfettered urban development, particularly in the larger islands of Santa Cruz and San Cristóbal. Ironically, on these islands surrounded by the vast shining expanse of the Pacific, and blessed by green forests and low-hanging mists, it is water that may ultimately be the limiting factor on their continued colonisation, and the element that saves the wider ecosystems from ruin.

The floor throughout the house was made up of smooth tiles, which had a pleasing cooling effect, but I knew from bitter experience would become entertainingly slippy when wet. This would happen a great deal, as a few paces into the backyard revealed just how close we were to the sea. The yard was nothing more than a large square of white sand, with a few straggly plants in one corner being slowly incinerated by the sun. Surrounding the entire area was a rather bleak breeze-block wall about eight feet high. This was a very good thing in that it meant the girls would be incarcerated and kept out of trouble, but very bad in that I could hear the surf pounding away on the other side. It struck me as a wanton act of denial to erect an impenetrable barrier between the house and one of the most beautiful beaches in the world, and I hooked my hands over the top of the wall, scrabbling inelegantly with my toes to steal a brief glimpse of swaying palms and white sand. Maybe the person who built the place hated the sea, or loved their privacy – either way, Isabela seemed a strange choice as a home. Secretly, I was rather pleased that our 'garden' was essentially a chunk of beach, as I was certainly not the most green-fingered of people. The girls, who had now sorted out the bed dilemma, were equally delighted that they lived next to what was essentially a colossal sand pit, and immediately began construction of a giant castle. The presence of a great many lava lizards on the hot faces of the wall made it even more exciting for Molly – as ever, they were all red chin and attitude, and she ran round the yard shouting and pointing, leaving an oval trail of small footprints as she did so.

'It's a bit bleak, that wall,' said Tam beside me. 'Let's paint it. I think we should record our experiences on it while we're here.'

This was a splendid idea, and I particularly looked forward to the girls' interpretation of island life. I didn't know precisely what this would look like, but was confident that they wouldn't be constrained by biological accuracy, and that pink would predominate. Despite all this excitement – or perhaps because of it – we suddenly felt weary to our bones, and collectively the family moved inside and towards their beds. We passed quickly into a dreamless slumber, lulled by the sonorous boom of the surf, and what I thought at first was rain drumming on the window. It was only in those final moments just before sleep that I realised it was the noise of the wind rustling the palm fronds that hung over the house, which seemed as good a soundtrack as any to send me to sleep on our first full day back on the great seahorse-shaped island of Isabela.

Early the next morning we decided to take a short walk along the beach, just to acquaint ourselves with our extended front yard. We turned right out of the front door, and immediately passed a small shop. The owner smiled at us, and, much to the girls' delight, a colossal dog bounded out of the door to say hello. He was a dashing grey-and-silver bear, with a bit of husky in there for sure, and a few other breeds too. Judging by his size, the husky had incorporated those other breeds into his own DNA by eating them.

'Okay?' I asked the owner rather nervously, as Molly wrapped her arms around the considerable circumference of the dog's neck.

She was a short, rather rotund lady, who dismissed my concerns with a wide smile and a wave of the hand.

'Hey, Ron, *ven aquí*,' she said, and the dog immediately turned and trotted obediently to her side. I thought it was fantastic that we would be living immediately next to a large, well-behaved dog – although obviously not ideal on the 'invasive species' front. I thought it was even better that the dog in question was called Ron. It's quite a thing to travel 6,000 miles to find your next door neighbour has a dog with a name about as British as they come. Looking at his great lolling tongue and amiable expression, I decided it rather suited him.

The lady made her way back into the shop, with Isla and Molly pressing their noses up against the glass of the door. This revealed a line of refrigerators containing ice cream. For them this meant that our new home was ideally placed, although for us parents it would present a few challenges in the months ahead, and Tam looked at me with a somewhat resigned expression. Living next to an ice-cream shop with Isla and Molly is akin to living with two crack addicts next to a very large facility that sells nothing but crack. Policing this could be quite exciting.

We turned right again, and after following a narrow white sand track, were almost immediately on the beach itself, with the coast stretching away on either side, and the sea leading to a wide horizon directly ahead. To our left was the town jetty, and to our right the shoreline swept in a beautiful parabola leading to a lava reef. And, purely coincidentally, to Pablo.

'Monty, hey, good to see you and your lovely family!' He smiled broadly and strode towards me, barefoot on the sand, hand extended to grip mine. 'I'm here with Laura and my boy, come and say hello.'

Isla and Molly had already sprinted ahead, dancing in and out of the shallows, shrieking as the sea snatched at their ankles. We followed in their footsteps, and Pablo waved to a tall girl standing next to the reef, watching a flaxen-haired boy pick his way through the rock pools.

'Laura, this is Monty and Tam,' he shouted, gesturing her towards us. She looked up, waved back, and made her way across the sand.

'Welcome,' she said 'welcome to Isabela. We're so excited that you're here. You'll soon find out that it's an easy place to love . . .' she paused for a moment, 'but can be a difficult place to live!'

She laughed, delighted at our slightly non-plussed reaction to her greeting. She had a warmth about her that immediately put us at our ease, with long brown hair framing an attractive, open face.

'Oh, don't worry, you'll love it here. And me and Pablo will look after you, just you see.'

What was most striking was not so much what she said as the fact that it was delivered in perfect English, with a hint of the southern counties accent thrown in. She saw my puzzled expression.

'Oh, I'm English. Didn't Pablo tell you?' She glanced at him fondly. 'I came out here on holiday ten years ago, and snogged my wildlife guide! Very unprofessional of him, I must say. And now here I am, and we've got a son who is a proper islander.'

With this she gestured to the boy, who by now was standing directly beside her.

'Kian, meet the Halls family,' she said. 'You'll be looking after them for the next few months, so it's very important that you introduce yourself properly.'

By now Isla and Molly had joined us, and eyed this new arrival rather like viewing a rare and exciting new species. Kian looked every inch the beach boy, with a shock of blond hair, board shorts and a physical poise and confidence that belied his years. He was whip thin, and plainly as fit as a butcher's dog.

'Hello,' he said, and peered more closely at the girls. Isla and Molly smiled shyly back, and glancing down I thought I saw the hint of a blush rising in Isla's cheeks. I felt my paternal hackles rise, the first occasion I had ever seen her somewhat awkward in the presence of a boy (and undoubtedly not the last). But Kian immediately put her at her ease.

'Hey, do you want to come and see some iguanas with me?' he asked, which struck me as a terrific first line for later in life, if nothing else. The girls nodded, and within moments the three of them were tiptoeing across the lava rocks towards the shoreline.

'Come and have a drink with us,' said Pablo, 'and we'll tell you a little about living on the island.'

Next to the beach was a ramshackle little bar, with a painted sign hanging askew above it. The 'Bar de Beto' was to become our regular haunt during our time in the islands, and was less of a well-appointed hostelry than a collection of chairs, a hammock, and a counter where the owner – Alberto – would serve drinks. But it occupied maybe the best position of any bar I had ever encountered, at the head of the reef, in the bullseye of the beach that spread away on either side, and affording a ringside seat to the daily iguana commute into and out of the sea.

We sat and sipped coconut water from the husks, as we watched the children play in the shallows.

'It's not an easy life here, but it is paradise, it really is,' said Pablo, taking in the sea, the reef, and the distant headland shrouded in spray and the shimmer of the morning sun. 'Here we are so close to nature, and maybe that is the reason we on this island are fighting so hard for it. You'll soon learn, Monty, that Isabela is a battleground in many ways, but I think it's a battle we can win, I really do.'

With that, he smiled, rose to his feet, and walked on to the beach. We followed, with Laura and Tam already hatching plots about getting together, and the children a shimmering mirage at the reef's edge, all awkwardness and introductions a distant memory.

A few days after our arrival, Laura mentioned that there was to be a fundraising event at the beach for the local school.

'Everyone will be there,' she said, 'so it'd be a great idea if you took the girls. Good chance for them and you to make some friends.'

Tam was away in northern Isabela for a few days, having been invited to join a project that was sailing along the coast to gather data on the impact of oceanic plastics on marine life. This had left me home alone with the girls, something I enjoyed immensely. They were less sure about the entire process, understanding at a basic level that the finely honed routines and administrative excellence of their mum had been replaced by the slightly more scatter-gun approach of their dad. They found this 'muesli for dinner' lifestyle entertaining, but slightly disorientating, although it did give them the opportunity to make hay while the paternal sun shone. The pulsing jugular of a man making it up as he went along hadn't gone unobserved, and they were ready to exploit the opportunities that represented.

Saturday morning dawned, and the three of us ambled the short distance to the beach opposite the centre of town. It is undeniably part of the magic of Isabela that the roads remain thoroughfares of white sand, essentially just a piece of the shoreline that has been corralled between houses, shops and restaurants. This meant that you could walk everywhere barefoot, and watching the girls skip ahead of me, their cotton dresses swaying in the breeze, straw hats askew, whilst unselfconsciously holding hands, I felt a moment of giddy pride. Any dad has moments when his children take his breath away, although this time the sensation ambushed me somewhat. Perhaps it was the simple contentment of my two little girls, miles from the gentle rolling shires of their Devon home, each made wholly secure by the mere presence of the other.

By the time we arrived on the beach, the festivities were just beginning. Laura saw me and waved me over.

'Hello, Monty. How lovely that you've come. This is Señor Julio Garcia, the headmaster of the island school.'

Julio looked precisely how you'd expect a school principal to look – impeccably turned out, and slightly bookish, with glasses balanced on the tip of his nose.

'Ah, Monty, how lovely to meet you and your girls.'

Both Isla and Molly were sheltering behind me by this stage, possessing as they do that rare ability to spot a headmaster at a hundred paces.

'Thanks so much, Julio,' I said, narrowly avoiding calling him sir.

'Please, do make yourself at home here. And come, join in the games.'

He steered me by one elbow to the edge of a square of fluttering coloured flags in the sand, surrounded by locals and young children, and then wandered off to continue organising the day.

The adults surrounding the square shared the universal look of any parent with young children – slightly careworn, deeply fatigued, but with continuously swivelling eyes scanning the immediate locale for anything dangerous/embarrassing/edible. In the midst of the square a game was underway, one which looked impossibly complex, involving as it did tiny multi-coloured chairs connected apparently randomly by bits of string. The game was just concluding when I made my appearance, and evidently someone had just won, as there was a brief moment of uproar from the spectators, and one of the children raised their arms in triumph.

'You next?' said Julio, who had the singular skill (unique to headmasters) of suddenly materialising beside you.

'Ah, um, okay. What do I have to do?' I asked, eyeing the tiny chairs and string rather nervously.

'Oh, it's very easy. Molly will feed you, but she will be blind-folded. It is very fun.'

I looked down at Molly, who was staring up at me with a look of unbridled joy. If ever there was a definition of 'very fun' for her, then it's competitively smashing foodstuffs into her dad's face. She had the look of a little girl who had been waiting for this very moment, on this very beach, all of her young life.

We duly lined up with the other parents – each parent on a tiny coloured chair, each child corralled by a tramway of string (aha, I thought). Molly had her blindfold applied, and we were handed a bowl of yoghurt and granola. The hooter sounded, and Molls spent the next three minutes shoving it gleefully into my mouth/nostrils/eyes with all the vigour of a stoker keeping a roaring furnace alive on a (slightly behind schedule) Flying Scotsman.

Surprisingly, and massively undiplomatically, we won. Molls whipped her blindfold off to see not only an applauding crowd before her, but also her dad pebble-dashed with breakfast. Both of these things made her inordinately happy, and she whooped in triumph. The fact that the prize was a voucher to a local pizza house made the day pretty much complete, and we'd only just got there.

Isla, meanwhile, was irresistibly drawn to the surf, and had cast off her best dress to jump waves in her underwear. This was a habit I hoped she'd grow out of before she reached adulthood (or, then again, perhaps I didn't – it was as good an expression of joy and freedom as you're ever likely to witness), but certainly, as a seven-year-old, it was something of a hit with the local kids, who soon joined in. I have always thought that the sea is a great common denominator, something that binds us all regardless of race, culture, or background. To see Isla cavorting in the waves, shrieking with glee as her skin glistened and her hair flew, surrounded by local children doing precisely the same, was to bear witness to a medium and a moment that effortlessly surmounted all cultural boundaries.

And so the morning passed. The locals, one and all, were welcoming and generous with me and the kids; my lack of Spanish and their lack of English not a hindrance in the slightest as we occupied the common ground of wanting to have a great day with our children. Before I knew it, the events were drawing to a close, and everyone was being waved into the square for the final event.

This involved some large plastic bins of seawater, lots of disposable plastic cups, and some plastic bottles. There was a theme emerging here, and it wasn't a good one, but nonetheless I took my seat at the back of a row of people and waited to be told what to do.

The compère – bearded, wearing some wacky glasses and a big bow-tie (some things, annoying things, are truly universal) – was shouting in Spanish and repeatedly gesturing that we should get ready to pour water over our shoulder. Happily, Laura was directly in front of me, and translated through the side of her mouth.

'It's a relay race,' she said. 'One person fills a glass at the front from the big bin, then runs back. We all have a plastic glass each, and use it to pass the water to each other over our shoulders. You're at the back filling the big plastic water bottle with what's left. Simple.'

It actually turned out to be rather complicated, and rather ingenious. The snag is that as you fill the bottle through the very small hole at the top, using the very large plastic cup on your hand, the person in front of you has no idea whatsoever whether you're paying attention. As it turned out, I invariably wasn't, and much to the delight of the watching locals had several cups of seawater poured over the back of my head as I bent to my task. A ragged cheer from one of the other teams indicated that they had filled their final bottle, and general back-slapping and merriment followed.

'Sorry,' said Laura, as she turned round to see a man who looked very much like he'd just had five pints of sea water thrown over him.

'No problem,' I said moistly. 'My fault entirely.'

And so the day passed in a technicolour, mildly (and enjoyably) chaotic medley of sand, sea, socialising and sun. At the end of the day the organisers, weary and hoarse (that was their condition, not their names), gathered up the cups, the bottles, and the general detritus, placing it all in bin liners for disposal. And it was here that the big issue of the day emerged.

The predominant substance in the bags was, of course, plastic. Indeed, it was the reason that Tam was not with us on that particular day, scouring the shallows of the uninhabited shoreline to the far north on her micro-plastics survey. Such is life nowadays: the familiar scene that, regardless of location or occasion, our waste products are plastic. But as the bags were hefted into the back of a pick-up truck to be taken away, it seemed to me a particularly poignant scene. As the pick-up drove over the footprints of the children of Isabela in the sandy road, I reflected – in this of all places, on this of all days – why it was here in the first place. Surely in the midst of such a delicate World Heritage Site, contained and controlled, it should be a thing of the past.

We are all 'plastic aware' these days, but it is genuinely worth noting the scale of the problem we face. Repetition does nothing to dilute the horrifying statistics, and the exponential nature of the challenge it represents.

In short, when it comes to people and plastics, as we head into the second quarter of the twenty-first century, there are a lot more of us using a lot more of it. This might seem an overly simplistic viewpoint, but it is an unavoidable truth. In 1950 the world's population of two-and-half billion people produced a mere 1.5 million tons of plastic. Fast forward to 2016, and a global population of 7 billion people (in itself a terrifying statistic) produced over 320 million tons of plastic. This latter figure is set to double by 2034.

And the big issue is that all of the plastic produced to date, unless it has been burned, is still with us. It often occurred to me as I explored the islands that, should Darwin have stepped ashore in 1835 and eaten, for example, a flapjack in a plastic wrapper, and then dropped it, said plastic wrapper would still be there, hidden in the sand, or shredded within the marine food chain. But still there nonetheless.

There are no marine environments anywhere on the planet that do not contain traces of plastic. The sea is replete, we've filled a repository we always thought was limitless, and now all we can do is cram more in. It is estimated that there may now be around 5.25 trillion macro- and microplastic pieces floating in the open ocean, weighing up to 269,000 tonnes. That's an estimate, of course, but what we do know is that 60% to 90% of all man-made marine debris is now plastic. Like diamonds, plastics are forever being broken up and degraded by ultra violet light, being shattered, being ingested by animals large and small, but never, ever going away.

The impact on marine life has yet to be truly understood, but plainly it is grave. A study by the University of Plymouth esti-mated that 700 species in the sea, or relying on the ocean as a food source, face extinction directly because of plastic pollution. This is, once again, speculation, albeit based on the best data, but what we do know is that there are already 100,000 marine mammals and turtles, and one million seabirds, killed by plastic pollution annually.

Just in case we feel this is a problem we have to deal with as higher beings, as though we are somehow removed from the issue and therefore only operating at a philanthropic level, it's worth noting that we ingest about 70,000 bits of micro-plastic per year, with hitherto untold effects on our long-term health. We're in a spot of bother, and we're all in it together – seabirds, plankton, whales, fish and us.

Sure enough the Galapagos have passed legislation to address the issue, banning plastic straws in May 2018, then forbidding single-use plastic bags in June, and Styrofoam containers in July of the same year. It was notable though that throughout Puerto Villamil plastic bags still proliferated, such is the ingrained culture in so many parts of the world that any object bought or sold has to be wrapped in a flimsy bag, soon to be borne away by the wind or shredded against a fence. As I looked at the bin liners full of plastic being carted away from a school fundraising day, here on Isabela island at the heart of a World Heritage site, it reminded me forcibly that, much the same as in many other regions around the world, this will take time.

But there is another factor at play here. There was never a walk along the beach on Isabela that didn't see Isla and Molly bend down to pick up a piece of plastic, to return home clutching refuse and detritus in their little pink fists. For them it is completely standard, ingrained in their psyche – if you saw plastic, you picked it up and put it in the bin. Something rather wondrous is happening, with this new generation walking behind ours, picking up what we have left behind, clearing up in our wake. By this means, 22 tonnes of plastic was cleared up by local people in the Galapagos throughout 2018 as the population of the islands took matters into their own hands.

During our first sojourn on the islands two years previously, the girls had actually taken part in a beach clean organised by the local community. We had all turned up in flip flops and shorts, ready to stroll along the white sand of Tortuga Bay, picking up the occasional piece of plastic detritus, before returning triumphantly to the town centre at Puerto Ayora, noble eco-warriors flushed with pride at having 'done our bit'.

Sadly the day hadn't quite turned out that way. We had been directed to an area of dense mangroves next to the main highway, with the interlocking branches creating an impenetrable matrix over the top of thorns and scrub that coated the ground beneath. Molls, being Molls, had turned on one flip-flopped heel and strode wordlessly back to the car, signaling that her day was done. Isla was made of sterner stuff, and plunged into the dense thicket like a woman possessed, emerging periodically over the next few hours clutching various items of plastic, old bits of rope, fishing buoys, and – rather fittingly – an old broom.

The mangroves have always acted as a giant sieve for the sea, catching silt and waterborne debris in their roots. Today such debris is invariably man-made, with the vast bulk of it being plastic, a tide line of refuse washing in on the great ocean currents. Over the course of the day, here at the fringes of this most unique and precious set of islands, our little girl collected bag after bag of refuse, hobbling about on cut and bruised feet until I had to order her to stop, and then physically carry her back down to the car. In retrospect I think part of her urgency was a touching desire to 'clean it all up', a childishly simple notion that if she just picked it all up then the area would be safe for the animals that called it home. Of course, the next tide would bring more, and the next, and the next, until her efforts would be eradicated completely. But there was something so very heartening in her indefatigable desire to put this right, a sentiment shared globally by a new generation. As I patched up her feet on the pavement next to the car, I reflected on what a potent force this is, and certainly not one to be underestimated.

Tam returned a few days later from her trip to northern Isabela, much to the delight and considerable relief of the kids, now tiring of unidentifiable sandwiches and suspicious things in omelettes. We sat in the backyard, watching Isla and Molly painting the wall – a large tortoise seemed to be the theme, although with their exuberant and impressionist painting style it was always difficult to tell until a particular work was complete. The wind rustled in the great hanging fronds of the palm behind the house, and a frigate bird swept past on black satin wings, head turning from side to side, seeking mischief.

'It was pretty horrendous,' said Tam, still with the flush of the sun on her cheeks after several days at sea. 'The really hard bit was exploring the bays where there are mangroves. They're like . . . they're like . . . '

She struggled for the words, attempting to recall the scenes of previous days.

'It's awful: everything to do with us, with human existence, is there on the shoreline,' she said finally. 'It's shocking to be in these remote, really beautiful places, and just see this tideline of bottles, bags and plastic bits.'

She had not undertaken this trip idly. Tam had always been passionate about the natural world – ferrying small beetles to safety in her back garden as a little girl, and irresistibly drawn to the woods and the sea on holidays to Cornwall. Now, as a relatively new mum, she was viewing the world through the powerful lens of a maternal drive to protect her offspring – surely the most potent conservation force of all. Over the last few years, and following our first visit to the islands, she had become even more active, more engaged, and more determined that something could, and must, be done.

Her trip had been as a member for a survey team, led by local scientist Juan Pablo Munoz, and Cathy Townsend from Queensland University, which was attempting to assess how much plastic waste was being used in the building material of flightless cormorant nests – an iconic endemic species, and one that spends its entire life particularly close to shore.

'The nest we analysed was at least 30% plastic material,' said Tam. 'Fishing line, colourful bits of bags, anything the cormorant had found floating on the surface, or trapped in the mangroves. It was pretty awful really – and that's just the stuff we can see. Juan Pablo told me that they've found plastics in at least eighteen different species here.'

She shook her head.

'Makes you feel terrible, doesn't it?' She looked at the girls putting the finishing touches to what was indeed a tortoise. A purple one. 'Pretty crappy that we're handing such a mess over to them.'

At that precise point, Molly glanced at her paintbrush, then Isla, then her paintbrush again. Plainly an idea was taking shape. She suddenly started to chase Isla round the yard, waving a brush overhead and shrieking in delight.

'I don't know, Tam,' I said, watching their energy and exuberance, 'I sometimes feel that the future might not be in bad hands. Better than ours anyway . . .'

I smiled, stood up and stretched, and walked over to the girls.

Molly now had Isla cornered, and was advancing on her with a look of absolute delight, paintbrush to the fore, with Isla trying to climb the vertical wall behind her. I intervened, much to Moll's crushing disappointment, and led them hand in hand back to the house, the mural on the wall behind an unfinished work, a long, complex painting leading to an unknown future.

Sharks and San Cristóbal

I shifted in the seat, trying yet again to get comfortable as the outboards roared behind me and the bow slammed into the great Pacific swells that surged between the islands. Isla and Molly were both asleep, a remarkable feat in the circumstances. The sedative effects of a long boat journey never failed to amaze me, and as we rose up the face of each wave, then surged down its back, they experienced a moment of negative gravity, with their limbs rising and heads lifting, before slamming back down into the cushioned bench on which they slept. Each time they landed in a slightly different position, a tangle of limbs, hats all askew, and faces made content by dreams, I presumed, of roller coasters and funfairs.

We were travelling across the fifty miles of open sea to San

Cristóbal, a journey of about three hours. The island was the setting for some particularly exciting shark science, which I was keen to witness first hand. The journey, although long and taxing, would I hoped be eminently worth it.

San Cristóbal has the second largest population of any island in the Galapagos, at approximately 10,000 people. This is an estimate, because of the constant flux of tourists that come here, and the changing numbers of people to support them. It is a hugely popular destination, with a bustling seafront in the main harbour at Puerto Baquerizo Moreno acting as a gateway to a myriad of different attractions in the interior. It has a somewhat laid-back feel, lacking the commercialism of Puerto Ayora, although, much the same as the rest of the Galapagos, it continues to be developed at a phenomenal rate.

And much the same as the other populated islands, the modern benign manifestation of tour boats and pizza bars is in stark contrast to a barbaric past. Many of the first settlers on San Cristóbal came from the failed colony on Floreana. Brutalised and broken by their experiences there, in 1879 they sought a new life working for an entrepreneur called Manuel J. Cobos. Under the initial leadership of an Englishman by the name of Thomas Levick, ninety-four men and five women made their homes on the island in order to exploit a species of lichen that grew in abundance there, used for the creation of purple dye. Cobos had already run a lucrative business in Mexico creating and exporting the dye, and saw San Cristóbal as a golden opportunity to exploit the market further.

He founded a colony called El Progreso, more than 300 metres above sea level. His energy and industry were truly remarkable, and soon he was employing 400 people and had laid railroads, built a dock in Shipwreck Bay, and created successful plantations of coffee, sugar cane and fruit trees in an area that covered three thousand hectares. They were here to stay, and the presence of people on San Cristóbal would be continuous from this point until the present day.

The sugar mill was so successful that it supplied the entire Ecuadorian nation with sugar for the next twenty-five years. Cobos had two schooners which plied the seas back and forth to the mainland, which for three decades were the only vessels to make this crossing. He even created the currency that was the only one in use in the fledging republic of Ecuador.

Cobos truly was a remarkable businessman and pioneer. The snag was that he was a terrible, terrible human being. He had created his own fiefdom, and he ruled it through terror and intimidation. During his reign – and that is a fair description, as he enjoyed absolute power over his subjects – he ordered the exile of 15 people (taken to deserted islands and an unknown fate), had six men executed, and even reached the horrifying extreme of inflicting punishments of up to 600 lashes.

The end was inevitable. On 15 January 1904, after ordering a punishment of 400 lashes for one of his workers, Jose Prieto, he was shot by their leader, Elias Puertas. He survived these initial wounds, but in the words of Hugh Idrovos' outstanding book *Footsteps in Galapagos*, he was then 'lynched to death'.

There is something about these islands that drives men to extremes of violence and depravity. The pioneering history of the Galapagos is a patchwork of brutality, of mini-despots, of murder and of subterfuge. Perhaps it is a combination of the isolation and the promise of great riches, or the harsh climate and the severe landscapes. Whatever it was, it drove men to madness and dark deeds. Echoes remain to this day, in the mildewed ruins, the history books, and in the memories of the direct descendants from those dark days, striving to build a new identity and a new future for the Enchanted Isles.

There is something irresistible about the hour before dawn, even when that hour happens to be drizzly and rather bleak. Noises are softened by the darkness, and our most basic senses become heightened – I could smell the proximity of the sea in the gloom, and felt the rain soft on my cheek, causing me to hunker down into my coat. I glanced down to see Isla beside me, her hand held in mine, her body pressed against my legs as we walked. Molly – much to her highly vocal chagrin – had not been allowed to come, as she was too little. Isla was therefore basking in some exclusive dad time, an emotion that was entirely reciprocated.

We carefully made our way along the jetty, walking through the stepping stones of light cast by the neon lamps overhead. Ahead of us a damp pelican sat at the water's edge, squat and immobile, chin drawn to chest and feathers ruffled. It looked out over the limpid pool of the shallow water by the jetty, illuminated by the industrial glow of the street lights. A solitary sea lion twisted and spun over dark basalt rocks, an early riser chasing fish drawn to the eerie artificial glow of civilisation.

We reached the edge of the jetty and dropped our bags. The *Sea Quest* was already alongside the steps, her flared bow rising in an elegant curve, her deck covered with the equipment required for the day ahead – bags of nets, robust plastic cases of scientific gear, and a large measuring board. The skipper was bustling about in the stern, preparing the outboards for the day ahead. He glanced up, gave us a flashing smile and a wave, and then returned to his work.

Isla edged even closer to me, and wrapped one arm around my leg. This was the earliest she had ever been awake, and to see her world shrunk to her immediate vicinity as a pool of light, knowing that imminently we would be heading out into the darkness beyond, rendered her silent and watchful.

'Hi there,' said a voice, with an undertone of mid-western drawl, 'you must be Monty and Isla. Sorry I'm a little late.'

I looked back along the jetty and striding towards us was a tall, athletic-looking girl carrying a dive bag over one shoulder. She had tightly curled hair held back in a bandana, and olive skin which accentuated the whitest and widest of smiles.

'I'm Lauren. And you must be Isla,' she said, bending down to shake her hand. 'Are you going to help me tag some sharks today?'

I glanced down at Isla, who was staring open-mouthed at Lauren with something approaching awe. Dimly aware that there was a chance I was doing exactly the same thing, I stepped forward, and introduced myself.

'Hi Lauren, I'm Monty. Thanks so much for having us along today. Isla and me are chuffed to bits. Aren't we, girl?'

I glanced down once again, to see that Isla had still not moved a muscle. Then, as I watched, she solemnly extended a hand, which made Lauren snort with delight, and grasp it in her own.

Isla was looking at her ultimate hero made real. Not only an actual marine biologist, but one who tags sharks, is a girl, and has a cool accent and great teeth. As a young girl raised on a visual diet of mermaids, Barbie and the Octonauts (an animated underwater rescue squad – essential viewing in our house, even before we had kids), she was, at last, meeting one in the flesh.

Lauren looked at Isla quizzically. 'Come on, then, let's get the equipment on board and get cracking, shall we?'

Isla nodded slowly, eyes the size of searchlights, and slavishly followed Lauren down the steps into *Sea Quest*. I lagged a few paces behind, abruptly relegated from marine legend to bag carrier.

It is said that you have to be at sea at dawn to really know where the morning comes from, and as we sped away from the harbour we could just see the first glow of the sun touching the sky. I breathed deep, and briefly closed my eyes, entirely happy at the prospect of the day ahead. Isla was now sitting beside Lauren, although she kept her eyes fixed firmly forward lest the spell be broken. Lauren chatted away happily to her, receiving the occasional slow nod in return.

Accompanying Lauren was her field assistant, Bridgett, and it dawned on me how wonderful it was that the two people conducting this important research were both young women. This might seem insignificant, but shark research can be a bit of a male bastion, and I was delighted that their presence showed my own wee lass that such prejudices were on the ash heap of history. Having said that, one of the greatest shark scientists of all time was a woman, although even she faced male chauvinism and prejudice in the early stages of her career. Dr Eugenie Clark was a giant figure in marine biology, and was something of an idol of mine when I was a young boy. Lauren and Bridgett were her successors, and worthy ones at that.

The work they were undertaking was, for me, some of the most significant shark science in the entire island group. Protecting sharks is an emotive subject, with much of the effort focused on the adult animals being taken for their fins. These conservation efforts come in many forms, either through legislative and political pressure to stop the consumption of shark-fin soup, or in efforts to protect key populations of the animals while they are still alive. But a sorely neglected area is understanding where the young sharks congregate, and ensuring that they can reach a size that at least gives them an odds-on chance of survival in the big bad blue world of the open sea.

Shark nurseries are therefore extremely important in the future survival of the species as a whole. And hammerhead shark nurseries particularly so in the future of the Galapagos population – of both people and sharks. The latter will swiftly die out if the adult sharks are fished out and the young are deprived of habitats in which to grow. In turn the human population will suffer, as shark tourism is one of the staples of the Galapagos economy. Deplete one and you radically impact the other.

Lauren's work was attempting to identify the location of several shark nurseries, with particular emphasis on juvenile hammerheads. This work is well advanced, and today we were heading to just such a location, to take part in the sampling process and witness what may well be the final pieces of the jigsaw fall into place.

We travelled for half an hour, before the skipper turned *Sea Quest* into a quiet cove. The shoreline was a mixture of mangroves and dark lava peninsulas, with the occasional white curve of sand between. By now the whole scene was illuminated by the golden light of dawn. Offshore the great mass of Kicker Rock glowed like a sentinel, harvesting the sun's rays amid a leaden sea.

Whenever I visit these coves, I always think of Darwin. They are effervescent pools of life, with boobies and frigate birds overhead, turtles surfacing to breathe, stingrays exploding out of the sand beneath the boat, and oyster catchers picking their way delicately along the water's edge. Surely even a man sated with four years of travel to some of the most wild and beautiful locations on earth must have come alive as his boat nosed into these coves, the water around him pulsing with energy and promise.

Mangroves have long been acknowledged as key nursery grounds for a range of different marine species. The interlocking roots make them difficult places for large predators to operate, and create a perfect sanctuary for young animals to shelter, to grow, and to learn to hunt. They also support a huge range of species above the water, being a favoured haunt of numerous different types of birds, invertebrates and insects. All of this means that mangroves are some of the most productive ecosystems on earth. Add to this their ability to maintain the integrity of coastal regions by binding silt and sand in their roots, and you'd think they'd be a truly sacrosanct environment.

And yet it is the mangroves that fall away first as mankind continues a relentless march along coastlines around the world, clearing them for industry, for housing, for aquaculture, and for recreation. The long-term costs of this are yet to be fully understood, but can easily be imagined. By tearing up vast tracts of mangroves, we are stripping away the basic architecture of our shorelines, while simultaneously removing the kindergartens for countless marine species. And this doesn't even begin to consider the impact for resident larger species. It is estimated that every hectare of mangrove is worth US $33–57 thousand per annum in terms of the biomass it produces. And yet they are being destroyed at a rate of 1% of the total global coverage per year. As such, by 2100 they will be functionally extinct, and with them so will countless other species that rely wholly on them to survive.

This meant that the work we were doing that day was something of a race against time. There would be three phases. The first would involve dropping a baited camera trap on to the sea bed, to be retrieved at the end of the day. As the outboard stilled and the boat glided to a halt, Lauren lifted a hatch beneath the deck, and pulled out a truly Heath Robinson contraption. It had a familiar look to it, one I couldn't quite place.

Lauren noted my quizzical expression.

'It's from my fridge,' she said, lifting up what was suddenly and obviously a fridge drawer.

'We attach cameras to it, put some bait in the bottom, and chuck it in to see what comes along. Oh, there's this as well,' She grabbed what looked suspiciously like an old broom handle.

'It's an old broom handle,' she said, all matter-of-fact and scientific rigour. 'We use it to get baits a bit further away from the basket.' Attached to each end were two sugar shakers, in which more bait had been placed. She tied the whole assembly to the basket.

'Is there anything at all left in your kitchen?' I asked.

'Not really,' she said with a smile. 'If I could figure out a scientific use for the cooker, that'd definitely be on the boat too.'

The final piece of this glorious contraption was a large lump of lava rock, chucked in the bottom of the basket to weigh it down.

'Right,' said Lauren, 'Isla, let's get these cameras on and throw it over the side.'

The cameras were turned on, and the entire system was unceremoniously consigned to the depths.

'Now, Isla, this is where the real fun begins. Let's go and catch us a shark.'

I looked at Isla, and had a genuine concern that she might explode. Such excitement is not easily contained in only one seven-year-old, and I thought it important that we get her in the water sooner rather than later.

The boat edged closer to the beach, and Lauren leapt out into the shallows. Bridgett began feeding the end of a dark net to her, emerging in odorous folds from the hold of *Sea Quest* like scabrous innards. The boat moved slowly forward, creating a perfect crescent of marker buoys under which the net hung suspended, an ominous barrier between the shallows and the open water. Soon Bridgett also jumped in, and they began to haul the net towards the beach. As the ring of buoys tightened, so a smaller and smaller pond was created, and within it we could soon see the darting, frantic shapes of small fish, flashes of silver ticker-tape corralled upon one another in glittering shoals.

This proved a bit too much for Isla, who leapt overboard and swam towards the net. It also proved a tempting spectacle for the local brown pelican population, who up to this point had been observing all this activity with idle interest. The shimmering mass now held in the close confines of the net were the equivalent of a colossal dinner gong, and they descended in raucous squadrons to begin attacking the perimeter.

This same perimeter was precisely where Isla happened to be standing, and I felt a twinge of alarm as she was briefly surrounded by very large birds and flashing beaks.

'Shark!!' Isla roared, pointing at a distinctive shape gliding back and forth at the base of the net. I took this as my own cue to jump into the water, and began wading at some speed from the boat to shore to join in the mayhem, urged on by visions of my daughter being devoured from beneath while simultaneously being pecked to death from above.

When I finally got to the edge of the net, Isla was still bouncing up and down with glee, further exciting the pelicans, who came sculling over to see what all the fuss was about. As we all peered over the edge, I could see that, far from being an adult shark, this was very much a juvenile, and felt immediate sympathy for it. One moment it had been swimming sedately in the mangroves, safe, secure, and very much getting on with the business of growing up. The next the world had closed in, and the new, smaller version of the sea contained lots of pelicans and a shrieking little girl.

The poor animal dashed back and forth, desperate to escape the clamour. Lauren was beside us in an instant, and expertly folded a section of the net around the shark, lifting it from the water in one swift movement.

'Ready, Bridgett, ready!' she shouted, as she ran through the shallows to the beach. Here Bridgett waited with the measuring board, some scales, and a pen poised over a clipboard. Lauren arrived, with Isla and myself panting in her wake, and placed the shark on the board, holding it firmly in place as she did so.

Before us was a perfect, tiny shark, an exact replica of the magnificent animal it would eventually become. Its skin glowed like a copper ingot, its gills quivered, and its flanks flexed with muscle tremors as it twisted and writhed in Lauren's grip. The

The riot of fish life on our first dive at Darwin (*left*) and an inquisitive hog fish coming over to inspect me as I explore the reefs at Wolf (*right*).

Isla meets the neighbours on Isabela.

The Halls family – represented in two and three dimensions.

The kids explore the lava reef in front of the beach house on Isabela.

Lenny the lobster gets repatriated. My feelings are mixed
at this point (unlike Lenny's).

Exploring the shallows of Floreana.

The clear night skies over the Sierra Negra volcano,
a dramatic back drop to the pig hunt.

'Bowie' the hunting dog.

The hunters – Luis, Freddie and Charlie.

A man and a horse in total disharmony. It is no coincidence
that Buttercup is looking longingly towards home.

Charlie prepares to transport the pig off the slopes of
Sierra Negra the morning after the hunt.

Pablo Valladares – a man possessed of an implacable will
to restore the islands to their former glory.

Pablo, Luis and their families enjoy my re-enactment of Buttercup at
full gallop (*above*) and some last goodbyes (*below*).

tips of the shark's fins ended in a perfect jet-black ellipse, as though dipped in ink.

These young sharks are predators from the moment they are born, emerging from the womb as sleek, swift hunters. Sharks have been swimming in our oceans for millennia, and such longevity is a monument to their senses, their instincts, and their ability to dominate their environment. Such is their efficiency as apex predators that they have become slow growing and reproduce late in life, otherwise they would dominate the food chain to such a degree that their own food resources would deplete to dangerously low levels. Such strategy, devised and implemented by the forces of natural selection so beloved of Darwin, now mean that they cannot reproduce fast enough to counter over-exploitation by man. Should this particular shark grow to maturity, at our current rate of depletion, there is every chance she would be one of the last of her kind.

'Can I touch her?' asked Isla, overwhelmed to the point of sudden timidity.

'Of course,' said Lauren, still busying herself with measurements and note taking. 'We'll have her back in the water in two minutes, so make the most of it. There aren't a lot of little girls who have this chance, you know.'

Isla reached out and gently stroked the burnished flank of the shark, smooth as silk, brushing her finger over hydrodynamic perfection. A shark's skin is made up of what are essentially tiny teeth, called denticles, each of which channels water to create a fluidity of movement and hydrodynamic efficiency that is unrivalled by anything produced by the hand of man.

'Right, done, back in the water with her,' said Lauren. Isla ran ahead, strapping on her mask and snorkel as she did so. Lauren jumped aboard the boat to release the shark in slightly deeper water, and Isla, with me alongside her as the dutiful mothership, pounded out to the point where the release would take place. The boat drifted towards the shallows, and Lauren lowered the young shark into the water. She moved it gently back and forth, allowing water to move over the gills, and then released her grip.

The shark twisted out of her grasp, a detonation of energy, accelerating from a standing start to flat out in the space of a metre. Moderately significantly from my perspective, at the end of that metre was Isla's face. She had snorkelled closer and closer, drawn in by the magnetic appeal of this exquisite young animal, and now found herself very much in the flight path. There was nothing she could have done about it even if she wanted, but happily for all of us the shark had only one thing on its mind: escape. It wanted to flee, back to the murky comfort of the mangroves, to a kingdom of tiny fish and interlocking roots. To a place it knew, and had always known, was safe.

The shark gave the most imperceptible dip of a delicately turned pectoral fin, and cannoned past Isla's face at a range of an inch, buffeting her with a shining wake of tiny bubbles, a moment seared on her consciousness for ever.

We spent the rest of the morning catching more sharks, and reviewing the footage from the baited cameras (showing two small hammerheads, much to everyone's delight), but nothing could match that explosive, life-changing moment as the shark brushed past Isla's face.

As we motored home, replete and entirely spent by the day that had passed, I reflected on the experience as a whole. For me as a father, it was priceless; for Isla as a young citizen of a new world, it was seminal. I was aware, of course, of how very fortunate I was to have these chances in the islands, but I was also so very pleased that Isla had been shown the way by two young women. As we left the bay behind, I glanced over and saw them reviewing the footage from the camera traps on Bridgett's phone. In this moment there was a gap of a couple of decades between them, but little else.

There is a wonderful poem written by a mother to her daughter, and it came to my head unbidden, based on the fact that I hoped Isla's path was now set. But soon the hard work would really start, typified by the two young scientists with whom Isla had shared one extraordinary day.

> 'Never play the princess when you can
> be the queen:
> rule the kingdom, swing a scepter,
> wear a crown of gold.
> Don't dance in glass slippers,
> crystal carving up your toes –
> Be a barefoot Amazon instead,
> for those shoes will surely shatter on your feet.'

Flamingos and Hot Flushes

Just behind Puerto Villamil, tucked into an emerald green hollow, is an extensive area of wetlands. I would catch glimpses of it as I walked along the sand road towards the beach bar or into town, a cool, lush environment with tranquil water reflecting the blue skies above. Every time I did so, I would always resolve to take a stroll over the wooden walkway that cut through the mangroves and reed beds, and yet I never quite got round to it.

It was Isla and Molly who finally persuaded me, albeit for a reason that had nothing to do with tranquility and finding their inner chi. They too had spotted glimpses of green, but they had also seen a flash of pink. And no ordinary pink – this was the kind of deep, garish, Alice-in-Wonderland pink that was very much making a statement: I'm here, you can see me, and I just don't care. Set like outrageous coral jewels in a jade sea, the wetlands were alive with flamingos.

There are certain species (Galapagos is full of them) that defy description. I've often reflected on that very first attempt of that very first person who ever saw a flamingo to describe them to their friends back home.

'It's pink. But, you know, really, really, really pink. It's got a ridiculous hooked bill that is bigger than its head. And it stands on one leg a lot. Its neck is so long it looks like a very camp snake. And it dances with all of its friends in close formation when it's feeling horny.'

I can imagine the nods and the smiles and the 'let's not send him away on another trip for a while' muttered conversations. Flamingos sound like an absurd construct of a fevered mind. And yet there they were, right on our doorstep, in all their magnificent, absurd, garish pomp.

As we left the house for the short walk to the lagoon, Molly decided that the first-aid kit was essential for this trip. She could not be dissuaded, and clutched it in one fist as we ambled along the white-sand street. I had no idea why this was the case, but plainly, as far as she was concerned, she was entering a deeply hostile environment inhabited by an animal that could turn on you at any point, so medical cover was a must.

We soon hit the start of the wooden walkway, meandering its way across the mangroves and mudflats of the lagoon. The sun was high in the sky, and the water shone like a mirror. Of flamingos there was no sign whatsoever, but Molls was not placated and clutched the medical kit ever tighter, eyes darting from place to place, waiting for one to pounce. A couple of pintail ducks, a species from the Caribbean blown in on tropical storms many years ago that quite reasonably decided to stay, busied themselves in the reedy margins. I was surprised to see what to all intents and purposes looked like a moorhen, akin to a visitor from a chalk stream in Hampshire. My suspicion that this local variant – known as a *gallinule* after its Latin name – was closely related to our home-grown species was confirmed when I saw it having a vigorous punch up. Moorhens are psychotically territorial, and do not take kindly to other birds wandering into their patch of pond. The one we were watching had embraced this fully, and was hysterically assaulting anything that strayed innocently within range. We could still hear it as we rounded the corner of the walkway, screeching obscenities at a passing duck.

Exposed as we were on the raised slats of the walkway, the sun was doing its damnedest to broil us, and Molly and Isla were rapidly losing interest in the hunt. To restore morale, I took a moment to remind them that they were walking over what is basically a massive lavatory. As there's nothing quite like a story about poo to engage a five- and a seven-year-old, they perked up immediately, standing on tiptoes to peer over the edge of the railing in an attempt to spot any passing floaters.

The lagoons of Puerto Villamil are beguiling, evocative, tranquil and soothing. They have also been ingeniously utilised to filter waste from the town.

This is a relatively recent development, with the system only being introduced three years ago, but already it is reaping rewards. The main one of these is the prevention of serious sewage ingress into the local ecosystem. Wherever mankind expands his presence, wherever populations boom, there will be waste. Affluence invariably leads to effluence. The challenge, particularly on an island in a World Heritage Site, is how to deal with this waste with minimal impact, and in doing so even create something positive for the local environment.

There is a precedent here. The truly extraordinary East Kolkata wetlands in Calcutta produce 10,000 tonnes of fish each year, and almost 50% of the fresh fruit and vegetables in the city markets. This is done by using waste water, essentially the by-product of the first stage of sewage filtration, to feed vast reed beds and artificial ponds. Natural processes break down the contaminants, and the nutrients produced provide a rich soup in which plants and animals prosper. The result – at 125 square kilometres – is the largest sewage-fed aquaculture project on earth, and makes Calcutta one of the cheapest places in India to buy fruit and veg.

The Kolkata wetlands model did not escape the attention of the authorities in the Galapagos, and they set about engineering the lagoon behind the town in Isabela. In 2016 they created five new areas of wetland, and began to pour in the water that was a by-product of sewage treatment. The result is a small, super-efficient filtering and recycling system – the kidneys of the island. It also provides a terrific talking point for small children.

'I can see one! I can see one!' shouted Molly. I looked up, expecting to see riotous shades of pink and bobbing heads, but instead saw what – in all fairness to Molls – did look rather like a poo. Isla joined her at the rail, and began an animated discussion about the veracity of the sighting.

Moving the kids along hastily, I was relieved as we rounded the next corner to see that unmistakable outline, that flash of iridescent plumage, and that absurd neck bending low towards the water. It was a lone flamingo, standing at the centre of concentric rings of ripples, a shining jewel in a vast cistern.

'A flamingo, a flamingo! It's a flamingo!' shouted Molly frantically, her feet pattering on the weathered decking as she sprinted to the rail. As I watched her breathless progress, it struck me that there are very few animals on earth that seize the imagination of young people quite this way. These odds are improved massively, of course, if you happen to be pink and ridiculous, and standing in the centre of a massive toilet.

Everything about the flamingo is rather splendid and absurd. There are six different species globally, but it's thought that the Galapagos version is a variant of the American flamingo. They are somewhat smaller, and, interestingly, are also somewhat pinker than their cousins on the mainland.

The coloration comes from the carotenoid pigment in their food, which includes tiny crustaceans and plant material. They find this by stirring up silt with their feet, bending their heads low, and vigorously sieving water through their bills. The more food they eat, the pinker they become, and judging by the lone flamingo before us, it was an all-you-can-eat diner here in the Puerto Villamil u-bend. Even their egg yolks are pink, which would make a flamingo omelette a magnificent way to start the day (although the authorities at the Galapagos National Park might take a dim view of this). There are only 500 or so individuals throughout the islands, but they add a touch of brilliance and eccentricity that belies their low numbers.

We watched our flamingo for ten minutes or so, all three of us rapt at the delicacy and poise of the animal before us. Molly even put the first-aid kit on the ground, although she kept it within arm's reach in case one was sneaking up on us, the bird we were watching being just a diversionary tactic.

Hot, sweaty, but very much content, we eventually retraced our steps. It was a particularly satisfying morning, all in all, mainly due to two simple things: one was a beautiful bird, and the second was the place that had become its home. An entirely natural, rather elegant solution to an age-old problem.

The Front Line:
The Battle for the Hills

The mist hung heavy in the air, seeping into my clothing and turning the figures before me into silent wraiths moving slowly in the half light of morning. I turned up my collar and tucked my chin into my chest, stamping my feet to get the blood flowing. The feeling of my senses coming alive in the moments after dawn added to the mystery of the scene before me: ghosts of flat, monochrome men, horses and dogs. Even the sounds of their preparations were softened, losing direction in a world made uniform by the newness of the hour. I was watching a timeless scene, as men prepared their animals for the hunt.

Several days before Pablo had asked me if I wanted to be part of the ongoing efforts to remove feral pigs from the highlands of Isabela.

'This is no tourist trip, Monty,' he added. 'You'll be going with local hunters who have been doing it all their lives, and their fathers before them. It's hard work, and dangerous too – on horseback for several days. But I think you should see it.'

I agreed wholeheartedly, and nodded in assent.

Pablo looked thoughtful, as though faintly surprised that I had agreed to come along.

'How are you at riding a horse? That's the only way to get to where the pigs are, and it's not an easy route by any means. The horses can be pretty wild – this okay with you?'

This was a surprisingly perceptive question, and I wondered if it had been my blank expression when he'd first mentioned the horses that had given me away, a slight blanching of the skin and a flicker of alarm in the eyes. I did have riding experience, but it was in two forms. The first was of the holiday trekking variety, riding a bored pony that was simply staring at the backside ahead of it, and wanted above all other things to get it over with and be back home. These ponies were generally so small that my toes trailed through the grass on either side, and falling off would take place from a lower altitude than if I'd fainted standing up.

The other was an ill-judged attempt to gallop a horse through the surf in the Outer Hebrides. This had always been an ambition of mine, and having slightly exaggerated my experience at the local stables, I was given a lovely old horse called Webster. He was, according to the manager, 'completely bomb proof. No one ever falls off Webster.'

The fact I fell off Webster four times that afternoon therefore counts as something of an achievement. The festival of sudden stops, abrupt changes of direction, and snorts of mirth indicated to me quite early on that Webster was having the best day out he could remember. Horses know, they just know, that when I'm on their back it's open season. Maybe it's the clenched buttocks and trembling knees, or the terse and occasionally falsetto commands. Either way, I've never ridden a horse that hasn't thoroughly enjoyed the experience.

'I'll be fine Pablo,' I said. 'If nothing else I can just hang on. Try to get me a nice horse if you can though?'

He smiled and nodded, and said that he'd 'have a word'.

As an experience it might well prove to be grim and possibly life threatening, but I had very powerful reasons for wanting to witness this process. This really was the front line of the conservation efforts on Isabela, but in my own mind the rationale for the hunt itself was far from clear cut. It was well known that the highlands on Sierra Negra – the volcano where we would be hunting – were alive with feral pigs. It was also very clear that they were having a devastating impact on the native species there, digging up tortoise nests, even venturing down to the coast to dig up turtle nests, and dramatically re-engineering the landscape as they foraged.

But I couldn't help but question the real motivation for the hunting process itself. My limited experience with 'hunters' in other nations had not been favourable. For me, they tended to veer towards the alpha end of the spectrum, carrying unnecessarily big knives and a few extra kilos. They seemed to be exclusively male, and hunted because they were seeking something – and that 'something' was rarely their quarry. Perhaps they needed personal validation, perhaps it was peer approval, but I had consistently found that the conservation bluster that invariably accompanies the pursuit and death of a large animal is baseless. In fact, I would admire the protagonists more if they simply admitted that they liked killing animals because it made them feel more manly, and gave them an excuse to have some beers round a camp fire with their mates as they all oiled their guns.

So here, in the Galapagos of all places, I wanted to see if this still held true. If it was simply a social event built around an excuse to use dogs to chase down a terrified pig, then for me it would indeed be a bitter revelation. Even a moment reflecting on the problem raised all manner of other solutions – trapping, shooting, poison? I wanted to find out the real story, as for me it represented something approaching the very soul of the local people's approach to the conservation issues that surround them.

The scene before me on that misty morning didn't augur well. As the hunters strapped bottles of water, sacks of supplies and personal camping gear on to their horses, I noticed huge machetes in abundance. There were also smaller, lethal sheath knives on their belts. The men themselves looked capable and purposeful, intent on the business in hand. One of them pulled a bandana up over his mouth and nose, and a battered cap low over his eyes. If I had bumped into him on a remote jungle track, I would have immediately handed over my watch, wallet, and then the children. I raised an uncertain hand in his direction to give a tenuous wave, which he acknowledged with a brief lift of the chin, before looking straight at me for a disconcertingly long time. I assumed he was selecting an aiming point that wouldn't damage anything of monetary value.

'Monty, meet Luis,' said Pablo. 'He is leading the hunt and will pick your horse. So be nice to him, eh?'

Beside Pablo was a powerfully built man of medium height, with immense shoulders and flat features. He was smiling broadly, causing his eyes to become deep slits, and bulldog creases to appear in the folds of his face.

'Monty, welcome, welcome,' he said. 'Thank you for coming on our hunt.'

He reached out and shook my hand in one of his own, a great meaty paw entirely enfolding mine.

'We call him "Big Buffalo",' said Pablo, with an affectionate sideways glance. 'His family have hunted in these hills for gen-erations.'

'Come, Monty, I will show you your horse,' he said, gesturing me towards the row of horses tied to the fence a few metres away.

This was where my plan could come badly unstuck. These were not the gentle steeds of quiet stables frequented by visitors to the islands. They were half-wild horses descended from stock handed down from the original settlers. Before my arrival, the men had caught them on the hill behind the homestead, corralling them using a line of beaters and a lasso. As such, the horses were pretty annoyed before I even got there, and what's more they were now having all manner of equipment strapped to their backs. The addition of a trembly-kneed hacker with a very high centre of gravity could be the final straw.

As I looked down the row of horses, I wondered if they had anything as prosaic as names – an essential part of owning a horse back home. I thought that this was probably not the case, so I decided to give them names based on their appearance. There was Hurricane, shifting and snorting right next to Fury, who just looked livid at the entire process. A little further down the row, Satan tossed his head and stamped a foot. Bronson twitched in outrage and shook his mane, ears flicking and muscles tensed, rear hoof cocked like a loaded gun. Beyond them were the mules and half-breeds that were our baggage animals, looking like a gang of hoodies on day release. And there, at the far end, stood Buttercup.

Buttercup was staring at a passing butterfly with an expression of benign interest. A blonde mane flopped over gentle brown eyes, and she looked so relaxed I thought she was about to pass out.

Luis led me down the line of horses, with me muttering fervent prayers as we did so. And then, triumph and joy, we stopped at Buttercup. She looked round, and gave me a look of amiable welcome, like a hippy snapping out of a dope-fuelled haze. She then turned back round to see if the butterfly was still there.

This introduction cheered me up no end, as it meant that I had at least a vague chance of surviving the next few days. I was fairly confident that some sort of injury was inevitable, but, looking at Buttercup, I was heartened that it might not be of a type that the mainstream media are fond of describing as 'catastrophic'. We might even get away with 'serious', or 'nasty', but hopefully the words 'stable' and 'almost full recovery' would also feature if Buttercup and I got along.

Luis left us to get to know one another, and headed back up the line to make the final preparations before our imminent departure. This involved releasing the hunting dogs, a moment that changed the atmosphere completely. It was a trigger, an immediate transition from relaxed preparation to urgent action. With the pack unleashed, the hunt was on, and everyone knew it. The horses tossed their heads, pulling and bucking against their traces. They rolled their eyes, lifting their heads and whinnying at the pack, urgent to be on their way. Buttercup glanced around, vaguely aware that something might be happening, then decided to continue her examination of the six inches in front of her nose.

The dogs themselves were a collection of breeds and differing colours, but were all of a similar body type – lean, rangy and long of limb. They looked in good condition, far from anyone's idea of the clichéd farm dog, and all immediately fell in behind what was clearly the alpha. The pack charged up the track in a tangle of tails, sniffing at the morning air, bounding and spinning in exhilaration as their ancient heritage was realised – they were a pack, seeking a kill. The lead dog had the most extraordinary coloration, with a russet brown coat overlaid with what can only be described as a tiger's stripes. He bounded ahead unchallenged, ears pricked and tongue lolling.

'*El Tigre*' said Luis, who had noticed the direction of my gaze. 'The boss.'

Several of the dogs had one brown eye, with the other a startling ice-blue. This gave them a particularly menacing appearance – evidently there was a sire somewhere in recent island history who had been a busy boy. I hoped beyond measure that he was called 'Bowie', as otherwise this represented a missed opportunity of criminal dimensions.

And so the moment had arrived. I moved towards Buttercup, undid her head rope, and grasped the metal bar at the front of the saddle, a curved piece of iron plainly used for attaching bags and stores. I duly mounted, and Buttercup glanced around to welcome me aboard. She shifted from foot to foot, adjusting her stance to cope with the sudden arrival of her passenger – for that's undoubtedly what I was, as 'rider' would be grossly exaggerating my credentials – and then bent her head to take a quick mouthful of grass before departure. I picked up the reins and gave an experimental swish to the left, bracing myself for the inevitable outraged buck and abrupt acceleration, only to find that she moved slowly round and ambled after the other hunters, who were by now following the dogs along the track. This was a splendid start, and I soon found myself slouching in the saddle in the approved gaucho fashion. This was undermined somewhat by the fact that I was wearing a newly purchased helmet – a gigantic plastic dome that tripled the size of my head – and what can only be described as a bum-bag to give me easy access to my camera gear. The rest of the group, all wearing battered sun-hats or beanies pulled down low on their foreheads, looked appropriately menacing, a group of men heading into the mountains to fulfil their birthright as hunter gatherers. The helmet/fanny-pack combo made me look like someone called Tarquin on his way to the Budleigh Salterton gymkhana.

By now the mist had begun to burn off, and the rise in temperature made the air heavy with the vegetative scent of the undergrowth alongside the track. We had a long ride ahead, following the track to the flanks of the Sierra Negra volcano, and then pushing into the pampas of the true highlands. I shifted uncomfortably in the saddle, and tried to adjust to Buttercup's easy, rolling gait. I would have several hours to reflect on the hunt ahead, and the monumental challenge that the eradication of large invasive species represented to the Galapagos.

The big problem that invasive species present to any island

ecosystem is that the battlefield is so confined. There is simply nowhere for the terrestrial animals and plants to go should they find themselves at the wrong end of a super-competitive new arrival. There is no move to pastures anew, no 'further afield'. As an animal or plant, you stand and fight for your own tiny patch of real estate, and most are pitifully equipped to do so. Lose this fight and extinction beckons. This might be viewed as a normal process, all part of the evolutionary process beloved of Darwin, but there is nothing natural about the arrival of new plants and animals with which the native species of the Galapagos now compete.

Plants are a good example of this rapid acceleration of incoming competitors, fuelled, of course, by our colonisation of the islands. Since 1535 and the arrival of our good friend the Bishop, the rate of new plant species arriving has been about two a year, leading to the present number of 750 new plants with which the endemics have to do battle for resources. This compares to the natural rate of one new plant species coming to the Galapagos every 10,000 years without the vector of man.

Added to this is the presence of larger factors that do not provide direct competition, but weaken the very foundations on which, as a native plant, you do battle. And the most significant of these is the introduction of domestic animals.

Approximately thirty species of vertebrate have been introduced to the Galapagos in the last two hundred years. Considering there are only 145 native species of vertebrate on the islands anyway, that is a huge number, representing a third more large animals competing for scant resources on a group of islands where survival can be precarious at the best of times.

But it is the nature of these introduced vertebrates that has proved so devastating. These are either domestic stock, and so they are supported, fed, and nurtured by the people who rely on them, or they are predators that have run amok.

At the very top of this apocalyptic list are goats. Ironically, these are the absolutely perfect Galapagos animal: they can eat anything, survive and indeed prosper in the harshest of environments, get their moisture from their food, and are agile enough to access even the most remote areas. Introduced by the first settlers, goats adapted very quickly to the Galapagos, and soon were running amok through the archipelago. Nothing is spared when a herd of goats passes through an area – even the tiniest plants that hold together the thinnest layer of topsoil are eaten, and so the topsoil that has taken centuries to accumulate is blown back into the sea. No seeds are left, no buds, no shoots and no hope. The only endemic animal to prosper from the goat's presence has been the Galapagos hawk, foraging off the carrion in their wake, and hunting its traditional prey more easily on the bare earth that remains after the scorched-earth passage of a large herd. The realisation soon dawned among the scientific community that, unless the goats were removed from the islands, all that would remain were the dark silhouettes of the hawks watching over the dust clouds beneath them, harbingers of the death of one of the most extraordinary land-based ecosystems on earth.

Perhaps the most poignant symbol of this future, nothing short of Armageddon for the Galapagos, was in the form of a single tortoise. Lonesome George was the last of his kind, a single messenger from an ancestral line that stretched back millions of years. At the time of his removal to the safety of the Charles Darwin Research Station on Santa Cruz in 1972, there were no tortoises except him left on his home island of Pinta. But there were 667 goats per square kilometre. That figure is worth a moment of reflection – for every 1,000 square metres of this exquisite, remote, entirely unique and otherwise uninhabited landscape, there were 667 animals eating everything in their path, scratching at the top soil, removing the bark from trees, devouring cactus, seedlings, and exposing the hard rock beneath. In their midst stood one remaining tortoise, as the very essence of Pinta was carried away on the oceanic winds.

Written on a notice next to his enclosure in Santa Cruz was a simple inscription: 'Whatever happens to this single animal, let him always remind us that the fate of all living things on Earth is in human hands.'

When he died on 24 June 2012, a local café put up a simple, hand-drawn notice that was perhaps even more powerful: 'Today we have witnessed extinction.'

Perhaps this seminal event in the very heart of a community, under the mournful gaze of the wider world, was the moment of realisation that this fight for Galapagos was going to be one to the death.

And just to show that there is always hope, that nothing is insurmountable, even as George passed away in his enclosure, so his island home was making a tentative recovery. The efforts that have been made over the years to remove the goats from remote islands have been nothing short of heroic, and have achieved remarkable results.

The saga of the goats would make a stirring Hollywood film, right from the moment of 'let's resolve the problem once and for all' in the early 1960s, through to the triumphant and hard-won conclusion almost fifty years later in 2008. Such were their numbers on the islands that initially it was simply a case of herding them from horseback, then humanely destroying them. Following input and advice from New Zealand, helicopters and marksmen were then used to shoot any escapees that had fled into the more remote areas of the islands. But although this was effective in the smaller islands with sparse vegetation (which, of course, was due to the goats in the first place), it didn't work on the larger islands where forests and undergrowth remained.

Hunting dogs were then used, which had to have special boots made as their feet were cut up by the lava rocks over which they ran. Once again this was effective to a degree, but limited time and resources meant that herds of goats remained in remote areas. These herds couldn't even be located, let alone eradicated. And so the final phases played out, a monument to the ingenuity and indefatigable will of those conservationists involved, who simply refused to give up. The solution was the rather elegant (albeit rather ungentlemanly) strategy of using goats against goats.

These are animals that naturally seek out their kin, so goats with tracking collars were released, which duly sought out the hidden herds. In their wake followed the hunters, and at last many of these final pockets were located. But these 'Judas' goats were still not 100% effective, and there was no denying the daunting fact that even after all this effort, all that had to remain for the programme to be considered a failure were two goats – a male and a female. There was a real danger that once the hunting ceased, the cycle would simply begin again, meaning that all of this effort would have been for naught.

And so the final chapter played out, and like all good final chapters, it involved secret agents and sex.

Following the 'Judas' goats, came the 'Mata Hari' goats. These were females, sterilised but chemically induced to appear receptive, that were released to lure out the males. Where the males roamed, so the rest of the herd tended to follow. This proved remarkably effective, and by 2008 the last goats had been eradicated from many of the islands. The numbers are staggering, with 268,000 goats killed from ten major islands. Given the scale of this problem, one does wonder if the programme would have even started had those involved known just how massive the issue was. But, as ever, it had taken a few hugely driven individuals, who in turn mobilised an international effort, and then simply refused to give up over several decades of being thwarted. Looking back on this extraordinary feat of conservation, one is reminded of the Nelson Mandela quote: 'It always seems impossible until it's done.'

And so to this particular day, eleven years later, riding into the mists of the Sierra Negra volcano with a group of hunters, tracking down the other great environmental vandal of the islands – the pig. There is actually a connection between the eradication of the two animals, as a few goats were left deliberately on the island of Santiago to graze down vegetation and therefore allow the pig hunters to access their quarry. This led to the complete eradication of wild pigs on Santiago by the year 2000, at the time the largest successful project of its kind anywhere in the world.

But Isabela is an altogether different matter. The sheer scale of the island makes the task so much harder, requiring any hunting expedition to head deep into the interior, where there is ample vegetation and a vast number of inaccessible nooks and crannies to hide your average pig.

And it's worth noting at this juncture that even your average pig is above average when it comes to most other animals. They are barrels of muscle, equipped with a fearsome array of senses – smell being the most predominant – with which to seek out food. This they do with ruthless efficiency, using their great strength and persistence to burrow, snuffle, chew and snort their way towards anything that smells vaguely interesting. They are also highly intelligent and learn fast – this factor above all others makes them difficult to hunt. Researchers at Penn State, intrigued by so much anecdotal evidence of the pig's ability to adopt new skills, created what was essentially a video game for them. The pigs they used in the experiment learned to control a joystick, which moved a cursor on a screen to a specific location, which in turn led to them being given a treat. The only other animal that has ever successfully done this are chimpanzees. This was no clichéd 'dumb' animal we were hunting.

They are also extremely well equipped to defend themselves. The boars have fearsome tusks, and when combined with their power, aggression and agility, it makes them formidable foes. Stories abound of dogs and hunters being badly gored – not unreasonable from the pig's perspective, of course – but this just added to the feeling that I was involved in anything but a jolly.

As we rode higher and higher into the hills over several hours, still on the wide track but approaching the point where we would turn off into the thick vegetation that surrounded us, I had the chance to introduce myself properly to my fellow hunters. They were Charlie (stout, unsmiling, shy), Freddie (the bandana-sporting chap of my first acquaintance – lean, compact and, as it turned out, very friendly), and Kevin (skinny, young, entirely focused on the task ahead). Bringing up the rear were myself and Pablo, with him increasingly alarmed as my lack of horsemanship became more and more apparent. And last of all was the rear gunner, called – incongruously – Peachy. He was older than the rest of the group, and rode with an ease that spoke of many decades in the saddle. He had a snow-white moustache that sat like an alabaster caterpillar above the warmest and widest of smiles. As he was right at the back of the line he got to watch me ride, a form of in-flight entertainment that seemed to keep him thoroughly amused.

After an hour and half we halted in a large, circular area of dark gravel, our launch pad into the great slopes of Sierra Negra. Pablo rode up beside me, doing the equivalent of a handbrake turn so we were knee to knee. His grin could only be described as wide and wolfish.

'Okay Monty. Well done, my friend, but now the riding really begins. I've been watching you, and it is very important now that you . . .' he struggled briefly for the right words . . . 'try hard to stay on your horse.'

I nodded solemnly, and Buttercup chose that exact moment to snort in agreement. It's not only pigs that have great intelligence and can spot when the game is afoot.

'You see, we will be heading into the pampas zone soon. This used to be a beautiful area of wild grasslands and low bushes, but now has been taken over by guava forests. You will have to control your horse . . .'

'Buttercup,' I interrupted. 'She's called Buttercup.'

'Ah, yes, okay, Buttercup,' said Pablo, not batting an eyelid. 'You will have to control Buttercup, because if you fall and injure yourself out here there is only one way out. And that is on your horse. I mean Buttercup. Okay? You understand?'

'I do, Pablo,' I said. 'I'll be fine. I think we've come to something of an agreement.'

And I was right. Over the last hour and half, Buttercup and I had worked it out. Essentially, the agreement was that I wouldn't bother her, and if that happened she wouldn't bother me. Having sent her a series of completely baffling and contradictory instructions on the ride up the track, she had quickly decided to just amble onwards. I had also begun to understand that she knew her way round these hills way better than I did, and so had assumed the role of intelligent freight. This was working splendidly for both of us.

'Let's go, then,' said Pablo. 'Good luck! And Buttercup, be nice, hey?'

He smiled once more, and wheeled away – a man and a horse in perfect harmony. We followed – a man and a horse who just happened to coincidentally be on the same hunting trip, with one of us sitting on the other.

As we left the track, the landscape changed almost immediately. Once we had cleared the dense vegetation that ran parallel to us, we broke through into a spectacularly verdant scene. Undulating slopes of bracken and grass spread away from us, vanishing into the mists of the higher ground. Dotting these great, open volcanic slopes were copses of dark green guava trees, a precursor to the dense forests through which we would soon be travelling.

'Imagine this pampas with hundreds, maybe even thousands,

of giant tortoises feeding here,' said Pablo, looking back over one shoulder to speak to me. 'It must have been the most amazing sight. But even by the time Darwin arrived most of them were gone. Maybe one day we will see it again.'

The dogs raced and coursed through the dense bracken, agitating the undergrowth like torpedo tracks in a green sea. We were still an hour or so away from the hunting grounds, but the pack was already alive to the potential presence of prey, running hither and thither, pausing only to raise their heads and sniff the air.

We soon saw a thick green line on the slopes ahead, a demarcation point between pampas and forest. These were guava trees, with twisted interlacing branches, heavy with dark moss that hung in dark, tangled masses. Guava is also an invasive species, and ironically provides the perfect food for the pigs that forage beneath its branches, as well as a refuge that is akin to a fortress. Both species, if left unchecked, would soon dominate the landscape entirely.

As soon as we entered the forest, I understood the scale of the challenge ahead, both for me personally and for the hunters in their quest for the pigs. My serene and passive approach to riding had to abruptly change, and I found myself constantly twisting and leaning in the saddle, one moment hunkered down by Buttercup's neck, the next lying flat on her broad backside. The colossal helmet, up to this point a rather embarrassing hindrance, became a perfect battering ram, and I quickly found myself using it like the bow of a supertanker, carving a passage through the undergrowth before me.

There was one particularly exhilarating moment when, while limboing under a stout branch, I managed to get it caught under the rim of the helmet. Buttercup ploughed on in her indomitable style, and I found myself being scraped out of my saddle in what would have been the most embarrassing fall in equestrian history.

Fortunately, just at the point when I had my toes hooked under Buttercup's chin, and was lying entirely flat on her back and eyeing a suitable landing spot with wide eyes, she stopped and allowed me to haul myself back upright. Having disentangled myself, and now returned to the more conventional upright position, I noticed that something extraordinary had happened. Buttercup had grown longer. I was looking at considerably more horse in front of me than I had been moments ago. Perhaps this was a trait unique to Galapagos horses, some evolutionary quirk that extended the spine to allow them to push through dense undergrowth.

I thought this worth mentioning to Pablo.

'Hey, Pablo, I think my horse is getting longer,' I said over one shoulder. 'Is that normal?'

'No, Monty,' came a weary voice from the rear. 'It's just that your saddle got scraped along her back as you got caught on that branch. You're now sitting on her backside.'

'Oh, righto,' I said, and stopped so Pablo could make the appropriate alterations.

As we continued on, the forests thickened even further. We now moved through a world of cloying proximity, as the tangled growth around us snatched at our clothing and whipped our shins. The horses kept their heads low, leading with their foreheads in order to push aside branches and dense bunches of leaves. Far from providing shade and comfort, the canopy seemed to contain the rising heat of the day, creating a claustrophobic tunnel through which we laboured. The thought of trying to dismount and chase a barreling boar through this was absurd, and suddenly the use of the dogs made perfect sense. To catch an animal sprinting and twisting through otherwise impenetrable undergrowth, you had to match its speed and agility, and have the keen senses to seek it out when it went to ground. There could have been a pig the size of a caravan six feet away from me as I rode, and I simply would not have seen it.

There was one glorious, vivid moment that brightened the day no end. As I paused to take a drink, Pablo whispered to me, *sotto voce*, but urgent with excitement.

'Monty, look, look . . .' he pointed at a tree directly overhead, eyes wide and smile broad. And there, sitting on a branch, peering at me with genuine curiosity, was a vermilion flycatcher.

This is a tiny bird, that not surprisingly given its name, eats small insects. But the thing that sets it apart so dramatically is its plumage. It is a blood-red droplet with wings, an absurd ruby flashing bright in the dark backdrop of the canopy. Not for nothing is the local name '*brujo*', or 'sorcerer'. To see a vermillion fly catcher is indeed a moment of magic.

What's more, I had always wanted to see one, and in twenty years of visiting the islands, had never done so. For this moment alone, the ride had been worth it. I mentioned as much to Pablo.

'Ah, Monty, congratulations!' He looked genuinely pleased on my behalf. 'To see one of these is a great moment. But you know what, it is also a good symbol as to why the conservation of the islands is so complicated. You see, they really like the guava forests. So if we get rid of the guava, which many people think we should, then until the scalasia forests grow back, the flycatchers would have nowhere to nest. That is why management is so important, as opposed to complete eradication.'

We both admired the flycatcher for a moment longer, until it tired of us and vanished into the forest, an iridescent spark on the wing.

We stopped for lunch in one of the open patches, giving me the opportunity to stretch my legs, massage my backside, and (covertly) examine my inner thighs. As red as a letter box – or indeed a vermillion flycatcher – thank you for asking.

We were soon underway once again, this time breaking clear of the forests for a sustained period, as we were nearly at the rim of Sierra Negra. It was glorious to be clear of the suffocating embrace of the undergrowth, and to see the ridge of the main caldera of the volcano drawing ever closer, a sharp line meandering across a clear blue sky.

And then, abruptly, it was upon us. The ground fell away at our feet, causing even the amiable Buttercup to stop and then skip backwards. The slope plummeted into the vast, dark heart of Sierra Negra, a blasted apocalyptic landscape, dotted with fumaroles still smoking moodily after her last eruption only twelve months previously. The scale was absurd, as was the feeling of proximity to such basic creative might. The magma driving the engine of this immense mountain was a mere two kilometres beneath the hooves of our horses. We stood over the epicentre of the incomprehensible forces that had forged the Galapagos, the crater before us a monument to the pressure and heat that had made the very earth convulse.

As the afternoon drew on, it became obvious that there was a problem. And that problem was me. Although the hunters remained courteous and genial throughout, I could sense their growing frustration at the speed of my progress through the forests. I tried encouraging Buttercup in the approved manner, but no amount of digging my heels in to her ample midriff, squeezing with my knees, 'Hah! Hah!'-ing, or vigorous movement of my pelvis, would get her to accelerate beyond a sedate walk. It did allow Luis a moment of considerable mirth as I moved past him, shouting and bent low over Buttercup's neck, as though approaching the final furlong at Aintree, but at walking pace. But something had to be done, and that something was myself and Pablo heading back to camp, leaving the main hunt to carry on at something approaching a normal pace.

I would love to say that it was with considerable regret that I turned Buttercup back along the path. But that would be a terrible lie. I was delighted, particularly as I didn't want to write off the possibility of Tam and I ever having more children. My nether regions had taken a fearsome pounding, my legs ached, and my back was killing me. Even Buttercup perked up, breaking into a canter in one of the open areas, which seemed to surprise her as much as anyone else. Peachy also agreed to tag along, mainly to keep an eye on me it seemed, and so the three of us headed slowly back down the slope.

The camp was a simple affair, at a location that had plainly been used for many years. A small grove of guava trees created a quiet glade, with shorter grass and ample shade for the horses. On arrival we wearily dismounted, pitched our shelter, and began to prepare dinner prior to the eventual arrival of the main hunting party. I sat with Pablo as the sun set, the landscape coming alive with glorious, golden light. It didn't take a huge leap of imagination to picture the shapes of giant tortoises moving slowly across the pampas before us, and I asked him just how realistic he thought this hunting effort was in terms of eradicating the last of the pigs.

He took a sip from his water bottle and carefully considered his answer.

'Well, Monty,' he said finally, 'when I was younger I would come up hunting to this very camp, and we could see pigs and cows all around us. Hunting was easy, we just set the dogs on the pigs then went home.'

He paused for a moment, looking at the ground at his feet, before picking up a blade of grass to twirl between his fingers. He studied it intently before continuing.

'But now, the hunting parties have to ride for two, sometimes three hours from here to even get to the areas where the pigs can be found. That is, at least for me, proof that the hunting is working. We may never rid Isabela of feral pigs, but what we can do is control them. And, for now anyway, that is enough.'

The words, and the sentiment, were heartfelt. It struck me that although the war may never be truly won here, and the slopes of Sierra Negra may never again see thousands of giant tortoises, at least the individual battles should still be fought. The alternative was too awful to contemplate. There was one outstanding question though, something that had bothered me ever since we set out.

'But why not just use poison, Pablo? Or traps?' I asked.

'Well, to poison an animal is a horrible death. They die slowly, and in terrible pain. You may also impact other species – it is very difficult indeed to create a system where only the pigs will eat the poison. And trapping? Pigs learn, Monty, they learn really fast, so trapping would be very difficult. We would also have to transport the traps up here, disguise them, check them regularly, and even then, we still have to kill the pig that is inside.'

He paused once more, by now the sun's glow creating a molten line across the horizon. The end of another day on the vast, ailing island of Isabela.

'We've been hunting in these hills a long time,' he said. 'The knowledge we have, the horses, the dogs, the quick kill – it really is the best way to do this, I think. I love animals. I even like pigs, but if you gave me a choice between a feral pig and a giant tortoise, then there is no choice. I'm sure you agree.'

And agree I did. This was the front line of conservation on Isabela, and on the front line it is a fight to the death, with both sides in an arms race to thwart the other, with survival the glittering prize of the victor.

Soon the sun had set entirely, and night was upon us. As was the way in the Galapagos, straddling the equator, darkness descended abruptly, a fact that seemed heightened by the remoteness of our camp. But this did create the bonus of an immense sweep of sky, entirely devoid of any light pollution and strewn with stars. In their midst, rather appropriately, hung a hunter's moon.

Pablo and I talked for a while, with Peachy joining us to sit in companionable silence. I was just contemplating turning in for the night, and bracing myself for the stiff-legged walk to my small tent, when I glimpsed a flickering light in the distance. It was soon joined by another, and then more, weaving through the night towards us. Moments later two dogs came bounding into the camp, an advance party to the main group. Next was Kevin, materialising out of the darkness with his head torch bobbing overhead, and then the main hunting party clattering in his wake.

'We got three,' shouted Luis, just behind him. 'Come and see.'

His smile shone wide in the gloom, and he gestured towards one of the pack ponies, over which was slung a huge dark body.

I walked quickly over to the group, and then stopped in my tracks. The pig was an immense, coarse beast, so far removed from the gently agreeable farmyard variety as to be another species entirely. It was covered in thick, dark hair, and although it was so big it hung down both sides of the horse's belly, this was no corpulent idler. It was a slab of hard muscle, with the neck in particular a great dark bulge, designed to drive the head deeper into the earth as it foraged for food. Its mouth gaped open, frozen in a last moment of defiance, exposing the tusks. These were relatively short – this was not even a fully-grown pig – but they were wickedly sharp. I hesitantly reached out to run my finger over the yellowed leading edge of one of them. It was an enamel razor, designed to slash and lacerate, driven by that power of torsion of the barrelling body behind. I could only begin to imagine the ferocity of an assault, a combination of huge strength, lightning speed, and primal rage. This particular pig had of course been fighting for its own life, a last stand in the face of the pack, and it had wreaked its own form of havoc as it went down under the hounds.

'Monty, come and look,' said Pablo quietly.

Nearby lay a dog with a wicked wound gaping on its abdomen, a deep slash that pulsed as the dog shifted and whimpered on the ground.

'Three of the dogs were injured,' said Pablo. 'The other two are not as bad as this one, and should be okay, but this one will probably not make it.'

The dog looked up at us as we spoke, and then lowered its head to the dirt once again. If ever I needed a reminder that this was indeed a form of warfare, here it was, panting and shifting on the ground before me.

The hunters had by now moved to the shelter, and were beginning to prepare their food. After the adrenaline of the chase, and the battle with their quarry, they now looked drained. Luis opened a huge Tupperware container, and began to listlessly spoon rice into his mouth, gesturing me over to come and sit with him.

He smiled as I joined him, and reached into a cloth bag to hand me a small camera.

'GoPro,' he said simply, raising his eyebrows and gesturing that I should turn it on.

The tiny screen flickered to life, and I was transported at once to the very heart of the hunt. Kevin had worn the camera on a chest harness to record the kill, and the sights and sounds of the final moments were suddenly revealed. I crouched over the screen, face illuminated by the ghostly glow of a scene of terrible drama and harrowing intensity.

The opening moments showed undergrowth being pushed aside as Kevin sprinted uphill to the site where the dogs were battling the pig. As he drew closer, the noise of the fight became apparent – the snarling and snapping of the hounds, mixed with the initially outraged grunts and then the terrified squeals of the pig in their midst.

The screen then showed Kevin bursting into the midst of the maelstrom. The footage was wobbly and frantic, moving this way and that as he tried to get his bearings, then plunged straight into the pack of dogs as they surrounded the pig. It was a confused mêlée of close ups, of wide eyes and snapping jaws, and in the midst of it all a head lifts into shot – the pig, twisting and turning, desperate for a way out, but anchored by the clenched jaws of the pack.

Then the camera stills, and Kevin's hands move into frame. He seizes the pig by the hind legs, drags it from the midst of the dogs, and puts it out of his misery with one swift cut of his sheath knife. This was a moment that was thankfully out of shot, but was signalled by a last frantic squeal from the pig, and then a quiet, wheezing grunt as it died. I paused the footage, and took a few deep breaths. From the initial noise of the fracas that indicated the dogs were on to their quarry, to the final merciful knife stroke, was two minutes and thirty-four seconds, a time indicated by the clock in the corner of the screen. Two-and-half minutes of unimaginable terror, of excruciating pain, of primal intensity – but still only two-and-half minutes. Would several days in a trap be preferable? Confused, frightened, and then terrified as the hunters approached to administer the coup de grace? Would hours and hours of pain as poison took effect be a better death? Crouched in the darkness, writhing and panting, an intelligent animal not comprehending what was happening to it, before meeting its death as organs failed and blood vessels haemorrhaged?

As I looked up, I realised that Luis was studying me closely as I watched. Over the course of the hunt it had become very apparent that behind the affable and easy-going façade, he was a deeply thoughtful and intelligent man. But there was something else – a resolve, an inner fortitude that had just seen him ride for fourteen hours to track down three pigs. My viewing of the footage was, he knew, a moment when the grim reality of the hunt would hit home. When the detached expression 'eradication of an invasive species' would be thrown into stark reality. He turned towards me to speak. His English was faltering, but the sentiment was entirely heartfelt.

'This – Isabela – my island,' he said, gesturing into the darkness around him. 'I want beautiful again. Understand?' He leaned forward as the question was asked, keen to hear my response, looking, perhaps, for validation from an outsider who had shared the rarefied world of the hunt.

I nodded, and smiled reassuringly. For me, the experience had been transformative. I felt I had been granted a glimpse into a culture of which I had no knowledge – accompanying a small group of local men who possessed a genuine sense of mission. I had been treated with courtesy, patience and respect. I had even managed to get a smile out of Charlie.

It would be naïve to say that there was no joy in the pursuit, that the men around me did not experience the thrill of the chase, or that they didn't share a camaraderie borne of generations of hunting in these hills. But it would also be entirely false to say that this was also a recreational outing. Perhaps this was after all a perfect marriage of conservation, local people, traditional skills, and the highly effective eradication of a pervasive and destructive invasive species.

Luis smiled in return, shook my hand, and heaved himself to his feet. He walked to the base of the large guava tree to which the shelter was secured, lay down, closed his eyes, and was asleep in an instant. I took this as a signal to make my way to my own small tent, and bade everyone good night. Before climbing in, I looked up at the night sky, arching up and over the great dark shadow of Sierra Negra, the latest battleground for the future of the Galapagos.

Santa Cruz Island:
The Clamouring Hordes

I gingerly assisted Molly off the water-taxi, glancing back reproach-fully at the driver as I did so. Most skippers of these small, fast boats are highly skilled, as the bulk of their work consists of hours of close-quarter manoeuvring in the crowded harbour at Puerto Ayora. But this chap, who looked only slightly older than Isla, was plainly new to the job, and had driven our boat at some speed directly into the pier. This it seemed was his way of 'stopping', and although highly effective, was less than ideal when one is holding a wriggling five-year-old. As I glared at him, he gave me a cheery thumbs up before reversing at full throttle back out into the main harbour, off to wreak a little more havoc.

Tam was waiting for me at the top of the walkway, and smiled encouragingly as she stood next to our teetering pile of bags. Isla was long gone, and I glanced to the end of the jetty to see her stress-testing the playground that stood next to the main square. I looked back at the bags, and as ever was profoundly impressed by the amount of kit required to support two small children for a week-long visit to another island. It seemed to me akin to a siege-style Himalayan assault *circa* 1921; one of those expeditions that proceeded upwards via an interminable series of base camps supplied by several hundred panting porters. At least for them the implication of forgetting something was merely death. For me it was a week, possibly more, of incandescent fury from a height of four feet.

A month had passed since our return to the Galapagos and we were in Santa Cruz, our old stamping ground, at the invitation of the Galapagos National Park. There was some particularly interesting science taking place in terms of animal husbandry, which was of course reason enough to make the thirty-mile sea journey from Isabela. But a chance to visit the island where we had first made our home in 2017 made the prospect irresistible. Two years is a long time in today's Galapagos, so I was particularly interested to see if I would notice any changes, even at a superficial level.

This did not take long. As we rode a taxi through the centre of Puerto Ayora, with the kids shouting out the names of their old haunts, I was immediately taken aback by what I was seeing. In our short absence, Puerto Ayora had grown up, and it didn't give a damn who knew about it.

Gone was the awkward adolescent, the grubby teenager with hygiene issues, unsure of itself and made gawky with growing pains. It had been replaced by a sleek supermodel, manicured and primped, sashaying along the shoreline of Academy Bay. At every junction was a new hotel, down every alley a boutique coffee bar. The shops were now of a more upmarket variety, selling art and crafts. The transformation in just two years was dramatic and striking. There were still plenty of t-shirts and tea towels, but the place had undeniably cleaned up its act. Puerto Ayora had scrubbed up and come out glowing, and the reason was simple – money. A great deal of money.

This modern Puerto Ayora, one I observed with mixed emotions as we drove to our accommodation, has restaurants that are packed, and permanent queues at the cash points. It exudes affluence and the giddy contentment that comes from seemingly limitless income. And it was not an end point by any means, it was simply part of the journey – there is still plenty of growing up to do. The scene behind the town reflected this, as on the slope rising towards Bella Vista was a vast building site, with the concrete shells of substantial houses and hotels rising from the earth. Not only was the town expanding, it looked as though it had absolutely no intention of stopping as it marched relentlessly towards the interior. The bucolic memory of Puerto Ayora as a fishing settlement was gone for ever, and perhaps part of the solution in terms of controlling this unfettered expansion is acknowledging that fact.

To understand what has happened here, it's important to appreciate the real impact of the last forty years on these islands – and indeed the truly seismic effect of the last two. There can be very few archipelagos in the modern world that have undergone such a profound change in terms of their population centres, and now a line had been crossed.

In 1979, a year after being declared a World Heritage Site, Galapagos received approximately 12,000 visitors a year. These were hosted by a resident population of 4,865 people. By 2017 – the year of our first residency – visitor numbers had gone up by 2,000% to 220,000. And the official population had increased by 616%. In terms of unofficial population, the people who travelled on Ecuadorian visas and simply never left, one could probably add another few hundred per cent on to that. But no one knows this particular figure, although everyone acknowledges that it is substantial.

As I looked out on the busy thoroughfares of Puerto Ayora once again in 2019, visitor numbers were now estimated at 275,000, with one local authority (who asked to remain anonymous) even putting this figure as high as 300,000. That is 3,500% higher than the original UNESCO-recommended tourist capacity for the islands.

These numbers are now so high as to be meaningless in terms of the original targets and aspirations for the Galapagos. And indeed the moment updated figures are issued, they are almost immediately surpassed the next year, and the year after that. Such thoughts made me rather gloomy as we checked into our hotel – aware, as ever, that we were part of the problem. But to blame the people who come here as tourists is a gross simplification, as it is the people who allow them to come that should bear the brunt of our ire. However, there is every chance that even this is a futile exercise. With the Galapagos tourist industry bringing in $150 million in 2005 alone, such rants – particularly from an outsider who has exercised the right to visit the islands several times – are rendered hollow and churlish.

There are a number of factors at play here. The first is that the popularity of the islands continues to rise. With the exponential growth in social media, the web is awash with images and videos of people realising their dreams in the Galapagos. It is a clarion call to those who have not yet made the journey to come, and never has it been easier to do so. The historical reasons for not going to the Galapagos – cost, the rigours of the journey, and limited tourist infrastructure – are now no longer relevant. Galapagos is open for business year round, can cater for virtually every budget, and is accessible from anywhere in the world.

To prevent environmental catastrophe on these islands, people must practise restraint; that much we know. And we also know that this seldom happens when there is a quick buck to be made – history has taught us that, if nothing else. For the continued expansion of human settlement in Galapagos to be halted or at least controlled, there needs to be a massive outbreak of collective conscience. And I'm not entirely convinced that will be forthcoming anytime soon.

But there is a far more basic problem. This is about boundaries and borders, and let's not forget that the Galapagos is 97% National Park. We tend to see, and to judge, the areas that have been heavily colonised by mankind, but the vast majority of the islands remain free of people and are the realm of wildlife. This is hugely commendable, and is a great example of that exact restraint that is so essential. But invasive species know no such boundaries and borders, and what's more they are a great deal more ruthless than we are. The chance to make a quick ecological buck might be a good analogy, and they will exploit each niche to its absolute maximum potential. And here lies the real threat:

by introducing so many invasive species, we have let the genie out of the bottle, and now they run rampant across almost the entire archipelago.

And so we are in the midst of a war for the soul of these islands. The enemy is not just human settlement and increased tourism, it is the armies that have been unleashed as a consequence – the Hill Raspberry, the feral pigs and the fire ants will not stop until they have completely taken over the Galapagos. Those are the battles that rage today, the conflict that simply must be won over the next few decades. The price of defeat is just too awful to contemplate.

Once we had arrived at our accommodation, I left the girls unpacking, as I had an appointment at the Charles Darwin Research Station. This meeting was with the head of the rather excitingly named Rapid Response Network (RRN), a group of specialists created to deal with the very modern issues around people and animals sharing the same spaces.

One of the (many) factors that demands attention with this increased footfall are the less desirable interactions between people and animals on the islands. More and more, as the famously laid-back animal population occupies the limited real estate of the islands with huge numbers of visitors and residents, accidents and incidents take place. Invariably when this happens, the animal comes off worse.

Eduardo was a short, powerful figure, who looked every inch like he should be in charge of something that responds to things. Ideally rapidly. He spoke excellent English, and had what can only be described as a compact muscularity. He wore sturdy boots while sporting a multi-tool on his belt. If our meeting had been interrupted by the clatter of helicopter blades and he had word-lessly vaulted out of a nearby window to clamber aboard, I would not have been overly surprised. Eduardo struck me as being very much ready to go.

In one of the meeting rooms at the Research Station, he talked me through the rationale behind the team.

'Well, Monty, like everything here, it is complicated. It is not simply a case of us going to the aid of every animal that is in trouble. We get images sent to us from wildlife guides and tour-ists all the time, but very often it's simply a case of the natural cycle of things. Animals pick up lots of injuries anyway inter-acting with one another and their environment, so often we have to explain that we cannot get involved. But if it is a problem created by us – by people – then we have to act straight away.'

'Do the local community call in as well?' I asked.

'That is a key aspect of the programme,' he said immedi-ately. 'It's really important that local people feel they're helping local wildlife. They are proud of the animals of the Galapagos, and know their value in terms of their livelihoods. The Rapid Response Network isn't just made up of the teams that head out to help the animals, it's also everyone who lives on the islands – they are our eyes and ears.'

The RRN had only been established in 2014, and had already been very busy indeed. It had also become more and more profi-cient as time progressed, and could now respond very quickly to incidents anywhere in the archipelago. Eduardo asked me if I'd like to see some images of the animals they had assisted over the past few months. With some trepidation, I said I would.

He opened a file on his laptop. The thumbnails showed a series of iconic Galapagos animals – giant tortoises, iguanas, sea lions – in various states of distress. It made for uncomfortable viewing.

'See this,' said Eduardo, enlarging one image, 'we get a lot of these. A young sea lion swims through a loop of line, or a plastic ring, and it sits on their neck and as they grow it slowly throttles them.'

The image showed a sea lion sitting on a beach with what looked like a collar. Closer examination revealed that it was actually a length of rope, acting like a garrote cutting into the skin. This was a particularly excruciating way to die, asphyxiation by millimetres over several weeks or months.

'We're proud of that one,' said Eduardo unexpectedly. 'As soon as we received that image, we deployed a team within a couple of hours, were at Floreana the next morning, and removed the line that same day.'

He closed the image and moved the cursor to another.

'This has just come in, actually.'

The picture showed a young sea lion on a pristine beach. It would have been an idyllic scene but for the wickedly curved fish hook sitting in the side of its mouth. The hook was huge, with a thick line trailing from it. It was a gruesome image, and particularly poignant in light of the beauty of the setting and the helplessness of the sea lion. There was an innocence in its demeanour, a kind of bewildered acceptance of its fate.

'We think it's a hook from a longline, as it's so large,' said Eduardo. 'We're actually heading out there tomorrow to try to remove it. Would you like to come?'

I said yes immediately, and after thanking Eduardo, headed back to see the family to explain about my mission of mercy. Isla and Molly were suitably impressed by their dad's derring-do.

'Wow,' said Isla, when I told her about the hook. 'So will you have to catch the sea lion, then?'

'I will, yes,' I said firmly, leaving out the minor details such as the fact that the accompanying team would do it, and I wasn't actually permitted to touch the animal, let alone wrestle it into submission.

'And will you need a plaster for it?' asked Molly. For her the answer to all of life's ills, both physical and emotional, was a plaster. Ideally with a cartoon character on it.

'I will Molls, definitely.' On hearing this she scuttled off to the medical kit, and came back to press several into my hand.

Still basking in the fraudulently acquired adoration of my children, the next morning I made my way down to the dock in Puerto Ayora to meet up with the team.

As I approached the quayside, as busy as ever at this early hour, with goods being unloaded and water-taxis cutting back and forth, I had no problem at all making out the team. Standing beneath an absolutely colossal net was a man with a ragged goatee, accompanied by a young woman and an older companion. The net was a vast loop on the end of a pole, precisely like a butterfly net might be if it was designed to catch a sprinting sea lion.

It was only as I drew closer that I realised that the net, although impressively large, was not quite as immense as I first thought. It was the fact that the man holding it, who introduced himself as Marcelo, was actually very small. But, much like Eduardo from the day before, he exuded a kind of elastic muscularity that I imagined made him an ideal character for pinning down distressed animals.

The girl with him introduced herself as Andrea, and in faltering

English explained that she was the vet. She was painfully shy, but had a wide smile and looked pleased and excited that we were about to set out. With her she had a medical kit in a large tool-box, as part of her role today would be to take blood samples and check the general condition of the sea lion once the hook had been removed.

To my great pleasure, the third person turned out to be Harry Reyes, my partner in crime from *The Queen Mabel* two years previously. We embraced, and quickly exchanged our news – or as much as was possible with my (very) limited Spanish and Harry's (somewhat) limited English. All was well with him it seemed, although something had happened involving an elephant, but that may well have been an anecdote lost in translation.

Introductions made, we climbed aboard the fast boat that would take us out to the distant island of Genovesa, where the sea lion had been photographed. This was another reason why I was delighted to be accompanying the team, Genovesa being one of the most beautiful and remote of the islands in the archipelago. It is famous for its bird life, with breeding colonies of red-footed boobies and frigate birds, as well as red-billed tropicbirds and swallow-tailed gulls. The entire area of the island is only 14 square kilometres, with the great curve of the bay at its centre speaking volumes for its volcanic origins. No one lives on the island, and there are only two landing spots, and thus it retains that pioneering atmosphere. Although I had visited the island once before, that had been many years previously, and I was very keen to reacquaint myself with what is, certainly in ornithological terms, something of a rare jewel.

Our arrival at Genovesa was signalled several hours later by the delicate forms of storm petrels massing in our wake. These were no individual, itinerant travellers: they were formed into a vast flock, squabbling and fluttering over the top of the heaving white water that marked our passage. The island had a large population of petrels, which in turn supported a great many short-eared owls. These wait at the entrance to the burrows where the petrels nest, timing their strike with absolute precision to snare the tiny birds as they flit past. Some owls have even learned to hide in the entrance to the tunnel itself, presenting a nasty and terminal surprise to any storm petrel making its return from foraging.

Our boat made its way to a mooring in the heart of the encouragingly named Darwin Bay, with the rugged shoreline of the island curving away on either side. This formed a perfect ellipse that ended in two headlands, with the gap between them acting as an entrance to the most entrancing of natural harbours.

Andrea, Marcela and Harry immediately set about launching a small tender off the side of our boat, and as soon as it was bobbing alongside, began loading it with all the equipment. We all squeezed on board, and the tiny outboard coughed into life before driving us forward with a reedy whine of protest. We headed towards a distant crescent of white sand, our tiny boat bobbing and weaving erratically over the blue chop of the water's surface. It was some relief to arrive at the beach, and we immediately leapt out to ferry the equipment ashore. This gave me, at last, a moment to take in my surroundings.

The sand of the beach was dazzlingly white, sloping gently into the sea to create a palette of blues from gentle azure to the deepest ultramarine. On one side of the beach rose a small cliff, which led enticingly inland, with dried scrub at its base, along with the various detritus washed up at the upper limit of the tide. I walked over, irresistibly draw by the flotsam and jetsam gathered by the immense curve of the island, and found a collection of bleached logs and scattered bones. The bones were the purest white, desiccated and honeycombed by the sun, and someone had arranged them into something approximating a skeleton. Plainly it had been some sort of small whale or dolphin, with the masts of the vertebrae standing proud creating a neat parabola along the spine, the elegant architecture of a marine giant.

The team were cautiously approaching several sea lions on the beach, checking them against the image Andrea had on her phone. Such caution seemed a little excessive to me, as this beach was used as a landing spot for tourists and so the sea lions were entirely accustomed to people peering at them from close range. I guessed that the price of scaring an injured animal into the sea was too high to take any risks at all – once in the water, there is zero chance of catching a sea lion. As such, the team crept about like they were stalking snow leopards, as opposed to approaching the yawning, scratching members of the colony on this particular beach.

Much to my delight, Marcelo approached me and indicated that the sea lion we were looking for was not here, and we would have to head off along the coast to search for it. This was very good news indeed, as it meant I would have the opportunity to pick my way through the nesting colonies that fringed the shoreline, a noisy mosaic of young birds in various stages of development. Such places present every facet of the life cycle, with squabbling hordes fighting for space, for food, and often for their very existence. It is an environment that is vivid and raw – anywhere in the world I enjoyed visiting a nesting colony, but here on Genovesa it was particularly special.

We moved off the beach in single file, with Andrea in front, Marcelo directly behind, having shouldered the net, Harry carrying the medical gear, and me loitering at the rear. Technically (and actually) I was supposed to stay close to the group, but this seemed such a rare chance to meander through the colony at my leisure that I decided to hang back a little.

Predominant amongst the nesting birds were red-footed booby chicks, which is no surprise given that Genovesa is one of the largest breeding colonies on earth for this species. These look, quite frankly, ludicrous, which is entirely fitting given that the name 'booby' is itself a translation of the Spanish word 'bobo', or clown. Even the adults have something comical about them on land, and, as I watched, one flew in to make a spectacularly ham-fisted landing, ending up with wings splayed, its face in the sand, and its backside pointing directly at the sky. The chicks around me were footballs of white fluff with vivid blue faces and beaks several sizes too large for their heads. Their eyes looked like marbles of darkest quartzite, and they stared out at the world around them with a bemused wonder. The chicks I passed were sitting in nests on low bushes, or in the dense sections of mangrove, with this fact alone making them notable among their kin. The red-footed booby is the only one of the three South American species that nests off the ground. It is also the only one that can perch, which seems an eminently sensible solution when feeding a large chick in a small nest several feet above a sharp lava reef.

The red-footed booby can travel prodigious distances to hunt, and has a particular penchant for flying fish, the most agile and elusive of prey. It was strange to look at the over-sized cotton buds dotted in the bushes around me and know that they would grow into such a highly effective aerial hunter, ranging ninety miles away from their nests, and even hunting squid at night.

By now the rest of the team were a little way ahead of me, so I hurried to catch up. It is a measure of the wonder of this island that, as I walked, I passed the only seagull on earth that is fully nocturnal – the swallow-tailed gull – and then immediately passed one of the rarest – the lava gull. Genovesa looks so arid and inhospitable from the sea, a long, low island that seems to epitomise barren oceanic rock flayed by the sun. And yet it is a vast depository of life, a restless hub that supports generation after generation of some of the most unique seabirds on earth, and in doing so recycles nutrients from the expanse of the surrounding ocean.

As we walked, I glanced down at the lava reef that fringed the coast, and was surprised and impressed to see that Andrea and Marcelo were now picking their way over the rocks in search of the elusive wounded sea lion. The waves were crashing in close proximity to where they tiptoed along the water's edge, peering under every overhang and into each crag and gulley. The surf hissed and boiled around them, for all the world like the lava on which they stood had retained its diabolical heat. Picking each step carefully, they reached the end of a rocky promontory, stood briefly in animated discussion, and then turned back.

By now I was standing beside Harry, who indicated with a jerk of his head that we should return to the original beach. As I looked back to check their progress, I noticed a flurry of activity just offshore. A red-billed tropicbird, a slip of a bird trailing a meteor tail of snow-white feathers, had been unwise enough to make a lone return from hunting out at sea, and was being besieged by frigate birds. It was a classic dog-fight, with the huge dark shapes of the frigate birds swooping down on the small alabaster form as it twisted and turned beneath them. We stopped to take in the spectacle, an acrobatic display of breathtaking agility in the clear skies over a tumultuous sea. One of the frigate birds grabbed the smaller bird by its long, delicate tail and hauled it upwards, shaking that great head with its broadsword beak. The tropicbird flailed desperately, breaking free to fall towards the sea with two more frigate birds immediately giving chase. I found myself clenching my fists and willing the smaller bird on as it drew closer and closer to the sanctuary of the cliff edge. And then, at the very last moment, one of its pursuers twisted in mid air and grabbed a single, pale, delicate wing-tip. This proved too much for the tropicbird, tipped up at full speed to tumble through the sky, and it disgorged its catch, which was immediately consumed by the dark squadrons in its wake. It's important to avoid anthropomorphism – very much frowned upon as it is by the scientific community – but as a representation of good versus evil, of a will o' the wisp, decent, hardworking bird being lynched by piratical villains while on the way home to the kids, it didn't come any better.

As we walked back to the beach, the path dropped down to sea level next to the mangroves, with each bush home to chicks and adult birds alike. The sand where the lattice of the roots intertwined was the point where the incoming tide raced in to meet us. Our timing was impeccable, with our arrival coinciding with rivulets of seawater making their way across the ground, seeking out every hollow and furrow, every gap and gulley. As the water advanced, now creating tiny wavelets around my feet and ankles, so the predators of the rising tide followed. Glancing along what had moments before been dry ground, I saw the distinctive shapes of two small stingrays gliding along the sand, while behind them a lava heron stalked resolutely up the path, like a stooped grey wizard driving the water magically before it. By now we had arrived back at the beach, and I saw the distinctive shape of a shark gliding along the edge of the surf, lurking in the shallows for whatever gifts the tide may bring. The surge of the incoming water had signalled a shift in the mood – the original sea change – and everywhere I looked there were predators on the prowl.

We dropped our kit in the middle of the beach, and sat down to sip from our water bottles and decide on our next course of action. This would, in all likelihood, involve clambering back on board our little dinghy, and then using the main boat to travel the entire coastline of Genovesa, putting ashore whenever we saw an area that looked suitable for landing. This would be a long afternoon indeed, and as I looked at the expanse of lava cliffs to either side of us, it also seemed somewhat futile – a search for a shiny dark body on shiny dark rocks while rocking wildly in a small vessel just offshore.

'What's that?' said Harry, suddenly sitting upright. He gestured towards a rock immediately next to where we had landed and there, curled up in the sun behind it and snoring contentedly, was a small sea lion. Andrea stood and walked slowly towards it, then dropped on to her haunches to peer at it, head on one side. She then stood up, and made her way briskly back towards us.

A quick conversation with the rest of the team, with me picking up one word in ten – which was quite enough in the circumstances – revealed that this was indeed our injured pup. The irony of the fact that it had been about four feet away from where we initially beached was not lost on me, although I cared not a jot, as it had meant a spontaneous tour of Genovesa, which in itself had made the trip worthwhile.

Marcelo immediately shouldered the net and strode purposefully towards the sea lion, with Harry and Andrea directly behind. I followed on, breathless with anticipation at the culmination of the hunt – capturing a wounded wild animal on a remote Galapagos beach. My expectations were high, and I hurried to catch up as I didn't want to miss a single moment of what I was sure would be an epic piece of high-octane conservation action. It was imperative that this happened as quickly and as efficiently as possible, and under no circumstances should the sea lion make it across the beach and into the sea.

As such, the event itself was somewhat anti-climactic. Marcelo simply walked up to the pup, they looked at each other amiably from a range of two feet, and then he very slowly put the net over its head. The pup looked up at him, somewhat baffled by this turn of events, and then decided to amble away. It seemed more embarrassed than anything at this lapse in people/sea-lion protocol. Its attempts to exit stage left simply entangled it in the folds that surrounded it, allowing Marcelo to then produce a towel. This he flourished like a matador, and duly vaulted on to the back of the sea lion, placing the towel over its body as he did so. The pup meanwhile let out a bark of protest, then sat with its chin on the sand, looking annoyed.

The tameness of the animal occupants of the islands has, of course, been well documented, but in the case of this particular sea lion on this particular beach, it would be magnified tenfold. This is a landing spot for the tourist boats that visit Genovesa, so this particular pup was probably one of the most photographed and fawned upon in the entire archipelago, and quite possibly the entire world. It was therefore entirely used to people crouching down beside it, although none of them to date had been carrying a vast butterfly net. Maybe in the future if this same sea lion came across something similar, it would take flight. But then again, knowing the islands and their animal inhabitants as I do, I suspect it wouldn't.

Andrea was by the sea lion's side in an instant, and cautiously lifted one side of its mouth to inspect it for the hook. This was, happily, absent, but where it had been embedded was a deep wound that gaped as she moved the pup's lip. This it took great exception to, and struck sideways with its head with viper-like speed. Andrea had plainly been expecting this, and quickly moved her hand, but even so the sea lion's teeth clamped shut only centimetres from her fingers. It is easy to underestimate these animals, to see them as fluffy accoutrements to the Galapagos theme park, but they are apex predators designed to do one thing: to lock on to the quicksilver forms of their prey using powerful jaws and dagger-like teeth. Anyone tempted to pet a sea lion might find their piano playing radically impacted for several months afterwards, and Andrea was suitably cautious as she continued to examine the pup.

After taking a quick blood sample, and making a further assessment of the wound, she nodded to Marcelo. She looked at me and said, 'He okay, he heal natural,' in faltering English, peering shyly up at me from under hooded brows.

Marcelo was also looking up at me, and gestured me away from the sea lion by simply raising his eyebrows and lifting his chin. I stepped back respectfully – the beast was about to be unleashed, it seemed. Then, with a suitably theatrical countdown – 'Tres, dos, unos!' – he jumped athletically off the sea lion's back while simultaneously whipping away the towel.

The sea lion didn't move a muscle, aside from lifting its head, and giving us what can only be described as a very hard stare. It was not happy, not happy at all, and seemed intent on letting us know. After it had treated each of us to a livid glance, it then stalked off back to its rock to slump back down precisely where it had been lying before, this time with its back to us. Seldom can a single gesture from an animal have been so very eloquent.

As we returned to Santa Cruz, the boat slamming and rolling through huge swells on a bone-shaking four-hour passage, I reflected on what I had just witnessed. I looked at the team around me, exhausted and grubby, spread-eagled on the deck and crammed into the corner of the wheelhouse as they tried to grab a few minutes' sleep. I had been profoundly impressed by their willingness to go the extra mile, to search every lava reef and boulder-strewn cliff face to find that injured young sea lion. The Rapid Response Network struck me as a particularly fine concept, and with park staff such as Andrea, Marcelo and Harry to the fore, one that is highly effective. It reflected two vivid truths. The first is that for any conservation initiative to prosper, it must engage the local people. And the second is that when the animals of the Galapagos are impacted by our presence, we have an absolute moral obligation to come to their aid. Perhaps in doing so we can begin to atone, inch by painful inch, for the sins of mankind's turbulent and destructive past here in The Enchanted Isles.

Sea Mountains and Forests
in the Deep

'And then one of the divers asked me "What do you think we'll see in the kelp?" and I laughed, and said "This dive IS the kelp, that's all there is about it!"' Salome shook her head in wonder at the memory, still aghast that anyone could see beyond the wondrous leathery fronds around which she had built her research.

I was drinking a coffee in the Acai bar, one of the many chi-chi little establishments that had emerged on the main street in Puerto Ayora. Sharing a skinny mocha (with extra cinnamon sprinkles, a real man's drink) with me were two young scientists, their eyes shining at the prospect of the days ahead.

Leading the conversation was Salome Buglass, who had started explaining just how important kelp forests were about twenty minutes previously, and had barely drawn breath since. If her explanation had been written down, there would have been no punctuation whatsoever, just a staccato, machine-gun delivery of interesting kelpy-related bits of information loosely bolted together by the occasional need to draw breath. One thing was very obvious indeed from the incessant barrage – Salome really, really liked kelp.

'Am I going on?' she said, suddenly self-conscious as our coffees cooled before us.

'Not at all, Sal,' I said, 'I was just . . . '

'And the sea mount itself? Have I explained about the sea mount?' she said. 'I've got to tell you about the sea mount. If you think the kelp is exciting, you wait until you hear about this . . .' and we were off again, hanging on to Salome's verbal coat tails as she charged off at breakneck speed.

Sitting quietly with us, nodding and smiling, was Isabela, a young researcher and diver who had been working with Salome for several months. They had found the kelp during a routine exploration of one of the many sea mounts, the tips of undersea mountains, that dot the Galapagos. These are, as Salome was explaining with some vigour, very much worthy of investigation, as there is strong evidence that they are submerged islands, having slipped beneath the waves due to the inexorable subsidence of the Nazca continental plate as it heads towards the mainland of South America.

They are also beacons for marine life, providing a focal point in an otherwise featureless underwater world. Their conical slopes cause deep water currents to rise sharply towards the surface, bringing all manner of good things with them as they do. Deep water tends to be cold, and the chemistry of seawater means that the cooler it is, the more oxygen it can hold. The ocean depths also tend to be nutrient rich, as most things that die in the sea ultimately sink towards the seafloor. This also applies to bits that fall off things, poop, airborne debris, and anything introduced from rivers and run-off from the land. The result is a rich soup. Imagine then, as this undersea river of delicious goodness hits a mountain in its path and thunders exuberantly upwards, it creates an upside-down waterfall delivering all the building blocks of the food chain to shallow water. It's even better if the mountain has a peak that is within reach of the sunlight streaming through the surface – known as the photic zone. In these cases it's open season, as every marine organism around tries to get a foothold in what is the oceanic equivalent of the leafy suburbs. Live here and you get sunlight, oxygen therapy, and your food is delivered to your door.

Salome had been involved in mapping the surface of the sea mounts around the archipelago using an ROV (a Remote Operated Vehicle). This is a mini-submersible attached to a tether that can be sent down to depths of seventy to eighty metres. It is about the size of a small suitcase, and allows exploration of these inaccessible and dangerous regions without putting divers at risk.

'Anyway,' said Salome, in one of her rare pauses to inhale, 'I was looking at Ro-Ro's screen . . .'

'Ro-Ro?' I asked.

'Our ROV: he's called Ro-Ro,' replied Salome, as though it was the most obvious thing in the world, which given the limited choice of names for something called an ROV, it probably was. 'Anyway, I suddenly saw on the screen what looked unmistakably like kelp. I mean. KELP. Here!!'

Isabela smiled, and looked wistfully nostalgic, savouring the memory. She closed her eyes, and nodded slowly. I was getting the impression that Isabela was also something of a kelp fan.

'It's exciting on so many levels,' Salome continued, 'a key ecosystem, right here in the heart of the islands, but also such a long way from where we expect to find kelp. It might even be a totally new species, and that would set the world of seaweed science alight.'

I had no idea what a group of very excited seaweed scientists might look like, but if Salome was anything to go by, it would be a scene of some intensity.

'But we had a problem. We simply had to get people down there to take samples, place equipment, and survey the area properly. Ro-Ro is only small, so couldn't do anything other than buzz about and shoot film, so that's where Izzy comes in.'

Salome, Ro-Ro and Izzy – thoughts of a 1930s music-hall act spring to mind. But at the mention of her name, Isabela sat forward in her seat, and took over the conversation.

'Well, the snag we face is that this is no ordinary Galapagos dive. It's at least fifty metres deep, with the possibility that we'll have to go as deep as sixty. And we can't get helium out here, so we'll have to do it on air. And it'll be cold, with big currents, and we're a very, very long way from help should something go wrong. So Salome has asked me to put a plan together.'

At this point it's probably worth expanding on the issues that were facing the research team, as they were genuine and life threatening.

Breathing air or indeed any gas underwater is a complicated business. This is due to the increased pressure at which you operate, with that pressure increasing dramatically the deeper you go. Dalton's Law and Boyle's Law – yep, those ones – show that, as this pressure increases, the various gases that make up air (nitrogen and oxygen being the main ones) will also increase in pressure and create all manner of issues for any diver. In other words, the deeper the dive, the more of these gases you take in with every breath. On a dive to fifty metres, every breath taken is the equivalent to six on the surface, and that brings a few problems.

The problems become very interesting indeed when it comes to nitrogen, and can be rapidly terminal when it comes to oxygen. With nitrogen it manifests itself in narcosis, described by Cousteau with typical Gallic flair as the 'Rapture of the Deep'. Beyond about thirty metres of depth, this can manifest itself in irrational behaviour, which, in turn, leads to life threatening errors of judgement. At fifty metres, narcosis will be intense, and no diver is immune from its effects (although there are plenty who claim they are). Increased nitrogen absorption also means risk of decompression sickness, which has to be mitigated by stopping on the way up. After only a few minutes on the seabed at fifty metres, the team would be operating in the equivalent of a cave, with no way to the surface without life threatening implications.

The effects of oxygen are less predictable, but even more

frightening. At about sixty metres – uncomfortably close to the depth at which the research team were planning to sample – it becomes toxic. This can lead to tunnel vision, twitching, respiratory problems and seizures. None of these symptoms are desirable at the best of times, but when battling currents on an undersea mountain-top a thousand kilometres off the coast of Ecuador, they can be very tedious indeed.

And the currents are also worth an honourable mention. Get blasted off the top of said undersea mountain and you face a long and lonely drift through blue water while you have a good hard think about your life choices. All you can do is fervently hope that you are a popular enough figure with the boat crew that they've kept an eye out for your bubbles or your marker buoy as you drift away into the immensity of the Pacific. Should they not have spotted you, there is a very reasonable chance of becoming part of the nutrient chain that you've just been researching.

For these reasons, the global limit for recreational diving has been set at forty metres. The research team would be heading a further 25% deeper into the unknown, the first ever divers to do so on this site, surrounded by blue water and unanswered questions.

Looking at Izzy as she explained the mechanics of the dive, I was struck by her youth, and also how slight she appeared. She had a wide smile and exuded confidence in the plan, but weighed about the same as a beer mat. Diving to these depths safely on air for any duration required four large cylinders – two for working at depth, and two more for decompressing on the way up – and looking at Izzy, I had no idea where they'd go.

'Oh, I know what you're thinking,' said Izzy, with a laugh, having read my expression with unnerving accuracy. 'I've done plenty of these types of dive before, just never here. That's the challenge, really, the location. If something goes wrong, we're in real trouble.'

She looked thoughtful for a moment, before finishing cheerily. 'That's all there is about it, and we have to come to terms with that, but it's worth it for the kelp.'

And much as I had reservations about the dive, and the safety of the team involved, I had to agree with her. Kelp is wondrous stuff. None other than Darwin himself recognised its extraordinary fecundity as an ecosystem, noting in his book about the voyage of HMS *Beagle*, published four years after his return:

'A great volume might be written, describing the inhabitants of one of these beds of seaweed. I can only compare these great aquatic forests with the terrestrial ones in the inter-tropical regions. Yet, if in any country a forest was destroyed, I do not believe nearly so many species of animals would perish as would here, from the destruction of kelp.'

Kelp can justifiably claim the title of being the fastest growing plant on the planet, driving upwards at a rate of 50 centimetres a day. Kelp forests support a dazzling array of other species, with one study in 1998 noting that: 'Kelp forests have been described as one of the most ecologically dynamic and biologically diverse habitats on the planet.'

Another research project on the west coast of Ireland noted 8,000 invertebrates living on each individual plant, akin to the scuttling masses of beetles living in the largest tropical trees. Added to this mind-blowing profusion of life is the value they add as producers of oxygen, and the introduction of key nutrients to the sea around them. For these reasons kelp is known as a keystone species, supporting a vast array of other plants and animals, so the discovery of the kelp bed on the seamount in Galapagos was a very significant one indeed. It was imperative that I wangled my way on to the trip by fair means or foul.

'How about this?' I asked. 'I'll act as your safety diver at thirty metres or so. I can hang on the line, and if there's any dramas you can get the diver to me and I can assist them to the surface? I'll be your guardian angel.'

Salome and Izzy looked at each other quizzically, then nodded.

'Okay, you're on,' said Salome. 'Meet us tomorrow morning at the dock. It'll be early, mind you – about 6am or so – but that's the best time for calm conditions. We'll arrange the dive kit for you.'

She smiled, and finished with a flourish by saying 'Welcome to the team!'

The next morning saw me standing on yet another quayside watching yet another dawn, as barrelling along the main street came a pick-up truck loaded with the research team and a truly absurd number of dive cylinders. They sat in a teetering pile, a great silver pyramid of colossal high pressure, clinking and rattling against one another like explosive wind-chimes. As the truck came to a halt, it dawned on me that if one went off it would set off all the others, creating a chain reaction that would blow Puerto Ayora back to 1905. I wondered if this would be such a bad thing.

Out of the back of the truck climbed Izzy and Sal, both of whom looked disgustingly fresh and bright-eyed for this ungodly hour. Accompanying them were the two other members of the dive team – Xavier and Jorge.

Xavier looked precisely as a deep diver should look, with a ragged goatee, and wild hair that flew in all directions from under a bobble hat. Jorge was the team leader, and walked up to wordlessly shake my hand before turning his attention to loading the dive boat with the vast amounts of kit required to get three divers to sixty metres depth in the middle of nowhere. It became immediately obvious that here was a man who knew his onions, as he directed operations with great clarity and confidence. In no time at all the boat was loaded, and he strode up to me with a big grin to properly introduce himself.

'Good morning, Monty,' he said. 'Sorry for not saying hello sooner – there's a great deal to do! I'm very happy that you are joining us today. I've got you a single cylinder and some recreational dive kit to go with it.'

He indicated the corner of the deck of our boat, *The Valesca*, that sat alongside the harbour wall. Next to a great heap of technical black neoprene and formidable looking silver aluminium sat my gear, looking rather insignificant and weedy.

'We'll do a detailed briefing when we get out there, but for now . . . vamoose!'

We all piled aboard the boat. One of the key characteristics of any seasoned diver is the ability to curl up in a very small space and go to sleep. It was no surprise at all to see Xavier fold himself up like a pen-knife, and immediately start snoring in a cramped corner of the cabin. Jorge, Salome and Izzy were deep in discussion about the day ahead, leaving me to watch the harbour retreat into the distance, framed by the widening rooster tail of our wake.

The trip to the site took about ninety minutes, long enough for the sun to rise fully and reveal a sea that looked like treacle, entirely flat and limpid, dotted only by the rise of an occasional fish or the dabbling feet of the storm petrels that faithfully followed our boat. Soon the tone of the engines lowered, and Salome made her way on to the bridge to assist the skipper to navigate to the precise point where the sea mount was shallowest. In this vast, vast sea, we were aiming for an area about the size of a tennis court, the absolute peak of the St Louis sea mount, and the only point shallow enough for the dives to take place. Salome had a sophisticated GPS, but she soon made her way back to the main deck with a rueful smile.

'The skipper says he knows where it is because there's a bulge in the surface of the sea! I'm going to take his word for it but check on the GPS as we go along.'

This might not be quite as fanciful as one might think. The skipper, an ex-fisherman, had generations of local knowledge interwoven into his DNA, and it is arrogant in the extreme to assume that modern technology trumps such painstakingly acquired local insight. To dismiss such knowledge is to discard a century of hard-won lessons out here on the open ocean, where the stakes for getting it wrong are as high as they can possibly be.

'Wow, amazing – I'd still check on the GPS though,' I said to Sal, hating myself just a little bit for doing so.

She laughed and waggled it in my direction.

After considerable amounts of circling, doubling back and heated debate, ancient wisdom finally met modern technology at a point that seemed to suit everyone.

'Time to wake up Ro-Ro!' said Salome, with a distinct twinkle in her eye. She opened a box at her feet, and pulled out a flat plastic box with an elliptical profile like a cross-section of an aircraft's wing. This was plugged into a roll of cable, and then Izzy produced the control console from the same box. There was much pressing of buttons and toggling of switches, and then Ro-Ro whirred into life. Her lights flashed, her small propellers whirred, and her camera beeped. Ro-Ro was wide awake, it seemed, and very much looking forward to jumping in.

Izzy lowered her into the water, and we all clustered round the small screen that showed her gallant progress through the water column, a faithful scout heading into a blue-green world with no horizon. And then, abruptly, appeared the top of the sea mount, coated in the unmistakable brown fronds of kelp. The team gave a spontaneous shout, leaving me to reflect on the fact that seldom can the appearance of some brown waving seaweed have illicited such a euphoric response. There was much back-slapping, and Ro-Ro was hastily retrieved, surfacing to a chorus of approval from the research team lined along the rail.

The next stage was marking this spot with a shot line, a fixed buoy to indicate the site for future surveys.

Jorge disappeared into the cabin, from where emerged sounds of weighty clanking. He staggered back out on to the deck carrying what appeared to be two car wheels filled with concrete. Closer examination revealed them to be . . . two car wheels filled with concrete, hence his somewhat pained expression. Several people immediately jumped up to help him, which became increasingly important as the car wheels were followed out of the cabin by a weighty chain. Eventually this was all piled on to the deck of *Valesca*, a great pile of ironmongery that was about to be hurled overboard.

'Big currents down there Monty,' he said, still puce of face and breathing hard, 'so the shot line needs to be a big one.'

'I know it seems a bit counter-intuitive,' said Salome, seeing my rather uncertain expression, 'but in this way we are assured of a single site where the survey can take place for a long time to come. A reference point, really. It has to be this heavy, as otherwise the marker buoy on the surface will drag it, and that would have a terrible impact on the kelp bed. In this way, only a single, very small area gets impacted.'

After a final bout of boat manoeuvring, Salome, who had been staring fixedly at the GPS in her hand throughout, suddenly shouted.

'Now, now! Let it go, this is the spot!'

Willing hands hoisted the clanking mass over the side of the boat, where it hit the water's surface like a depth charge. The line to which it was attached began hissing over the rail as though attached to a charging sperm whale, a moment that became doubly exciting when Xavier nearly got tangled in it. He Riverdanced his way out of trouble, showing commendable footwork, and ending up leaning on the rail smiling ruefully at us.

As soon as the line hit the bottom a marker buoy was attached to it in the boat, which was also thrown over the side. This quickly travelled some distance sideways across the surface, before coming up tight on the line and then rocking and heaving restlessly, a series of powerful ripples spreading away from it in a widening V-shape. The sea had wakened from its pre-dawn slumber, the current was beginning to run, and as such it was imperative to get the divers in the water quickly. Any further increase in the current would make an already difficult dive very dangerous indeed, with billions of tonnes of seawater sweeping over the top of the sea mount. Everything would become harder – holding position on the surface, the descent, crawling over the top of the sea mount, and then the long ascent back to the land of light and air.

The divers were one step ahead of me, and I glanced round to see that they were already pulling on their suits and preparing their gear. I started to do the same, although my own preparations were nothing compared to theirs. By the time I had checked my own cylinder and donned my suit, Izzy was just being helped to her feet with two huge cylinders on her back. It reminded me very much of a medieval knight being prepared for battle, as her courtiers bustled about her strapping on equipment and tightening straps before she entered the fray.

She caught my eye and smiled, as if suddenly aware of the absurdity of it all. She didn't look remotely concerned, in fact she appeared supremely happy and desperate to dive. Her confidence was a wonderful thing to behold, although it made me a little jealous to see her so carefree and full of *joie de vivre* at the great adventure ahead. 'Youth is wasted on the young', according to

George Bernard Shaw, and I would have loved some of her great pioneering spirit.

Instead I strapped on my own gear, largely ignored by the research team who were, quite correctly, concentrating on helping the technical divers. After glancing rather nervously at the vibrating and thrashing buoy behind me, I rolled over the side. It was akin to rolling into a river, and I was whisked quickly over the surface of the sea, just another piece of plankton in the grip of the tide, until I reached the shot-line. I clung to it just under the surface, waving like a flag in a stiff breeze, and waited for the proper divers to turn up.

This took some time, as they were still having lots of metal strapped to them, and various bits of sampling gear clipped on to whatever bits of them were still visible. Eventually they hove into view, three people looking like they'd walked through a dive shop wearing a suit made of magnets. Tanks, regulators, fins, weight belts and hoses all combined to make them look like astronauts drifting in a watery universe.

They hit the line just below me, conducted some final checks, and then began their descent. I followed them at a respectful distance, until we hit the point where I was due to wait for them. This depth coincided with a shimmering thermocline, a drastic difference of temperature that resulted in a hazy, pulsing layer of water, where two bodies of water meet but do not mix. It was a neat reminder for me that here was a barrier, a border that I was not permitted to cross with a single cylinder and simple recreational dive kit.

And so I watched them descend, and it was the most

wondrous, life-affirming, glorious vision of three young pioneers conducting the first ever technical research dive on to an
isolated undersea mountain in the Galapagos Islands, one that
had probably last seen the light of day four of five million years
ago. The underwater visibility was excellent, and I could clearly
make out their small figures, wreathed in bubbles, making their
way painstakingly across a landscape of waving kelp fronds and
sculpted rock.

My role was to watch them descend, make sure they arrived
safely on the sea mount, and then I would travel back up the
line to a shallower depth, before descending once again to meet
them on the way up. This I did, hanging in the current as it tried
extremely hard to wrench me from the line. My mask trembled on
my face, and my exhaled bubbles streamed directly away behind
me, whisked away by the ocean itself as it ebbed and flowed on
a timeless journey.

After twenty minutes, I descended once again, and saw the
dive team clustered once again around the line. Whereas before
they had been difficult to distinguish due to being draped with
astronomic amounts of equipment, this time it was even worse,
as they were shrouded in leathery fronds of kelp – the precious
specimens that they had been sent to collect.

I gave a gurgly whoop of triumph, and descended to check that
they were in good health. They then handed over the specimens
for me to take to the surface as had been previously agreed. This
had made me feel slightly guilty, as it felt like I was getting all
the credit for doing very little of the actual work. However, I
had quickly come to terms with it, having decided that they had
plenty of time left to get the glory, whereas, as the oldest man

on the team, I needed to make the most of such brief moments in the sun.

I broke the surface and gave a flamboyantly kelpy wave to the boat, a moment that was greeted with absolute pandemonium. It is important to understand that this whole venture was by no means guaranteed to end in success, and indeed walked a fine line in terms of the safety of the dive team (although not for me, of course, as I had only hung at a modest depth for a few minutes, something I chose to ignore as I triumphantly waved the kelp overhead and graciously acknowledged the cheers and high-fives of the crew). But my presence on the surface meant that the deep team were on their way home, the specimens had been collected, and a considerable leap in knowledge was about to be made about a new ecosystem in the Galapagos Islands. After days of preparation, weeks of planning, and months of careful research, success had been finally achieved.

As we rode *Valesca* home, with the sun sinking towards the horizon and the sea glowing like molten metal in our wake, I looked round the cabin to see everyone cocooned in their own thoughts. In this modern world, with every path well trodden, every angle covered, and every risk assessed, it is a rare sensation indeed to be involved in something new. Everyone had their own moment, their own memory of the day, all of which had combined to start what could be a momentous piece of research in these islands that hold surprises even today.

Xavier was once again snoring peacefully in the same corner of the cabin, Jorge was slumped on a bench, back resting against a lifejacket as he gazed out over the stern. Only Salome and Izzy were still talking, animatedly discussing the day and dive, the collection of the kelp, and the next steps in unravelling the story. Listening to them chat was to be inspired by such raw energy and drive, and a portent that this research project, at least, was in good hands. It was as good a sound as any to act as a backing track as I too drifted into a deep and dreamless sleep.

New Horizons, a New Generation and a Glimmer of Hope

I checked the house one last time, walking through it to make absolutely sure we hadn't left anything. I stood on tiptoes to peer into cupboards, and crouched down to look under beds. My footfalls seemed strangely muffled, leaden and flat in rooms now empty of our belongings, silent and devoid of life. Our residency was up, and we were leaving Isabela and the Galapagos for the last time. As the journey ahead involved a taxi, a boat, another taxi, another boat, a bus, three flights, and then a three-hour drive, I really didn't want to arrive back home in England and then find that we had left something entirely crucial back in Puerto Villamil, so I poked into every dark nook where little hands might have hidden things away. Living with Isla and Molly was a bit like living with two squirrels, with latent mammalian instincts meaning that they hoarded any precious (or recently pilfered) item, turning our lives into a litany of lost things. But with this one last nervous inspection, I was confident I had got the lot.

The previous few days had been a blizzard of goodbyes, the ground rush of our imminent departure taking us all by surprise. We had hastily organised a farewell party in the yard, inviting the hunters and their families, as well as Pablo, Laura and Kian. Luis had taken charge of the catering arrangements, turning up with the hind quarters of a pig, which had been duly butchered and then cooked over an open fire. He stood over the entire volcanic process, a stout island deity wreathed in smoke, stirring a gigantic pot with a long stick, periodically leaning forward to pour in some beer from the bottle held in one meaty fist. It was a scene redolent with the heady scent of meat and testosterone, and he would occasionally emerge from the billowing smoke to rub reddening eyes, wipe his brow, take a long pull on the beer bottle, and then head back into the gloom to continue the cooking process.

The resultant meat was delicious, pork with a slight hint of guava, and a slightly less slight hint of beer. We toasted each other royally, clinking bottles in the evening sun, nodding and smiling a great deal, and even re-enacting parts of the hunt. My particular charade about trying to get Buttercup to do anything other than walk went down rather well (I thought so anyway, although by that stage of the evening I probably wasn't the best judge), with Luis and Charlie nodding and laughing in fond recollection. At the end of the mime, Luis put his beer bottle down, and enveloped me in a colossal embrace – never had the expression 'bear-hug' seemed so very apt. Pablo darted everywhere throughout, filling glasses, slapping backs, and ensuring that everyone understood what everyone else was saying. As I watched him, it struck me what a hugely dynamic presence he was, galvanising those around him by the sheer force of his personality. Isabela and the wider Galapagos are lucky to have him, a true force of nature. He saw me looking over at him, raised his beer bottle, lifted his chin, and smiled.

The children played together, with Kian, Isla and Molly proudly showing the local kids around the full length of the mural on the wall. This now stretched all the way round the yard, and was – even if we do say so ourselves – rather good. Volcanos spewed lava, HMS *Beagle* sailed into a blue bay, and frigate birds, iguanas, boobies, tortoises and sea lions all jostled for position. At Molly's insistence, a large plastic bag was painted halfway along, with a red cross through it. The final section was of the family itself, completing the collage with the four of us holding hands on the last piece of the wall that led into the street.

I had asked them to make up a short poem so we could write it on the wall, something that summed up their time in the islands. After considerable thought, sucking on the end of pencils and surrounded by scribbled notes, they had finally approached the mural and, with white paint and wobbly script, Isla had written:

> *'From Isla's small land animals,*
> *To Molly's giant seabirds,*
> *All of the Galapagos is on this wall.*
> *So ssshhh,*
> *Or they cannot be heard.'*

As ever, they surprised me, my little girls. Throughout our time on the islands they had been observing us go about our business, they had watched, listened and drawn their own conclusions. The end result, the power and poignancy of those words, neatly summed up the parlous state of the local environment and the clamour and chaos that now surrounds every living thing on the Galapagos.

This is indeed a battleground, and one can argue convincingly that it is not just for the soul of the islands themselves, but for the environmental conscience of our generation. In 1978, by declaring the Galapagos one of the first World Heritage Sites, the human race put a marker down. We said that this place was so very special, so very delicate, and so very unique, that it must be protected by the world, for the world. In doing so, albeit unwittingly, we decided that we would be judged for ever on how we acted as its custodians.

First impressions today would seem to indicate that we have taken such a responsibility very seriously indeed. At present, 97% of the total land surface of the Galapagos – almost eight million hectares – is a National Park, and has been since 1959. A vast Marine Reserve around the islands was created in 1986, and extended to its current size of 133,000 square kilometres in 1998, making it one of the largest in the world.

And so it would appear, to all intents and purposes, that we have indeed honoured our collective vow to protect these islands, and entrenched that solemn duty in legislation. But appearances can be deceptive, and as we enter the second quarter of the twenty-first century, it has become apparent that we are failing in that duty. The numbers of visitors continue to rise at an astronomic rate, with a dramatic increase in land-based tourism being one of the recent and most alarming means of creating further footfall. According to statistics from the Galapagos National Park, the total number of visitors to the islands increased by 39% between 2007 and 2016, from 161,000 to 225,000. Significantly, during that same period, the number of visitors on land-based tours jumped 92%, from 79,000 to 152,000. This increase in those staying on the islands themselves, as opposed to residing on tour vessels, has required a huge increase in buildings and infrastructure. It has also meant a dramatic rise in the number of day trips between islands, in itself a concern because of increased boat traffic and transmission of invasive species. Whereas previously the islands had been the preserve of the intrepid or the well resourced, who invariably visited by ship, today the Galapagos is open to anyone who can travel, catering for almost every budget. This is not an elitist statement; it is a simple fact. With this seemingly uncontrolled and unregulated influx of visitors come invasive species, sanitation and infrastructure issues, and a whole host of new problems. Of the twelve terrestrial mammal species, ten are threatened or already extinct. Of the thirty-six reptile species, such a key part of the character of the Galapagos, most are classified as either threatened or, in the case of four species of tortoise, already gone, a footnote in history.

And yet, even in the face of overwhelming evidence of the negative impact of this uncontrolled influx of visitors and residents, the numbers continue to rise. The figure for 2019 is looking to be in the region of 300,000. To give this context, three years ago the WWF commissioned a study on tourist numbers, and the long-term impact on the island ecosystem. It created three scenarios – no increase in numbers, a moderate increase in numbers (3% growth year on year), and rapid growth (8% year on year). It concluded that long-term rapid growth would degrade the ecosystem to such a degree that in a few years two thirds of tourists would have no desire to return after a single visit.

Three years after this study, growth of tourist numbers for the last year has been 9%, just above the 'rapid growth' category. All visitors come with good intentions, the majority being passionate enthusiasts and vocal advocates for the natural world. It is simply the volume of people, and the infrastructure required to support them, that is pushing the ecosystem to its very limits. This is an issue that must be addressed at the highest levels of government both nationally and internationally if the islands are to be saved. And the time to do so is now.

During our time on the Galapagos, we had been treated with nothing but kindness and decency. The local people have, on the whole, an intense pride in their extraordinary home, and a code of cooperative behaviour that comes with living in a community where each so heavily relies on the others. And therein lies a glimmer of salvation, there and in the remarkable individuals it had been our privilege to work with. The great souls that we had met – Pablo, Roby, Luis, Maccaron, Lauren, Jacquie, Claudio, Salome – were motivated by something more than simple acclaim or civic duty. They have a higher purpose, one that drives them to extraordinary lengths, to feats of superhuman endurance and unstinting endeavour. They saw their role as protecting and preserving the islands for those still to come – in the words of an ancient Maori proverb, they were being good ancestors. On a more personal level they were, and are, my heroes. As long as they continue to fight, to trek into the hills, to dive deep, and to push ever on, and as long as those in power take a moment to listen, then there is always hope for the besieged and magical kingdom of the Galapagos.

And there are other forces at play here, great changes that mean, at last, that these individuals do not stand alone. Witnessing Isla and Molly explore the archipelago was to see in real time the rise of a new global consciousness, and a new resolve to address the problems of the world that they inherit. The girls were indicative of young people throughout the world, outraged at the actions of politicians, of big business, and of the system itself. In the last few years, children only a few years older than my small activists have taken to the streets, communicated on an international scale, and have made one thing perfectly clear – they will not stand, mute and obedient, as their birthright is denied them. They want to grow up in a natural world that has a chance of surviving, that can support them and their own children. They have realised, as they survey damaged ecosystems and vanishing species, that without them, there is no us. And so they have resolved to stand and fight. In ten years these militant youngsters, this noisy and troublesome rabble, will be the constituents that shape our political systems, in twenty years they will be the young professionals that shape our corporations, and in thirty years they will be the captains of industry that dictate our interactions with the natural world. Today we ignore them at our peril, for tomorrow they might just be our salvation. Charles Darwin – not only a great naturalist, but also a staunch humanitarian – would have been proud of them.

To me, there seem to be two urgent global imperatives that

must be addressed in order to counter the perilous position of the Galapagos in the modern world. The first is that we have declared this sacred archipelago a World Heritage Site, and yet we do not allocate global resources to protect it. By refusing to do so, we place the Ecuadorian Government, and the people of the islands, in a truly invidious position. In essence we tell them that they have to preserve the islands against the global forces of change that assail them, and yet deny them global money and resources to do so. This surely has to change, and quickly. The second is the need for an urgent response to young people around the world, and their passionate awakening to the genuine threats they face not just to their livelihoods but to their lives, due to environmental degradation in the decades ahead. Instead of challenging and patronising them, we should be enabling and supporting their efforts, doing everything we possibly can to prepare them for the challenges ahead and the changes they must force us all to make. We should learn quickly to be the good mentors they so desperately need now, so we can be the great ancestors they revere in the generations to come. A wonderful quote from an acquaintance in San Cristóbal summed this up perfectly for me: 'We all talk about creating an ideal world for our kids. But maybe it is more important that we create ideal kids for our world.'

All of this can be easily dismissed as philosophical speculation, as wishful virtue signaling. But what is undeniable is that the fight to save the Galapagos will be won or lost in the next twenty years. As we drove away from the little beach house by the sand road in Puerto Villamil, the girls clamouring and clambering as they attempted to catch a glimpse of Pablo one last time, I knew that one day we would return. I also knew that when we did, the islands would have transformed. The man in the rear-view mirror, and the raucous irresistibly energetic figures in the car – all powerful symbols of wider change – gave me real hope that such a transformation might just be for the better.

A Note from the Author

It can feel a little overwhelming at times, this relentless stream of negativity about the precarious state of the world around us. Such is the speed of change, and the scale of the issues, that one can feel helpless and impotent in the face of what feel like unstoppable forces. At lectures and events, the one question that I am asked again and again is 'What can I do? I know these issues exist, and I know that we need to try to live more sustainably, but what can I do personally?'

My answer is always the same. Never feel overwhelmed, because you can undeniably make a difference. It might not be the immediate, tectonic, epoch altering change we all wish to bring about, but all of our small actions can mount up to create significant impact and genuine momentum for global change. There are a great many things we can all do both to live more positively and to help protect the Galapagos. I've listed a few of them here.'

Conservation Groups

There are several conservation and research organisations doing good work in the islands, and invariably they are short of support and funds. Allying yourself to one (or indeed several) of them, either through offering your services as a volunteer, through formal membership, or by making a donation, has an immediate and genuine impact on their work.

One of them is, of course, The Galapagos Conservation Trust (GCT) (www.galapagosconservation.org.uk). This organisation identifies key projects in the islands and supports them through raising funds and assisting in research. If you have an interest in the islands (and I rather hope you do, having read this book!), then they also run events in the UK and overseas that celebrate and inform, arranging for experts to lecture about key issues on the Galapagos. They also arrange trips out to the islands, some of which are guided by our good friend Pablo, that directly raise funds to support particular projects. They are based in the UK but have contacts throughout the world.

Other fine Galapagos charities exist, of course, many of them doing great work on the islands, so if there is a specific area of interest for you, then it is often worth doing a decent internet search to drill down into these particular projects. However, the GCT covers a broad church under the banner of 'conservation, research and education', so it's a good place to start.

For anyone interested in shark conservation – a particular passion of mine, having witnessed the terrible impact of over-fishing first hand – The Shark Trust (www.sharktrust.org) is a splendid charity supporting various shark research and conservation projects globally. Another good one is Bite Back (www.bite-back.com), which does tremendous work in the fight against shark-finning and by-catch issues.

Visiting the Galapagos

I would never tell anyone *not* to visit the islands, but I would urge all visitors to travel well. When planning a trip, you should aim to ensure that your impact, as much as is humanly possible, will be positive not negative. You can start by ensuring that you are hosted by an operator who conforms to all of the rules within the National Park, and, indeed, is engaged in positive conservation activities with the funds they raise. A little bit of online research will tell you a great deal about the companies that are operating in a sustainable manner.

Whether to stay in land-based accommodation or explore the islands by a live-aboard vessel is a straight choice facing most visitors to the Galapagos. I would always favour the latter, as the long-term impact is undeniably less. One of the main factors creating the growth of land-based infrastructure has been the recent boom in more traditional tourism (i.e. staying in a hotel and exploring the islands through a series of day trips). It is undeniable, though, that cruising costs more, and is simply not affordable for many visitors. If this is the case for your visit, then limiting day trips to other islands makes a genuine difference – less boat travel, and less transfer of potential invasive species from one island to another. San Cristóbal, Santa Cruz and Isabela – the main inhabited islands – have everything you could possibly want to see within the confines of each island, so the inter-island trips are really not necessary to experience what the Galapagos have to offer, as it's all on your doorstep.

It is also imperative that you ensure you are not bringing any potentially harmful plant species into the archipelago. The biosecurity of the islands is a genuine problem, so making sure that your clothes and shoes are free of any mud or seeds caught in Velcro etc. really does make a difference. Over 14,000 items were impounded by the biosecurity teams in the year from 2015–2016. Virtually none of these items were brought in deliberately, but were attached to clothing or inadvertently hidden in luggage (the hay in my own case being a classic case in point). Making sure you are scrupulous about cleaning your kit (footwear in particular) when travelling between islands can also make a real difference.

Lifestyle

We all want to save the world, but it is completely unreasonable, and wildly impractical, to expect everyone to stop commuting, to become vegan, and to immediately cease using plastic (among the many other measures that would create immediate positive and wholesale change). But we can all make small changes. A couple of years ago, I decided I'd never drink from a plastic water bottle again. The average adult buys a startling 175 plastic bottles each year and, in total, some 7.7 billion plastic bottles are bought across the UK. The impact of removing myself from this statistic has had minimal impact on my life – I just have a metal water bottle that I fill from a tap – but it a) makes a difference, albeit a tiny one, and b) gives me a chance to flamboyantly swig from my metal bottle while feeling rather good about myself! The point here is that changes do not have to be hugely disruptive, but can instead be small and focused – and yet, when added up, do have an impact. Society is changing, with single-use plastic bags, straws and plastic water bottles all on the way out. That change has been driven by the little people like us.

It is also imperative that we 'make good kids for our world'. There is a hunger among the next generation to learn about how they can change the future, how they can re-write a script that predicts – at present – that they will inherit a dying planet. We should listen, advise, steer and help them in any way we can. The one thing we should not do is dismiss them. It is not too late to equip them for the battles ahead.

One of the best ways to educate our children is to get them outside. It genuinely does not take a great deal to inspire the little ones. A stream, a moor, a forest, a field, a coastline – deliver them there, let them off the leash, and let instinct and energy take over. The outdoors is genuinely transformative, and all we need to do as parents is announce that the adventure can begin. Looking back at your own childhood, your best memories will doubtless have a blue sky overhead and a wide horizon before you – very few of us recall with fondness a boring afternoon in the front room. I feel the least we can do for our own kids is help them make these memories for themselves.

I believe we are at a critical moment in terms of our interactions with the world around us. I also believe that we, as individuals, are faced with a straight choice – we either do something, or we do nothing. To choose the latter is to consciously accept the free ride we have all enjoyed for the last few decades, and to carry on in the clear knowledge that we are negatively (and possibly terminally) impacting the natural world. To choose the former, even through the smallest of lifestyle changes, means you are part of a movement that will make a real difference for the generations to come.

Good luck on your own travels.

Acknowledgements

To write this book, one must first explore the islands. This is an undertaking of some magnitude, so there are a host of people to thank. First is Martin Pailthorpe, for mooting the concept of telling the real story of Galapagos a few years ago. Many thanks to Channel 4 – Lizi Wootton, Sarah Lazenby and Sean Doyle especially – for agreeing to film the process, and for their support throughout. Thanks to Headline Publishing – a joy to work with, and to my editor Sarah Emsley in particular, who is definitely more excited about this book than anyone else (even my mum). Thanks, as ever, to Julian Alexander, my literary agent. I've been pestering the poor man for years about a Galapagos book, so at last he can now emerge from his office without checking the street first to see if I'm hanging around outside. Thanks to everyone at Seadog Productions – you are too many to name, and it would be wrong to single anyone out, such was the collective effort, but you have created a special TV series with such an important message. You have also been an absolutely delightful group with whom to work and to travel. Thanks to Suze

Scott – now moving on to pastures new after eleven years' meritorious service. You've been a wonder.

A huge thanks to the Galapagos Conservation Trust, partly for the extraordinary and important work you do, but also for being a constant source of advice and inspiration during our time in the islands. Thanks to Roby Pepolas – recently struck down by illness. We all wish you speedy recovery, Roby; the islands need people like you. Thanks to Maccaron, a truly amphibious creature if there ever was one. Thanks to Pablo Valladares, Laura and Kian – you were way more than our guides: you were (are) good friends, and took such great care of us while we were on your island. Come to South Devon, Pablo; be my guest, and I'll show you some proper surf! And thanks – a million thanks – to the people of the Galapagos, who were invariably generous, kind and hospitable at every turn.

And, finally, thanks to my girls. Tam was – as ever – our still point in a turning world. She has such extraordinary serenity, such a measured, calm, consistent approach to everything, that it is no wonder that we all turn to her in moments of crisis (which seem to occur on a daily basis). Everyone should have a Tam, and I'm very, very lucky that I'm with the original. And, lastly, Isla and Molly, my fearless, feisty, funny, mischievous, relentlessly curious little ones. I've done many, many trips to many, many places in my life, and they were all simply rehearsals for the main event, which was travelling with you two. You make me proud.

Picture Credits

Section 1

Page 1: Alastair McCormick (top); courtesy of the author (bottom)
Page 2: courtesy of the author (top); Tom Whitworth (bottom)
Page 3: Helga Berry (top left); courtesy of the author (top right and bottom)
Page 4: Helga Berry (top); courtesy of the author (bottom)
Page 5: courtesy of the author (top); Alastair McCormick (bottom)
Page 6: courtesy of the author
Page 7: Tom Whitworth (top); courtesy of the author (bottom)
Page 8: courtesy of the author

Section 2

Page 1: courtesy of the author
Page 2: Tom Whitworth (top); courtesy of the author (bottom)
Page 3: Tam Halls (top); courtesy of the author (bottom)
Page 4: courtesy of the author
Page 5: courtesy of the author
Page 6: Alastair McCormick (top); courtesy of the author (bottom)
Page 7: courtesy of the author
Page 8: courtesy of the author

Sources

Poem on page 156
reproduced with kind permission of Atticus

Verse from 'For My Daughter' on page 235
reproduced with kind permission of Sarah McMane

Quotes from Darwin's journals from:
Charles Darwin, *Journal of Researches into the Natural History and Geology of the Countries Visited During the Voyage of the H.M.S Beagle Round the World under the Command of Capt. Fitz Roy, R.A.*, 1860

Quote from the Bishop of Panama from:
Tomás de Berlanga, *A letter to His Majesty, from Fray Tomás de Berlanga, describing his voyage from Panamá to Puerto Viejo, and the hardships he encountered in this navigation*, 1535